OECD Regions at a Glance

2007

OECD

ORGANISATION FOR ECONOMIC CO-OPERATION AND DEVELOPMENT

ORGANISATION FOR ECONOMIC CO-OPERATION AND DEVELOPMENT

The OECD is a unique forum where the governments of 30 democracies work together to address the economic, social and environmental challenges of globalisation. The OECD is also at the forefront of efforts to understand and to help governments respond to new developments and concerns, such as corporate governance, the information economy and the challenges of an ageing population. The Organisation provides a setting where governments can compare policy experiences, seek answers to common problems, identify good practice and work to co-ordinate domestic and international policies.

The OECD member countries are: Australia, Austria, Belgium, Canada, the Czech Republic, Denmark, Finland, France, Germany, Greece, Hungary, Iceland, Ireland, Italy, Japan, Korea, Luxembourg, Mexico, the Netherlands, New Zealand, Norway, Poland, Portugal, the Slovak Republic, Spain, Sweden, Switzerland, Turkey, the United Kingdom and the United States. The Commission of the European Communities takes part in the work of the OECD.

OECD Publishing disseminates widely the results of the Organisation's statistics gathering and research on economic, social and environmental issues, as well as the conventions, guidelines and standards agreed by its members.

This work is published on the responsibility of the Secretary-General of the OECD. The opinions expressed and arguments employed herein do not necessarily reflect the official views of the Organisation or of the governments of its member countries.

Also available in French under the title:
Panorama des régions de l'OCDE
2007

Foreword

In recent years, regional development issues have returned to the policy agenda of many OECD countries. Higher integration driven by institutional processes (e.g. European Union, World Trade Organisation) and economic trends (i.e. globalisation) is eroding national borders and creating competition along regional lines in the world market. At the same time, the persistence of significant regional disparities challenges countries' capacity to promote economic growth while ensuring social cohesion.

To evaluate innovative strategies for regional development and diffuse successful policies, in 1999 the OECD created the Territorial Development Policy Committee (TDPC) as an unique forum for international exchange and debate.

The activities of the TDPC have generated new demand for statistical indicators at the sub-national level. Policy makers need sound statistical information on the source of regional competitiveness but such information is not always available. Sub-national data are limited and regional indicators difficult to compare among countries. This is why for some years the Working Party on Territorial Indicators (WPTI) has been carrying out statistical work on the measurement of regional economies.

OECD Regions at a Glance summarises the main results of this work. On the one hand, it illustrates the use of territorial indicators for the design and assessment of territorial development policies within the policy framework elaborated by the TDPC. On the other hand, it aims to diffuse the statistical tools elaborated by the WPTI for the analysis of regional economies.

Following the policy approach set by the OECD High-level Meeting on Innovation and Effectiveness in Territorial Development Policy (25-26 June 2003, Martigny, Switzerland), OECD Regions at a Glance is organised around three major themes:

1. regions as actors of national growth;

2. making the best of local assets; and

3. competing on the basis of regional well-being.

The first theme highlights that the factors of national growth tend to be strongly localised in a small number of regions so that promoting national growth would require improving the use of these factors within regions. The second theme assesses the economic performances of regions and identifies unused resources that can be mobilised to improve regional competitiveness. Finally, the third theme examines different dimensions of well-being in the perspective that well-being is a key factor to improve regional competitiveness.

Each issue of this series present a Regional Focus on a topic of prominent importance in regional development. In this issue, the Regional Focus is devoted to Geographic Equity in Health.

The series "Regions at a Glance" is coordinated by Vincenzo Spiezia, Head of the Statistics and Indicators Unit, Directorate of Public Governance and Territorial Development. "Regions at a Glance 2007" was prepared by Brunella Boselli, Carine Ferretti, Enrique Garcilazo and Vincenzo Spiezia, with the assistance of Angela Cataldi.

Table of Contents

IV. Regional Focus on Health

Source and Methodology

ISBN 978-92-64-00987-5
OECD Regions at a Glance 2007
© OECD 2007

Executive Summary

National economic performance is often compared across countries, and such comparisons are frequently used to highlight countries whose national policies appear to promote growth and development more successfully. However, national averages can hide wide regional differences in economic conditions and performances. *OECD Regions at a Glance* therefore presents a set of regional indicators – mainly in the form of graphs and maps – in order to identify those regions that outperform their country as a whole or the OECD area and those that lag behind. The patterns of development may differ widely in urban and rural areas, for example, and some areas may lag behind even when the national economy is performing well.

Population is unevenly distributed

Part I presents a number of broad macroeconomic indicators of regional development, including the dispersion of population, output, industrial concentration, employment growth and innovation. In OECD member countries, population is generally fairly unevenly distributed among regions: in 2003, approximately 40% of the OECD population was located in just 10% of regions. The concentration was greatest in Australia and Canada, where 10% of regions accounted for 64% and 61%, respectively, of the national population.

Urbanisation has increased concentration and non-urban dependency ratios

Moreover, in most countries, the concentration of the population has been increasing in recent years, partly owing to increasing urbanisation, a pattern that is reinforced by the greater availability of economic opportunities and services in urban areas. In 2003, almost half of the total OECD population (46%) was living in urban regions, and the concentration was particularly high in the Netherlands, Belgium and the United Kingdom. By the same token, the proportion of the population living in rural areas has declined. The fact that younger people tend to migrate from rural to urban areas to a greater extent than older ones has also contributed to an increasing concentration of the elderly population in rural and intermediate regions. In most countries, dependency rates (the ratio of the elderly population to the working age population) are already high in rural areas, with implications for the capacity of such regions to provide adequate heath care and other services as populations continue to age.

Regional economic performances

Part II looks at some of the factors that may explain regional variations in economic performance and GDP per capita. These include differences in labour productivity, degrees of industry specialisation, education levels among the labour force, and rates of employment and labour force participation. Although substantial, international disparities in GDP per capita are often smaller than differences among regions of the same country. In the United Kingdom, for instance, GDP per capita ranged from five times the national average in the richest region to just above half the national average in the poorest. This is by no means an isolated example; there are also significant territorial disparities in Turkey, the United States, France, Poland and Mexico. In these countries, income per head in the richest region was at least four times higher than in the poorest.

These differences are also linked to urbanisation. In 2003, GDP per head in OECD urban regions was 51% higher than the country's average; in intermediate and rural regions it was 77% and 64% of the national average, respectively. Higher GDP per capita in urban regions is a result of "agglomeration economies". The clustering of businesses and people in urban regions and large towns improves the efficiency of the local economy and leads to higher productivity.

Highly educated individuals tend to gravitate towards urban areas

In today's knowledge-based economies, a region's growth prospects depend in part on its ability to generate and use innovation. This capability, in turn, depends on skills level of the regional labour force. The proportion of the adult population with tertiary education – university-level education, from courses of short and medium duration to advanced research qualifications – is a common proxy for a region's skills level. Regional variations in educational levels are considerable. In France, Australia, the United Kingdom and Canada differences in tertiary educational attainments between the best and worst performing regions exceeded 30 percentage points. Differences were also considerable (between 20 and 30 percentage points) in New Zealand, Japan, the United States, Mexico, Hungary, Norway, Korea, Poland, Spain and Denmark. Here again, urban regions tend to fare better than intermediate or rural ones: on average, 57% of the OECD adult population with a tertiary education lives in urban regions, 19% in intermediate regions and 24% in rural ones. The concentration in urban regions is often the result of migration away from rural areas. The existence of significant differentials in the return to education between rural and urban areas is a major incentive for individuals with advanced education to migrate to urban regions.

Significant disparities in unemployment rates

Differences in regional performance also reflect the extent to which the regional economy is able to utilise available labour. Unemployment rates and labour force participation rates provide useful indicators of this ability. Unemployment rates vary significantly among regions, and, in many countries, regional disparities have persisted for long periods of time. Such persistent disparities should encourage individuals to move from regions with high unemployment to regions with low unemployment. Mobility is not without cost, however, and even if in the long run the return to a move to another region would exceed the costs, mobility may be restrained by imperfect capital markets, risk aversion or social ties. Wage inflexibility is another potential cause of regional disparities in unemployment rates. If wages are set at the national level, regional differences in productivity should in theory result in higher unemployment rates in regions with low productivity. In fact, the evidence is mixed, although in 17 of the 25 OECD countries for which data were available, there was a negative correlation between unemployment rates and productivity levels, suggesting that wage inflexibility may indeed be a cause of high unemployment in areas with low productivity.

The main drivers of regional growth

Part II is followed by an analysis of the key drivers of economic growth within regions, which highlights the different roles played by national and regional factors, economic policies and the existence of natural resources. Growth in regional GDP can be regarded as the joint result of several factors. First, regional performance is significantly affected by country-specific factors, such as national policies and the business cycle. Second, it depends on region-specific factors, such as demographic trends and natural resources. Finally, regional performance depends on regional policies, *i.e.* on the region's ability to increase productivity, change industry specialisation to seize new market opportunities, increase the efficiency of the local labour market and invest in skills and innovation. The performance of OECD regions in 1998-2003 suggests that region-specific factors play a significant role in producing above-average rates of economic growth, and that the reverse is also true, *i.e.* that regional factors can significantly undermine growth.

Quality of life

Of course, the relative merits of different regions depend not only on macroeconomic indicators such as growth, income and employment opportunities, but also on a range of other factors that contribute to the quality of life. Part III examines regional patterns in a range of such quality of life indicators, including travel times, education, crime rates, home ownership and the environment. This list excludes health, which is such an important and complex issue that it deserves separate treatment in Part IV.

Travel times vary widely among regions. Sparsely populated countries, such as Australia, the United States and Canada, have the largest variations in travel times (about 34, 30 and 25 hours, respectively). In most European countries differences in travelling time are narrower, but Turkey and the United Kingdom are exceptions. Not surprisingly, accessibility tends to be lower in rural regions. On average, travel times are more than 3.5 hours from rural regions, about 2 hours from intermediate areas, and just 37 minutes from urban regions.

Skill levels vary considerably

A highly educated labour force is a major factor in regional competitiveness, and enrolment rates in tertiary level education are a commonly used yardstick of skill levels.

These rates vary widely from region to region, but Korea stands out as having not only the highest national average enrolment rate, but also the region with the highest enrolment rate of all OECD regions. Moreover, Korea's lowest regional enrolment rate is above the highest regional rate in several OECD countries, suggesting that high levels of education have been a major factor in Korea's economic development. Safety is also an important factor in the relative attractiveness of regions, and regional statistics suggest that crime rates vary widely across the regions of a given country. However, crime statistics are difficult to compare internationally, as they are affected by how crimes are defined in national legislation and by the statistical criteria used in recording offences. In addition, the propensity to report offences varies greatly, not only among countries, but also among regions in the same country. That said, the regional data suggest that, perhaps unsurprisingly, crimes against property are most prevalent in urban areas.

Health indicators

Part IV examines a range of health indicators from a regional perspective, including mortality rates, premature mortality, the incidence of cancer, smoking and obesity, and health resources (numbers of doctors, nurses and hospital beds; access to medical technologies). One striking finding is that, in the majority of OECD countries, the male population in rural regions has the highest age-adjusted mortality rates. For females, with lower overall mortality rates than males, the pattern of adjusted mortality rates across types of region is not a clear one. Internationally, overall mortality rates were highest in eastern Europe, where smoking, obesity and alcohol consumption are quite prevalent.

Symbols and abbreviations

OECD (25) average	Unweighted average of 25 OECD countries.
OECD (25) total	Sum over all regions of 25 OECD countries.
OECD (25)	Range of variation over all regions of 25 OECD countries.
TL2	Territorial Level 2.
TL3	Territorial Level 3
NOG	Non Official Grid
*	Differences in the definition of data or regions. Please check the "Sources and Methodology" section.
PU	Predominantly Urban
IN	Intermediate
PR	Predominantly Rural
PPP	Purchasing Power Parity
USD	United States Dollar

I. REGIONS AS ACTORS OF NATIONAL GROWTH

1. GEOGRAPHIC CONCENTRATION OF POPULATION

2. GEOGRAPHIC CONCENTRATION OF THE ELDERLY POPULATION

3. GEOGRAPHIC CONCENTRATION OF GDP

4. REGIONAL CONTRIBUTIONS TO GROWTH IN NATIONAL GDP

5. GEOGRAPHIC CONCENTRATION OF INDUSTRIES

6. REGIONAL CONTRIBUTIONS TO CHANGES IN EMPLOYMENT

7. GEOGRAPHIC CONCENTRATION OF PATENTS

Population is unevenly distributed among regions within OECD member countries. In 2003, approximately 40% of the OECD population was located in just 10% of regions (Figure 1.1). The concentration was greatest in Australia and Canada, where 10% of regions accounted for 64% and 61%, respectively, of the national population. Iceland (50%), the United States (49%) and Mexico (47%) followed with around half of their population living in 10% of regions. In contrast, the territorial distribution of the population was more balanced in the Slovak Republic (12%), the Czech Republic and Belgium (17%) and Denmark (18%).

During 1998-2003, concentration increased by approximately half a percentage point (0.6) across all OECD regions. It increased most significantly in Turkey (by 1.8 percentage points), New Zealand and Canada (1.6) and Iceland (1.3), and decreased the most in Ireland (–0.7) and Hungary (–0.4).

Concentration is rising...

The geographic concentration index compares the geographic distribution of population to the area of all regions, not just the top 10%. According to this statistic (Figure 1.2), Canada (82), Australia (81) and Iceland (67) had the highest concentration in 2003. In contrast, population was more evenly distributed in the Slovak Republic (12), the Czech Republic (20), Hungary (21), Belgium (23), the Netherlands and Poland (25). During 1998-2003, concentration decreased in only seven countries and increased particularly sharply in Iceland (1.7), Korea (1.3), New Zealand and Turkey (1.1).

... and urbanisation has accelerated the trend

The geographic distribution of a country's population is determined by factors such as climatic and environmental conditions. These tend to discourage human settlement in some areas and favour concentration around a few urban centres. This pattern is reinforced by the increased availability in urban areas of economic opportunities and services. In 2003, almost half of the total OECD population (46%) lived in urban regions (Figure 1.3). Concentration in urban regions was particularly high in the Netherlands (85%), Belgium (83%) and the United Kingdom (70%).

Intermediate regions also attract a considerable share of the OECD population (31%), particularly in the Czech Republic (84%), the Slovak Republic and Iceland (63%), New Zealand (57%), Spain (52%) and Switzerland (50%). Predominantly rural regions account for a smaller, but still significant, proportion of the OECD population (23%). In 2003, the share (Figure 1.4) was particularly significant in Ireland (72%) and Finland (62%).

Rural populations are diminishing

During 1998-2003, the share of population living in urban regions increased by over 1 percentage point in New Zealand, Canada, Turkey and Finland, while it decreased by no less than 1 percentage point in Korea and Hungary. The share of population in intermediate regions increased by more than 1 percentage point in Korea, Iceland and Hungary and decreased by more than 1 percentage point only in New Zealand. Finally, the share of population living in rural regions increased only in Ireland, Hungary and the United Kingdom.

Definition

Total population is the number of inhabitants of a given region. Population can be either the average annual population or the population at a specific date during the year considered. The average population during a calendar year is generally calculated as the arithmetic mean of the population on the 1st of January of two consecutive years (it is also referred to as the mean population).

1.1. In 17 OECD countries more than one-third of the national population was concentrated in only 10% of regions in 2003

Per cent of national population who live in the 10% of regions with the highest number of people (TL3)

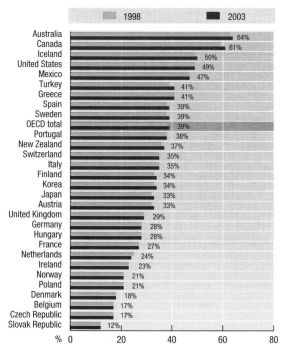

1.2. Canada, Australia and Iceland display the highest geographic concentration of population

Index of geographic concentration of population (TL3)

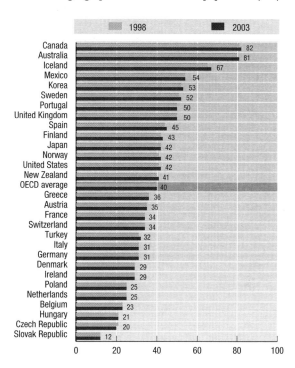

1.3. Between 1998 and 2003, the share of population living in urban regions increased in 18 out of 30 OECD countries

Distribution of the national population into predominantly urban regions (TL3)

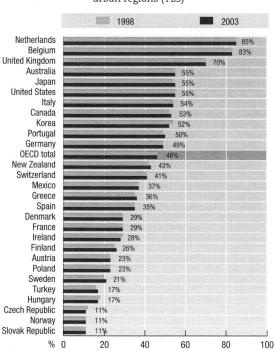

1.4. Only Ireland experienced a significant increase in the share of the population living in rural areas between 1998 and 2003

Distribution of the national population into predominantly rural regions (TL3)

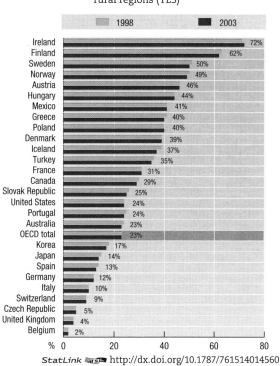

StatLink http://dx.doi.org/10.1787/761514014560

1.5. Regional population: Asia and Oceania

2003

- ■ Higher than 3 000 000
- ■ Between 1 500 000 and 3 000 000
- ■ Between 500 000 and 1 500 000
- ■ Between 200 000 and 500 000
- ■ Between 50 000 and 200 000
- □ Lower than 50 000

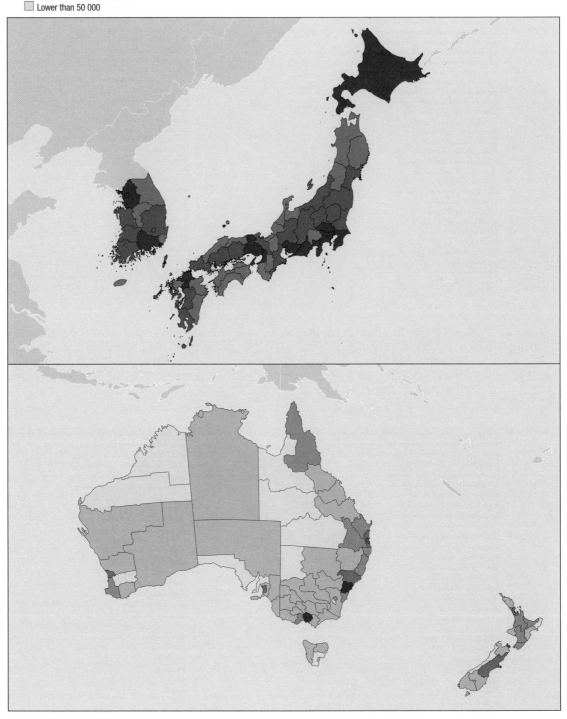

StatLink http://dx.doi.org/10.1787/318785005507

1.6. Regional population: Europe
2003

- Higher than 3 000 000
- Between 1 500 000 and 3 000 000
- Between 500 000 and 1 500 000
- Between 200 000 and 500 000
- Between 50 000 and 200 000
- Lower than 50 000

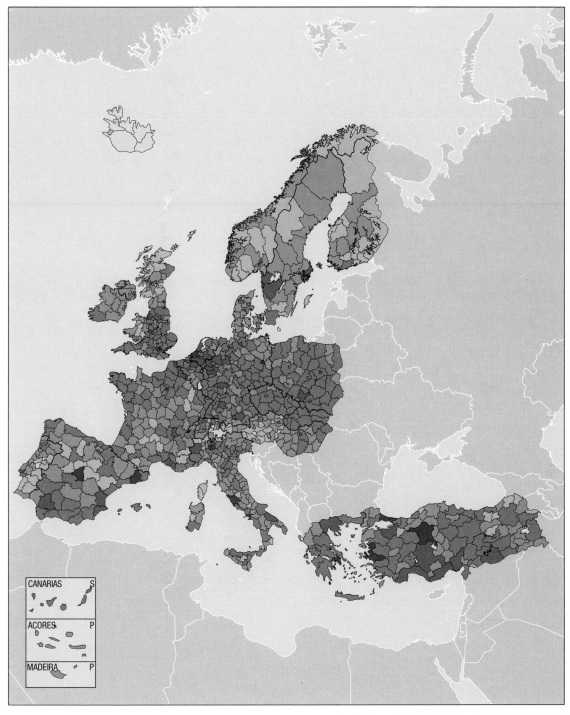

StatLink ⬛🔗 http://dx.doi.org/10.1787/318785005507

1.7. **Regional population: North America**

2003

- ■ Higher than 3 000 000
- ■ Between 1 500 000 and 3 000 000
- ■ Between 500 000 and 1 500 000
- ■ Between 200 000 and 500 000
- ■ Between 50 000 and 200 000
- □ Lower than 50 000

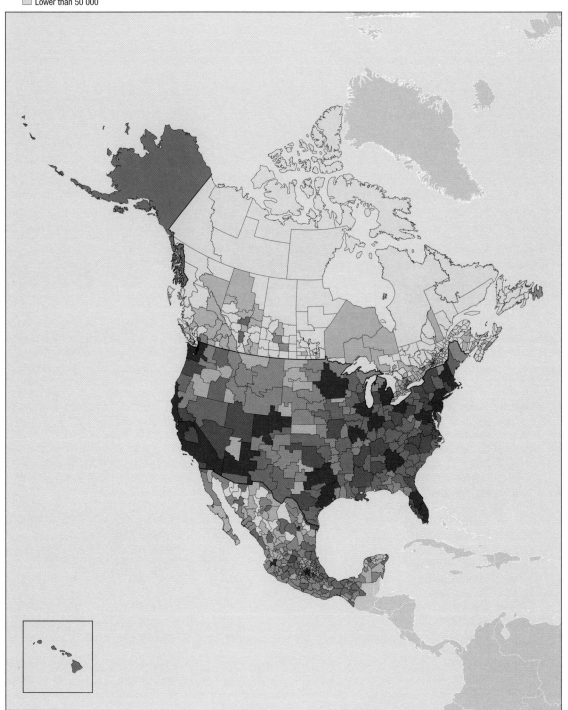

StatLink ⬛🖳 http://dx.doi.org/10.1787/318785005507

OECD REGIONS AT A GLANCE 2007 – ISBN 978-92-64-00987-5 – © OECD 2007

Large urban agglomerations: how much can they grow?

In OECD countries the population tends to concentrate in urban regions. In 2003, almost half of the total OECD population (46%) lived in urban regions. This concentration is mainly due to the benefits of "agglomeration economies". People want to live where firms – and therefore job opportunities – are concentrated. For their part, firms want to locate where demand – and therefore population – is large. Thus, the presence of firms and workers in an urban region will attract firms and more workers from other regions, thus increasing concentration.

This cycle is likely to continue up to a certain threshold, beyond which "diseconomies of agglomeration" tend to arise. When the concentration of people and firms in the same place is too great, increased pollution, traffic congestion, real estate prices and social tensions generate costs that eventually exceed the initial benefits from agglomeration.

In 2003, one-third of the OECD population lived in large urban agglomerations, i.e. urban regions with more than 1.5 millions inhabitants. The importance of urban agglomeration, however, varies significantly among countries. In the Netherlands, two-thirds of the national population lived in highly populated urban regions, while the share in Japan, the United States, Australia and Korea was approximately one half of the total (Figure 1.8). In contrast, there were no urban regions in 2003 with more than 1.5 million inhabitants in the Czech Republic, Denmark, Finland, Iceland, Ireland, New Zealand, Norway, the Slovak Republic and Switzerland.

With 22 million inhabitants, the region of New York has the largest population among all OECD urban regions, accounting for about 8% of the total population of the United States (Figure 1.9). The highest concentration of population in one urban region occurs in Greece, where more than one-third of the total population (36%) lives in the urban region of Attiki (Athens).

1.8. About half of the population of the Netherlands, Japan, the United States, Australia and Korea lives in large urban regions

Per cent of national population living in urban regions larger than 1.5 million inhabitants, 2003 (TL3)

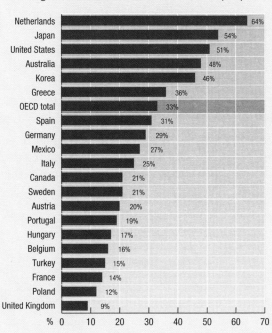

1.9. In six countries more than one-fifth of the population was concentrated in one large urban region in 2003

Per cent of national population living in the largest urban region larger than 1.5 million inhabitants, 2003 (TL3)

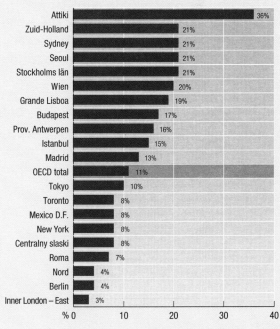

StatLink http://dx.doi.org/10.1787/761514014560

Over the last 30 years the elderly population (those aged 65 years and over) has increased dramatically in all OECD countries. In 2003, the elderly population in OECD countries represented 14% on average (Figure 2.1).

The burden of ageing is unevenly spread

As elderly people tend to concentrate in a few areas in each country, a small number of regions will face most of the social and economic challenges raised by an ageing population. In 2003, 35% of the elderly population lived in only 10% of OECD regions (Figure 2.2). The percentage was much higher in Australia (61%), Canada (58%) and Iceland (50%), where 10% of regions accounted for no less than half of the total elderly population. The elderly population was more evenly distributed in the Slovak Republic, the Czech Republic, Denmark, Belgium and Norway, where less than 20% of the total elderly population resided in 10% of regions.

The geographic concentration index compares the geographic distribution of the elderly population and the area of all regions, not just the top 10% (Figure 2.3). According to this index, Canada and Australia (82) were the countries with the highest concentrations of elderly people in 2003. In addition, the concentration index was significantly above the OECD average (38) in Mexico (52), Sweden (49) and the United Kingdom (47). In contrast, the concentration was lower in the Slovak Republic (14), the Czech Republic (20), Hungary (22), the Netherlands and Belgium (24), and Ireland (25). During 1998-2003 the concentration of the elderly population increased most in Japan (2), Korea, Greece, Portugal, Iceland, Spain, Turkey, and Italy (1) and decreased most in Switzerland, the Netherlands, the United Kingdom and Hungary (–1).

Dependency rates are higher in peripheral areas

The concentration of the elderly population may be a function of the total population – more population, therefore more elderly people – or it may be due to disparities in elderly dependency rates – same population but more elderly people.

A comparison of concentration indexes for the total population and the elderly population shows that in 2003, the total population was more concentrated than the elderly population in the United Kingdom, Portugal, Spain, Norway, Korea, Japan, New Zealand, Greece, France and Ireland (Figure 2.4). Dependency rates tend to be higher where the population is less concentrated, i.e. in "peripheral" regions.

Only in Poland was the elderly population more concentrated than the total population. This implies that Poland's dependency rate tends to be higher in areas where the population is more concentrated, generally urban regions.

Definition

The elderly population is the number of inhabitants over (and including) 65 years of age, with population considered either as the average population in a given year, or the population at a specific date during the year. The elderly dependency rate is defined as the ratio of the population aged 65 years and above to the working age (15-64) population.

2.1. The percentage of elderly people varies significantly among OECD countries

Population 65 years and over as a per cent of total population

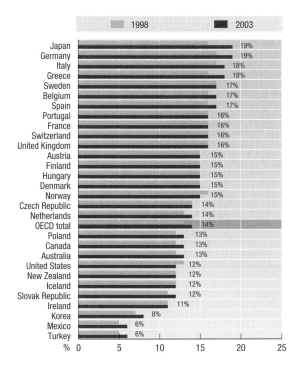

2.2. 35% of the total elderly population lives in only 10% of regions

Per cent of national elderly population who live in the top 10% of regions with the highest number of elderly people (TL3)

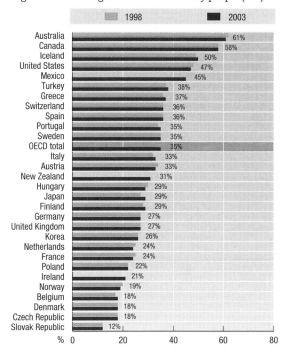

2.3. Canada and Australia were the countries with the highest concentration of elderly population in 2003

Index of geographic concentration of elderly population (TL3)

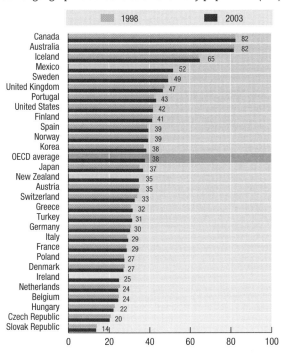

2.4. The elderly population tends to be less concentrated than total population

Concentration index, 2003 (TL3)

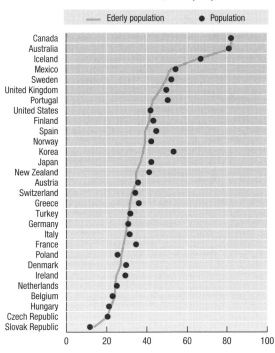

StatLink http://dx.doi.org/10.1787/133340106836

2.5. Regional elderly population: Asia and Oceania
Elderly dependency rate 2003

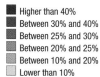

■ Higher than 40%
■ Between 30% and 40%
■ Between 25% and 30%
■ Between 20% and 25%
■ Between 10% and 20%
□ Lower than 10%

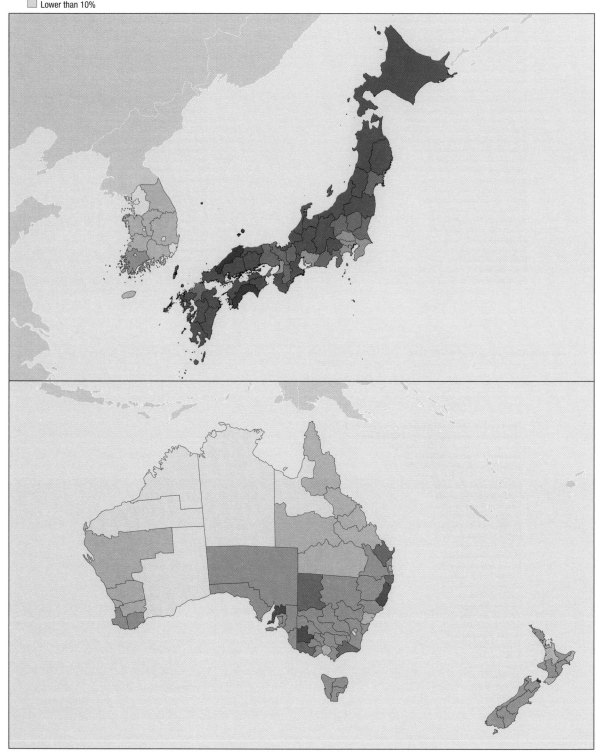

StatLink 🔗 http://dx.doi.org/10.1787/722331574356

2.6. Regional elderly population: Europe

Elderly dependency rate 2003

- ■ Higher than 40%
- ■ Between 30% and 40%
- ■ Between 25% and 30%
- ■ Between 20% and 25%
- ■ Between 10% and 20%
- □ Lower than 10%

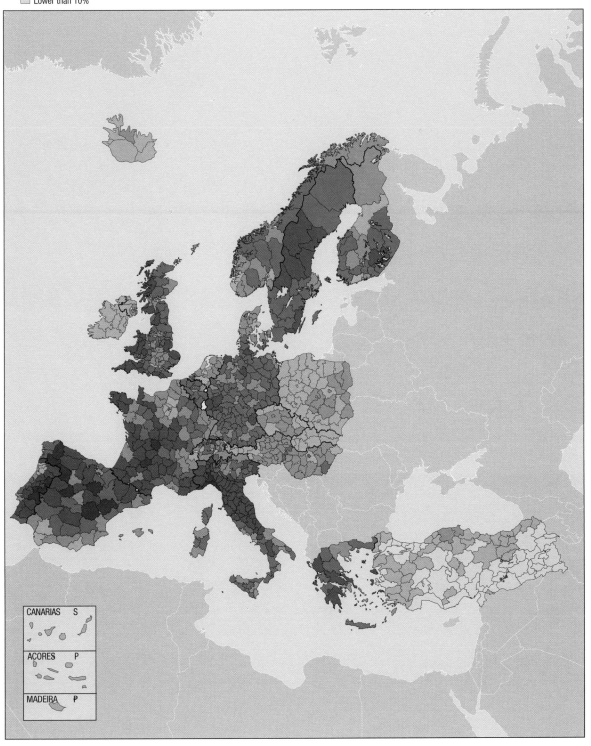

StatLink ⌗⌗ http://dx.doi.org/10.1787/722331574356

2.7. **Regional elderly population: North America**
Elderly dependency rate 2003

- ■ Higher than 40%
- ■ Between 30% and 40%
- ■ Between 25% and 30%
- ■ Between 20% and 25%
- ■ Between 10% and 20%
- □ Lower than 10%

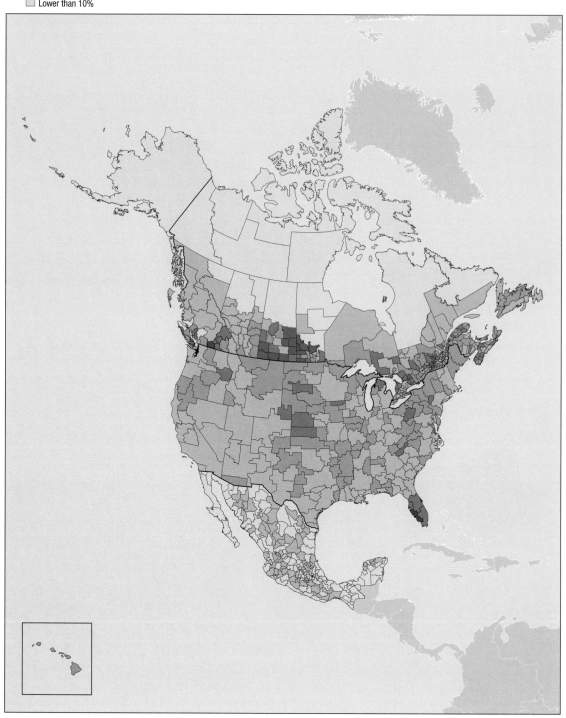

StatLink ⟐🔊 http://dx.doi.org/10.1787/722331574356

Rural and intermediate regions will face the challenges of ageing populations

Over the last 30 years the elderly population has gradually increased in all OECD countries. Some regions, however, are in a better position than others to meet the challenges of ageing societies.

The first factor is the region's capacity to generate sufficient resources to provide for the needs of elderly people (*e.g.* health care, assistance, homecare, transport). This capacity depends on the balance between those who are economically active and continue to generate wealth and those who are no longer active because of their age. The elderly dependency rate, *i.e.* the ratio of the population aged 65 years and above to the working age (15-64) population, provides a common statistical measure for this balance. To the extent that regional resources are insufficient, the provision of services for elderly people will depend on transfers from the national (*i.e.* federal) government.

In 2003, the elderly dependency rate across all OECD regions was higher in rural and intermediate regions (21%) than in urban regions (20%) (Figure 2.8). This general pattern was particularly pronounced in certain countries (Japan, Spain, Portugal, France and Italy) where the elderly dependency rate in rural regions was above 30%. The Czech Republic, Hungary and Poland were the only countries where dependency rates were highest in urban regions.

The second factor affecting a region's ability to cope with ageing is the concentration of elderly people. Regions with large elderly populations can exploit economies of scale in the provision of health care and personal services. By the same token, regions with small elderly populations may bear higher costs owing to the lack of economies of scale.

Consistent with the global trend towards urbanisation, in 2003 only a small share of the elderly population (23%) lived in rural regions. The majority lived in urban and intermediate regions (31% and 46%, respectively) (Figure 2.9). Therefore, owing to higher elderly dependency rates and lower concentrations of elderly people, the challenge of ageing is likely to be greater in rural than in intermediate and urban regions.

2.8. The elderly dependency rate is greatest in rural regions in 18 OECD countries...

Elderly dependency rate in urban, intermediate and rural regions, 2003 (TL3)

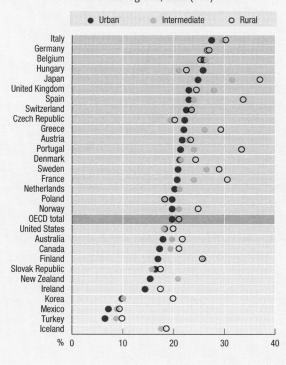

2.9. ... even though only 23% of the OECD elderly population lives in rural regions

Distribution of elderly population into urban, intermediate and rural regions, 2003 (TL3)

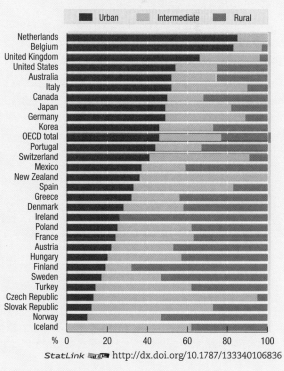

StatLink http://dx.doi.org/10.1787/133340106836

Gross domestic product (GDP) is unevenly distributed among regions within countries. In 2003, 38% of total OECD GDP was generated by only 10% of regions (Figure 3.1).

Economic output is highly concentrated

In 2003, GDP was particularly concentrated in Turkey and Portugal, where 10% of regions accounted for more than half of national GDP. In Sweden, Canada, Hungary, Spain, Austria, Finland, Greece, Mexico and Japan, the top 10% of regions were responsible for no less than 40% of national GDP. The territorial distribution of GDP was more balanced in the Slovak Republic, Belgium and Denmark, where the 10% of regions with the highest output contributed no more than one-quarter of the national total.

The geographic concentration index (Figure 3.2) compares the geographic distribution of GDP, and the area of all regions, not just the top 10%. According to this index, in 2003 Portugal (56), Sweden (55) and the United Kingdom (54) displayed the highest concentrations of GDP, followed closely by Korea (51), Australia and Finland (50). GDP was more evenly distributed in the Slovak Republic (24), the Czech Republic (27), the Netherlands (29), Belgium (33), and Denmark (35).

During 1998-2003, concentration increased most in Hungary (3), and Poland (2) and decreased most in the Czech Republic (–2), and Portugal (–1).

Predominantly urban regions appear to attract the largest share of economic activity (Figure 3.3).

In 2003, 53% of total GDP in the OECD area was produced in urban regions, which accounted for the largest share of national GDP in Belgium (88%), the Netherlands (87%), the United Kingdom (74%), Japan and Italy, (59%), Portugal (58%) and Germany (55%).

Rural areas generate the least income

Intermediate regions account for a smaller share, but still contribute 31% to overall GDP. In the Czech Republic (72%), the Slovak Republic (53%), Turkey, and Spain (47%), intermediate regions were responsible for no less than 47% of national GDP. For their part, predominantly rural regions accounted for only 15% of GDP. However, they contributed notably to national GDP in Ireland (62%), Finland (53%) and Sweden (43%).

Output is more concentrated than population

A comparison of the indices of geographic concentration for GDP and population shows that, in almost all countries, GDP is more concentrated than population (Figure 3.3). Only in Korea does the concentration of population exceed that of GDP.

These results provide evidence of significant "economies of agglomeration", i.e. that GDP per capita tends to be higher in regions where population is highly concentrated. This pattern is clearest in countries where large urban regions or capital cities (Attiki, Uusimaa, Dublin, Budapest, Grande Lisboa) have become the motors of their national economies.

Definition

GDP is the final result of the production activity of resident producer units. It is expressed at constant prices (2000) for comparisons over time, and in Purchasing Power Parity (PPP) for comparisons across countries.

OECD REGIONS AT A GLANCE 2007 – ISBN 978-92-64-00987-5 – © OECD 2007

3.1. In 11 countries more than 40% of national GDP is concentrated in 10% of regions

Per cent of national GDP in the top 10% of the regions when ranked by the GDP of regions (TL3)

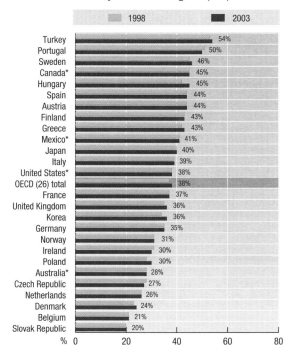

3.2. In 2003, Portugal, Sweden and the United Kingdom displayed the highest geographic concentration of GDP

Index of geographic concentration of GDP (TL3)

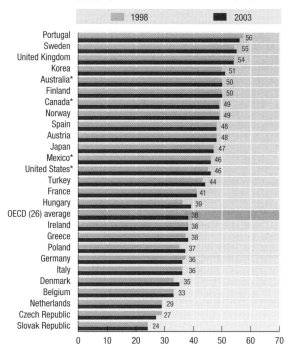

3.3. In 2003 more than half of OECD-area GDP was produced in predominantly urban regions

Distribution of the national GDP into predominantly urban, intermediate and rural regions, 2003 (TL3)

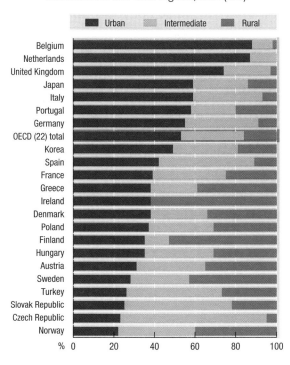

3.4. The spatial distribution of GDP does not reflect the geographic distribution of the population

Concentration index, 2003 (TL3)

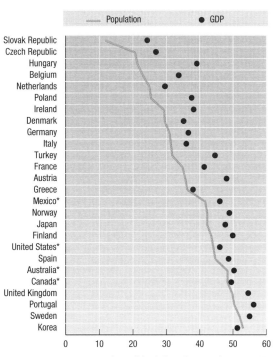

StatLink http://dx.doi.org/10.1787/825506767752

3.5. **Regional GDP: Asia and Oceania**

Millions of constant 2000 USD PPP, 2003

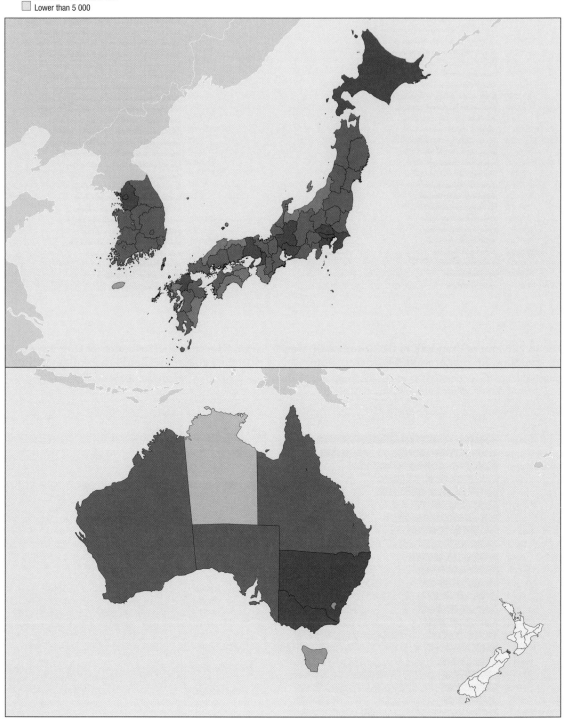

Higher than 100 000
Between 25 000 and 100 000
Between 12 000 and 25 000
Between 8 000 and 12 000
Between 5 000 and 8 000
Lower than 5 000

StatLink http://dx.doi.org/10.1787/365612755766

3.6. **Regional GDP: Europe**
Millions of constant 2000 USD PPP, 2003

- Higher than 100 000
- Between 25 000 and 100 000
- Between 12 000 and 25 000
- Between 8 000 and 12 000
- Between 5 000 and 8 000
- Lower than 5 000

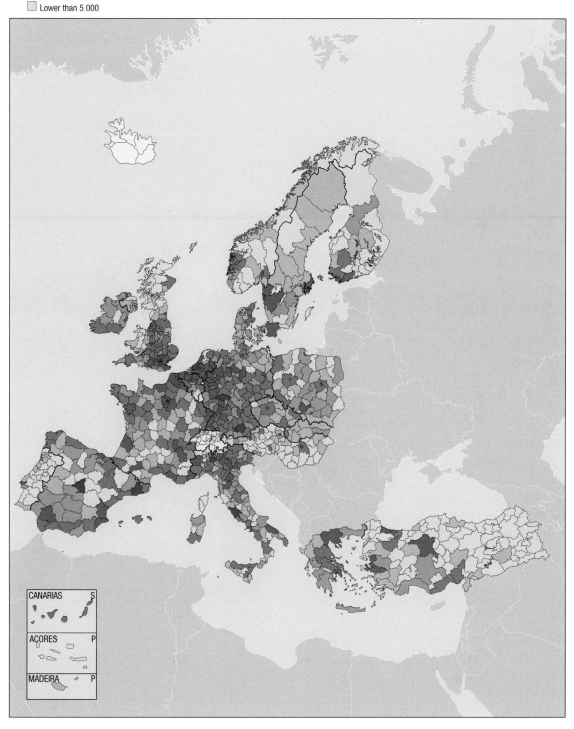

StatLink ᕫᒲᕋᒲ http://dx.doi.org/10.1787/365612755766

3.7. **Regional GDP: North America**
Millions of constant 2000 USD PPP, 2003

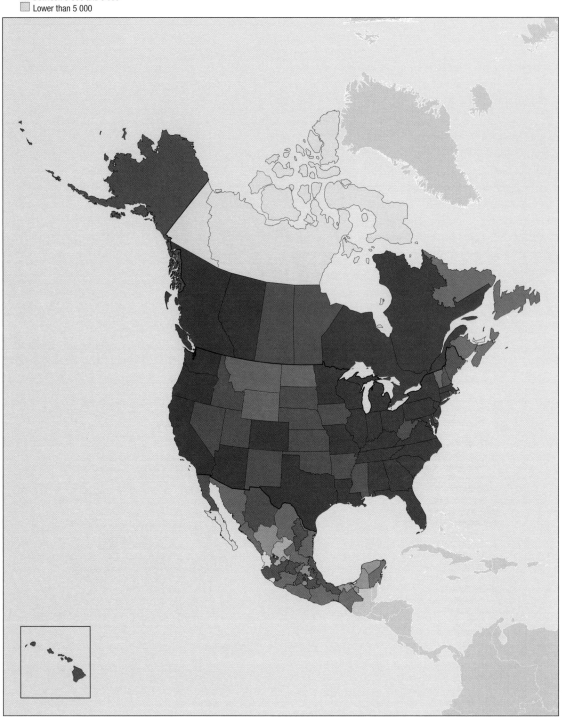

- ■ Higher than 100 000
- ■ Between 25 000 and 100 000
- ■ Between 12 000 and 25 000
- ■ Between 8 000 and 12 000
- ■ Between 5 000 and 8 000
- □ Lower than 5 000

StatLink ⟨⟩ http://dx.doi.org/10.1787/365612755766

Concentration of GDP and agglomeration economies

An interesting aspect of the geographic distribution of GDP is that it tends to concentrate in a small portion of the national territory. In Denmark, Ireland, Belgium, Norway, the Slovak Republic, Japan, Portugal and Poland, the 10% of regions with the largest share in national GDP accounted in 2003 for less than 5% of the national area (Figure 3.8). In countries where these regions represent a larger fraction of the national territory, it is still evident that a significant amount of national economic activity takes place within narrow zones or poles of development.

Urban areas and large towns in intermediate regions are prime zones or poles of development. The clustering of businesses and people in a small area improves the efficiency of the local economy and leads to the production of more output per capita. Figure 3.9 reveals that in every country the 10% of regions with the highest concentration of GDP enjoy a GDP per capita well above the national average.

Agglomeration economies are considered to be the main driving force behind the clustering of economic activity. The concept was introduced more than a century ago by Alfred Marshall who identified three sources of agglomeration. First, the advantages that large labour markets entail for firms (easier to find specialised personnel) and skilled workers (easier to find employment) alike. Second, the linkages between intermediate and final-goods producers, which allow firms to benefit from specialisation in some parts of the production process and from increased production volumes. Third, the knowledge spillovers that stem from the cross-fertilisation of ideas regarding innovation. Based on these ideas, modern economists have highlighted the role of sharing (infrastructure, risks, gains from variety, specialisation, etc.), matching (between business partners or firms and employees) and learning (knowledge creation, accumulation and diffusion) as the underlying mechanisms of agglomeration economies.

3.8. The 10% of regions with the highest concentration of GDP account for a small fraction of the national area...

Area share of the 10% regions with the highest concentration of GDP, 2003 (TL3)

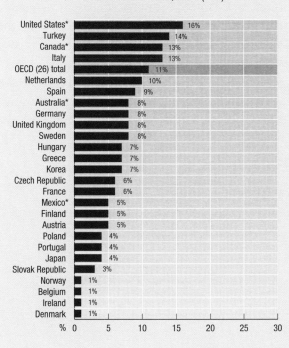

3.9. ... and their GDP per capita is well above the national average

GDP per capita (% of national GDP per capita) of the 10% of regions with the highest concentration of GDP (TL3)

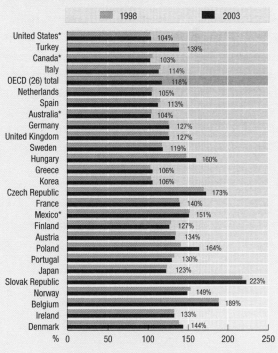

StatLink 🔗 http://dx.doi.org/10.1787/825506767752

Between 1998 and 2003, gross domestic product (GDP) in OECD countries grew at an average annual rate of 3.1% in real terms (Figure 4.1). International differences in growth rates were as large as 7.5 percentage points, ranging from 1% in Japan to 8.5% in Ireland. Although significant, international differences are rather small in comparison to differences among regions within the same country.

Differences in regional growth are largest in Turkey

During 1998-2003 the difference between the fastest and the slowest growing regions was largest in Turkey (19.7 percentage points), followed by Hungary (12.9), the United Kingdom (10.8), Canada (9.7), and Poland (9.4) (Figure 4.2). In Spain, the Czech Republic, Korea, the United States, and Mexico, regional differences were smaller but still considerable (6.2 to 8.6 percentage points). GDP growth was more even in the Slovak Republic (1.0), Denmark (2.5), Japan (2.7) and Belgium (3.3).

Regional variations are unrelated to national growth

Wide differences in regional growth rates do not seem to be associated with faster national growth. While Turkey had the largest regional variation in GDP growth, its national growth rate was among the lowest among OECD countries. For its part, Canada displayed one of the highest degrees of regional variation in GDP growth, but its national growth was one of the highest among OECD countries.

Large differences in regional growth rates imply that national performance is driven by the dynamism of a limited number of regions. On average, 10% of regions accounted for 43% of the total increase in GDP in OECD countries between 1998 and 2003 (Figure 4.3). The regional contribution was more pronounced in certain countries, where 10% of regions accounted for more than half of national GDP growth. This was the case in Turkey (88%), Hungary (56%), Sweden (55%), Norway (54%), Finland and Portugal (52%). Elsewhere, the 10% of regions that made the largest contribution to national GDP growth played a less pronounced but still significant role, ranging from 25% (Belgium and Australia) to 51% (Greece). Only the Slovak Republic (19%) and the Netherlands (23%) displayed a more balanced regional contribution to national GDP growth.

Declines in GDP are highly correlated with regional performance

Decreases in regional GDP are rare – declines were observed in only ten countries and tended to be localised. On average, 91% of decreases in GDP in the OECD area between 1998 and 2003 (Figure 4.4) were attributable to 10% of regions. In the Czech Republic, France, Germany, Hungary, Italy, Japan, Poland and the United Kingdom, the overall decrease in GDP was due to one or two regions.

These trends show that national GDP growth is fuelled by the performance of a few regions. Growth at the national level is often rooted in the specific assets of regions.

Definition

The gross domestic product (GDP) growth rate refers to the annual growth rate over the period 1998-2003 deflated at constant (2000) prices. GDP is the final result of the production activity of resident producer units.

4.1. From 1998 to 2003, GDP growth varied significantly among OECD countries...

Average annual growth rate in national GDP, 1998-2003

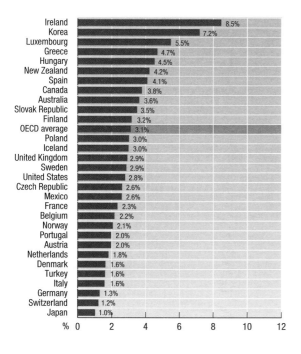

4.2. ... but the variation in GDP growth rates was even wider among regions within countries

Range in annualised GDP growth across sub-national regions, 1998-2003 (TL3)

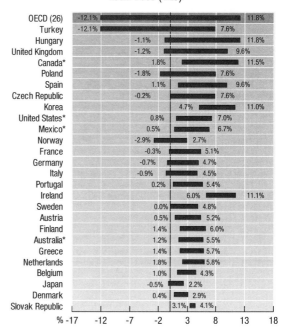

4.3. On average 10% of regions accounted for 43% of the overall increase in GDP

Proportion of increase in national GDP due to 10% of regions with the largest increase, 1998-2003 (TL3)

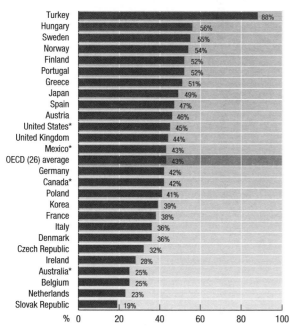

4.4. 91% of the overall decline in GDP took place in just 10% of regions

Proportion of decline in national GDP due to 10% of regions with the largest decline, 1998-2003 (TL3)

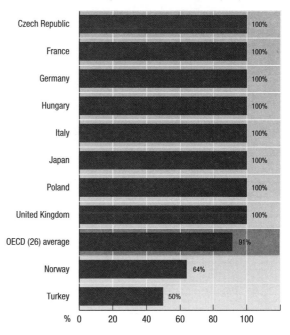

StatLink 🔗 http://dx.doi.org/10.1787/248868077163

4.5. **Regional GDP growth: Asia and Oceania**
Average annual growth rate in constant 2000 GDP, 1998-2003

- Higher than 5.5%
- Between 3% and 5.5%
- Between 2% and 3%
- Between 1.5% and 2%
- Between 0.5% and 1.5%
- Lower than 0.5%

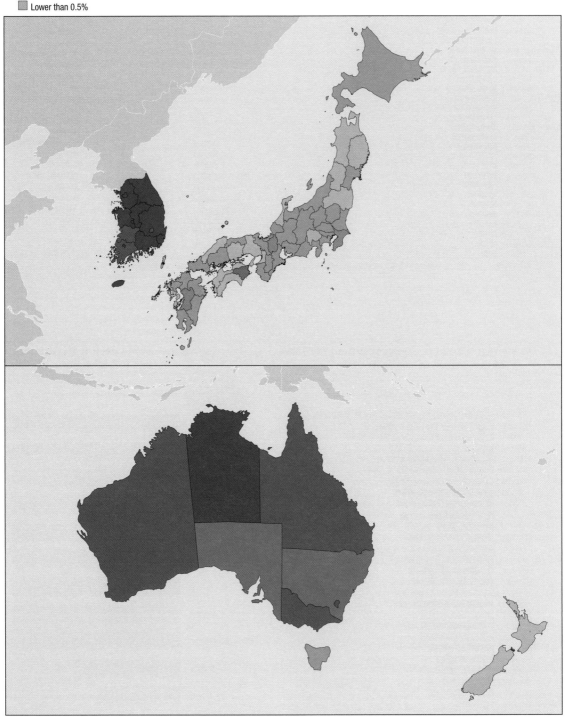

StatLink ᗰᑎᔕᒪ http://dx.doi.org/10.1787/078845266850

4.6. Regional GDP growth: Europe

Average annual growth rate in constant 2000 GDP, 1998-2003

- Higher than 5.5%
- Between 3% and 5.5%
- Between 2% and 3%
- Between 1.5% and 2%
- Between 0.5% and 1.5%
- Lower than 0.5%

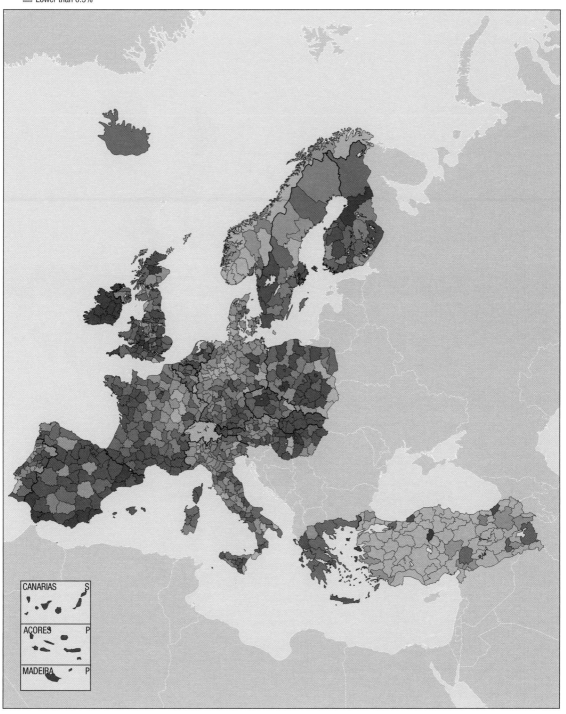

StatLink ⬛ᵐˢ▙ http://dx.doi.org/10.1787/078845266850

4.7. Regional GDP growth: North America
Average annual growth rate in constant 2000 GDP, 1998-2003

- ■ Higher than 5.5%
- ■ Between 3% and 5.5%
- ■ Between 2% and 3%
- ■ Between 1.5% and 2%
- ■ Between 0.5% and 1.5%
- ■ Lower than 0.5%

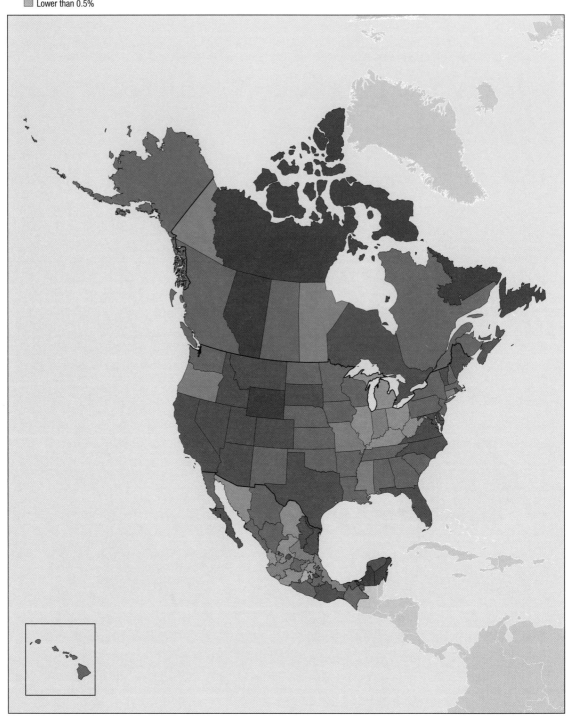

StatLink http://dx.doi.org/10.1787/078845266850

OECD REGIONS AT A GLANCE 2007 – ISBN 978-92-64-00987-5 – © OECD 2007

Is concentration good for growth?

Between 1998 and 2003, GDP grew faster, on average, in predominantly urban (2.4%) and intermediate regions (2.1%) than in rural regions (1.7%) (Figure 4.8).

Not only do urban and intermediate regions concentrate a very large share of national GDP (Chapter 3), they also tend grow faster than rural regions. This pattern of high concentration and fast growth seem to be driven by the benefits stemming from "economies of agglomeration".

First, firms benefit from lower transport costs when they are close to other firms and people (local demand). Second, information flows locally more easily than over greater distances so that firms have more opportunities to learn from each other and imitate more efficient methods of production. Third, the employment opportunities created by a concentration of firms attract skilled workers, while the greater availability of specialised skills increases the productivity of firms. Finally, more intensive use of infrastructure by a larger number of firms increases the overall productivity of the regional economic system. As a result, GDP tends to grow faster in urban and intermediate regions, where economic activity and the workforce are more concentrated, than in rural ones.

Urban regions displayed the highest average GDP growth rates in 8 out of 22 OECD countries (Figure 4.8), while intermediate regions performed best in 10 out of 22. Predominantly rural regions were the fast growing areas only in the Czech Republic, Germany, Ireland and the Slovak Republic.

Although GDP tends to grow faster in urban and intermediate regions, rural regions are not necessarily trapped in a low-growth path. In fact in 9 out of 22 OECD countries, the region with the highest GDP growth was a rural region (Figure 4.9).

4.8. **GDP grew faster during 1998-2003 in urban and intermediate regions than in rural ones...**

GDP growth rate averaged by regional type, 1998-2003 (TL3)

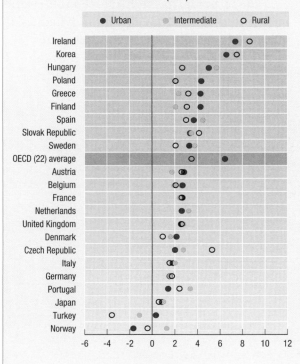

4.9. **... although in 9 countries the highest GDP growth was recorded in a rural region**

Highest annualised growth rate by regional type, 1998-2003 (TL3)

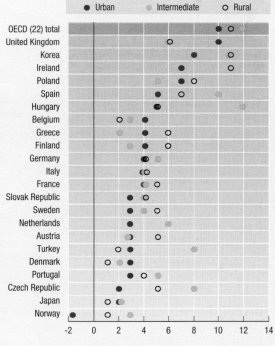

StatLink ⇌ http://dx.doi.org/10.1787/248868077163

Financial services are the most concentrated industry

Industries are unevenly distributed across OECD countries. According to the geographic concentration index, in 2003 the industry in which employment was, on average, most concentrated in OECD countries (Figure 5.1) was financial intermediation (45), followed by real estate, renting and business activities (43) and transport, storage and communication (37). In contrast, agriculture, hunting, forestry and fishing (20) and construction (31) displayed the lowest average concentration.

Agricultural concentration varies widely

These aggregate figures hide significant differences in industry concentration among regions within countries. Agriculture, hunting, forestry and fishing was most concentrated in Mexico, Sweden, the United States and Australia where the geographic concentration index stood at 46, 44, 42, and 38, respectively, in 2003 (Figure 5.2). In Finland (27), Belgium and Korea (26), Portugal and Canada (22), and Italy and Poland (21), this industry was more concentrated than the OECD average (20). It was more evenly distributed in Denmark, Greece (3), Ireland (9), Hungary and the Czech Republic (10).

During the last 30 years, the aggregate size of the manufacturing sector has gradually declined; nevertheless, it still employs 16% of the OECD workforce. According to the concentration index, in 2003 concentration in this sector was greatest (Figure 5.3) in Sweden (54), Australia (51), Iceland (49), Finland (47), the United States and Korea (46), Spain (45) and Mexico (44), while the lowest values were recorded in Denmark and the Czech Republic (15), the Slovak Republic (17), Poland and the Netherlands (20), Ireland (22) and Hungary (23).

Structural changes have had an impact

The structural change from agriculture and manufacturing towards services has affected regions diversely, particularly in financial intermediation, the sector with the highest concentration index on average in OECD countries. The sector was very concentrated in Mexico (80), Iceland (76) and Sweden (64) followed by Greece and Australia (58), Portugal (56) and Finland (55) (Figure 5.4). The concentration was above the OECD average (45) in Belgium (48), Denmark (47) and Spain (46). Only in Poland (26), Italy (27), Canada (29), Germany (31), and Ireland, the Netherlands and Switzerland (33) was the regional pattern of employment in this sector more balanced.

These patterns highlight considerable differences in the concentration dynamics of industries, and indicate that regional factors tend to play a dominant role in determining the national concentration of different industries.

Definition

Industries are defined according to the International Standard Industrial Classification (ISIC) Rev. 3.1 (one digit). Industry size is defined by the total number of people employed in that industry.

5.1. Financial intermediation is the most concentrated industry among OECD countries

Concentration index averaged across OECD countries for each industry,* 2003 (TL2)

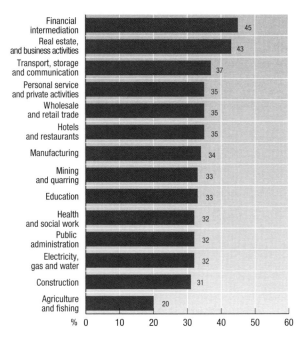

Industry	%
Financial intermediation	45
Real estate, and business activities	43
Transport, storage and communication	37
Personal service and private activities	35
Wholesale and retail trade	35
Hotels and restaurants	35
Manufacturing	34
Mining and quarring	33
Education	33
Health and social work	32
Public administration	32
Electricity, gas and water	32
Construction	31
Agriculture and fishing	20

5.2. In 2003, agriculture, hunting, forestry and fishing was most concentrated in Mexico, Sweden and the United States

Geographic concentration index agriculture, hunting and forestry, and fishing sector, 2003 (TL2)

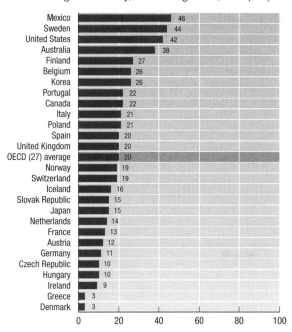

Mexico	46
Sweden	44
United States	42
Australia	38
Finland	27
Belgium	26
Korea	26
Portugal	22
Canada	22
Italy	21
Poland	21
Spain	20
United Kingdom	20
OECD (27) average	20
Norway	19
Switzerland	19
Iceland	16
Slovak Republic	15
Japan	15
Netherlands	14
France	13
Austria	12
Germany	11
Czech Republic	10
Hungary	10
Ireland	9
Greece	3
Denmark	3

5.3. The manufacturing sector is least concentrated in the Czech Republic, Denmark and the Slovak Republic

Geographic concentration index manufacturing sector, 2003 (TL2)

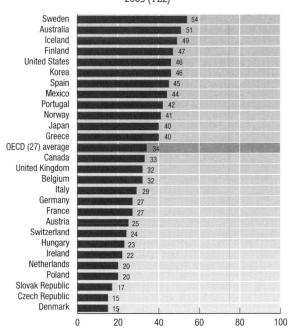

Sweden	54
Australia	51
Iceland	49
Finland	47
United States	46
Korea	46
Spain	45
Mexico	44
Portugal	42
Norway	41
Japan	40
Greece	40
OECD (27) average	34
Canada	33
United Kingdom	32
Belgium	32
Italy	29
Germany	27
France	27
Austria	25
Switzerland	24
Hungary	23
Ireland	22
Netherlands	20
Poland	20
Slovak Republic	17
Czech Republic	15
Denmark	15

5.4. Mexico and Iceland have the highest concentration in financial intermediation

Geographic concentration index financial intermediation, 2003 (TL2)

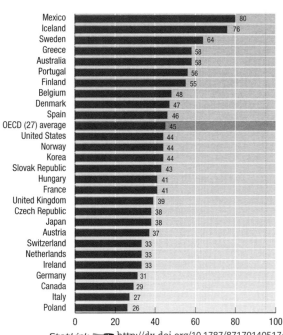

Mexico	80
Iceland	76
Sweden	64
Greece	58
Australia	58
Portugal	56
Finland	55
Belgium	48
Denmark	47
Spain	46
OECD (27) average	45
United States	44
Norway	44
Korea	44
Slovak Republic	43
Hungary	41
France	41
United Kingdom	39
Czech Republic	38
Japan	38
Austria	37
Switzerland	33
Netherlands	33
Ireland	33
Germany	31
Canada	29
Italy	27
Poland	26

StatLink ⬛ℐ⬛ http://dx.doi.org/10.1787/871701405174

5.5. **Regional employment in manufacturing: Asia and Oceania**

Total number of people employed, 2003

- Higher than 700 000
- Between 300 000 and 700 000
- Between 150 000 and 300 000
- Between 60 000 and 150 000
- Between 30 000 and 60 000
- Lower than 30 000

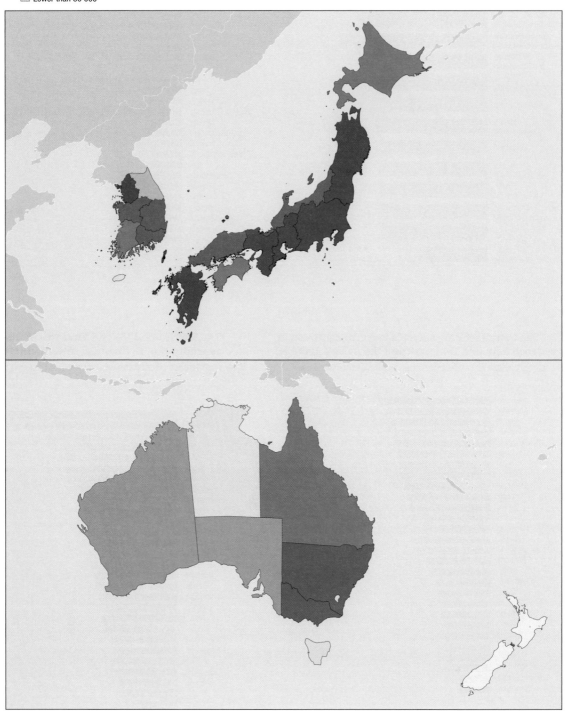

StatLink http://dx.doi.org/10.1787/615324323232

OECD REGIONS AT A GLANCE 2007 – ISBN 978-92-64-00987-5 – © OECD 2007

5.6. **Regional employment in manufacturing: Europe**

Total number of people employed, 2003

- Higher than 700 000
- Between 300 000 and 700 000
- Between 150 000 and 300 000
- Between 60 000 and 150 000
- Between 30 000 and 60 000
- Lower than 30 000

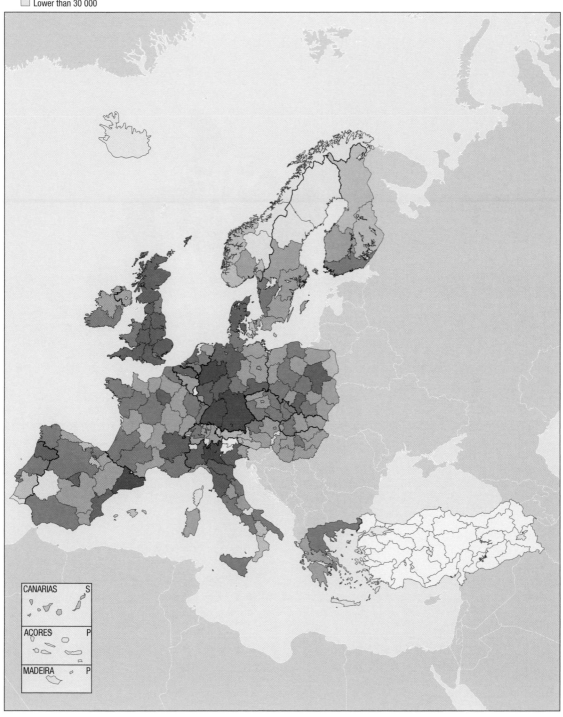

StatLink http://dx.doi.org/10.1787/615324323232

5.7. Regional employment in manufacturing: North America

Total number of people employed, 2003

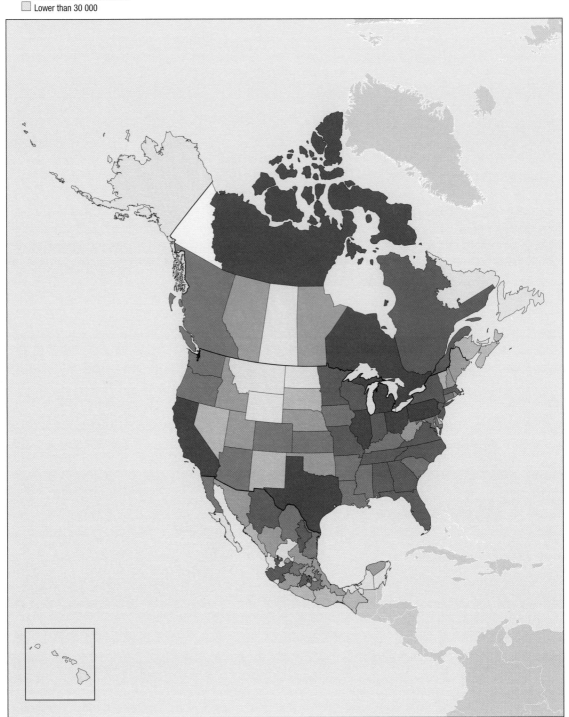

- Higher than 700 000
- Between 300 000 and 700 000
- Between 150 000 and 300 000
- Between 60 000 and 150 000
- Between 30 000 and 60 000
- Lower than 30 000

StatLink ᛗ᛫ᛢᛚ http://dx.doi.org/10.1787/615324323232

The concentration index varies significantly among industries and countries

The geographic concentration index varies significantly among OECD countries and among industries (Table 5.8). Agriculture, hunting, forestry and fishing (a + b) appears to be the industry that is most evenly distributed among regions; in 15 out of 27 OECD countries, it had the lowest concentration index, as well as the lowest OECD average (20). This result is partly driven by the larger regional grid (TL2) and by the small share of agricultural employment (less than 3%).

On average, mining and quarrying (c) also displays a balanced regional pattern; in 6 OECD countries it recorded the lowest index of concentration. Finally, hotels and restaurants (h) was the least concentrated industry in the United States (41); public administration, defence and compulsory social security (l) in Poland (17); education (m) in Italy (19), and health and social work (n) in the Slovak Republic (10).

In contrast, financial intermediation (j) appears to be the industry with the highest concentration index; it recorded the highest value in 12 out of 27 OECD countries, as well as the highest OECD average (45). This sector tends to concentrate in large cities and highly urbanised areas.

Real estate, renting and business activities (k), and mining and quarrying (c) are also very concentrated; they recorded the highest concentration index in 7 and in 6 of 27 OECD countries, respectively. Finally, manufacturing (d) was the most concentrated industry in Italy (29), and education (m) in the United States (50).

The countries with the highest concentration (average value) among all industries in 2003 were Iceland (60), Sweden (52), Mexico (48), Australia (46), the United States and Finland (44), while the countries with the lowest concentration were the Slovak Republic (21), Ireland (22), Italy (23) the Netherlands and Poland (25). The range between the industry with the lowest concentration index and the highest was largest in Iceland (62), Greece (55), the Czech Republic and Poland (51). It was lowest in the United States (9), Italy (11), Canada (12), the Netherlands (19) and Belgium (25).

5.8. **Concentration index by industry and by country**
Standard Industrial Classification (ISIC) Rev. 3.1

Country	a + b	c	d	e	f	g	h	i	j	k	l	m	n	o + p	Average	Range
Australia	38	20	51	50	47	48	48	49	58	50	45	47	47	47	**46**	**38**
Austria	12	16	25	28	24	26	26	28	37	41	28	27	30	32	**27**	**29**
Belgium	26	23	32	23	25	29	31	30	48	33	26	24	25	26	**29**	**25**
Canada	22	34	33	28	30	29	28	28	29	31	27	27	27	29	**29**	**12**
Czech Republic	10	61	15	25	18	21	24	24	38	33	22	18	21	28	**26**	**51**
Denmark	3	9	15	28	23	29	32	34	47	43	36	28	28	.	**27**	**44**
Finland	27	24	47	47	44	49	46	48	55	53	43	43	41	45	**44**	**31**
France	13	29	27	33	25	29	37	36	41	40	29	28	25	31	**30**	**28**
Germany	11	52	27	28	19	.	.	28	31	31	21	.	.	.	**28**	**40**
Greece	3	19	40	32	37	41	33	49	58	52	44	35	42	48	**38**	**55**
Hungary	10	38	23	17	29	32	26	32	41	49	24	22	24	38	**29**	**39**
Iceland	16	.	49	57	57	71	66	70	76	79	49	66	69	.	**60**	**62**
Ireland	9	6	22	24	19	23	25	28	33	33	22	23	21	23	**22**	**27**
Italy	21	21	29	22	20	20	26	24	27	25	21	18.6	18.8	25	**23**	**11**
Japan	15	20	40	30	28	36	39	39	38	45	.	45	33	.	**34**	**30**
Korea	26	21	46	30	40	43	39	44	44	55	33	37	39	.	**38**	**34**
Mexico	46	42	44	43	40	44	42	48	80	52	.	52	44	.	**48**	**40**
Netherlands	14	24	20	23	22	25	26	31	33	30	26	22	22	.	**25**	**19**
Norway	19	53	41	29	35	40	37	39	44	46	35	34	35	41	**38**	**34**
Poland	21	68	20	20	23	21	24	21	26	27	17.09	17.12	19	26	**25**	**51**
Portugal	22	14	42	40	36	40	41	42	56	54	43	36	36	41	**39**	**42**
Slovak Republic	15	36	17	18	15	17	17	18	43	32	20	11	10	26	**21**	**33**
Spain	20	31	45	41	39	41	46	47	46	52	35	39	39	45	**40**	**31**
Sweden	44	35	54	50	51	56	54	56	64	61	51	50	49	55	**52**	**29**
Switzerland	19	64	24	20	22	24	19	26	33	29	36	23	24	22	**28**	**45**
United Kingdom	20	48	32	25	32	33	30	37	39	41	28	31	29	35	**33**	**28**
United States	42	46	46	43	42	43	41	43	44	44	42	50	44	46	**44**	**9**
OECD average	**20**	**33**	**34**	**32**	**31**	**35**	**35**	**37**	**45**	**43**	**32**	**33**	**32**	**35**	**34**	**25**

Growth in employment varies significantly among OECD countries (Figure 6.1). During 1998-2003, international differences in employment growth rates were as large as 6.2 percentage points, ranging from –2.2% in Poland to 4% in Spain.

Labour market performance varies widely

Significant international differences in employment growth hide even larger differences among regions. In Italy (15 percentage points), France and Poland (11), Portugal and the United States (10), differences in regional growth rates were no less than 10 percentage points (Figure 6.2). In Australia, the United Kingdom and Canada (9), Germany (8), Korea (7), New Zealand, Spain and Sweden (6) the differences were smaller but still significant. Only Belgium (1), Norway, Denmark, the Czech Republic, Switzerland and Greece (2) had more regular patterns of regional employment growth.

Regional patterns shape national trends

Wide differences in regional growth rates do not seem to be associated with faster national growth. For instance, regional differences in Spain (6%), which had the highest national employment growth, were comparable to those in Germany (5%), which had one of the largest decreases in national employment.

Changes in national employment, therefore, do not result from an even pattern of growth across regions, but from the balance between growth in some regions and declines in others.

Employment growth at the national level appears largely driven by a small number of regions. Over the period 1998-2003, 51% of employment growth occurred in 10% of OECD regions (Figure 6.3).

Regions can contribute substantially to employment growth

The regional contribution to national employment growth was particularly pronounced in certain countries. In Japan, 10% of regions accounted for all of national employment growth. In Iceland, the Slovak Republic, Denmark, Japan, and the Czech Republic no less than 60% of the national employment growth was spurred by a single region.

The same is true of declines in employment

The pattern is similar for decreases in employment. During 1998-2003, 44% of all OECD-area reductions were concentrated in 10% of regions (Figure 6.4). In Austria and Korea, a single region accounted for the entire reduction in national employment, while in Australia and Italy, 10% of regions accounted for the total reduction. In Portugal the United Kingdom, Greece, Switzerland, Canada and New Zealand, no less than 87% of employment decreases were due to 10% of regions.

These findings suggest that changes in national employment are largely determined by a small number of regions. Regional factors therefore tend to play an equally important role as national factors in promoting total employment growth.

Definition

The employment growth rate refers to the average annual growth rate. Employed persons are all persons who, during the reference week, worked at least one hour for pay or profit, or were temporarily absent from such work. Family workers are included.

6.1. From 1998 to 2003 employment growth varied significantly among OECD countries

Average annual growth rate in national employment, 1998-2003

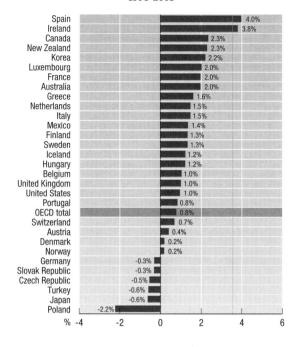

Spain	4.0%
Ireland	3.8%
Canada	2.3%
New Zealand	2.3%
Korea	2.2%
Luxembourg	2.0%
France	2.0%
Australia	2.0%
Greece	1.6%
Netherlands	1.5%
Italy	1.5%
Mexico	1.4%
Finland	1.3%
Sweden	1.3%
Iceland	1.2%
Hungary	1.2%
Belgium	1.0%
United Kingdom	1.0%
United States	1.0%
Portugal	0.8%
OECD total	0.8%
Switzerland	0.7%
Austria	0.4%
Denmark	0.2%
Norway	0.2%
Germany	-0.3%
Slovak Republic	-0.3%
Czech Republic	-0.5%
Turkey	-0.6%
Japan	-0.6%
Poland	-2.2%

6.2. Differences in employment growth among regions within countries were substantial

Range in annualised employment growth across regions, 1998-2003 (TL3)

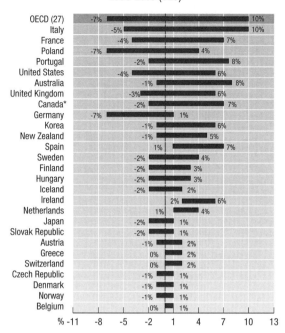

OECD (27)	-7%	10%
Italy	-5%	10%
France	-4%	7%
Poland	-7%	4%
Portugal	-2%	8%
United States	-4%	6%
Australia	-1%	8%
United Kingdom	-3%	6%
Canada*	-2%	7%
Germany	-7%	1%
Korea	-1%	6%
New Zealand	-1%	5%
Spain	1%	7%
Sweden	-2%	4%
Finland	-2%	3%
Hungary	-2%	3%
Iceland	-2%	2%
Ireland	2%	6%
Netherlands	1%	4%
Japan	-2%	1%
Slovak Republic	-2%	1%
Austria	-1%	2%
Greece	0%	2%
Switzerland	0%	2%
Czech Republic	-1%	1%
Denmark	-1%	1%
Norway	-1%	1%
Belgium	0%	1%

6.3. More than half of OECD-area employment growth during 1998-2003 occurred in 10% of regions

Proportion of increase in national employment due to 10% of regions with the largest increase, 1998-2003 (TL3)

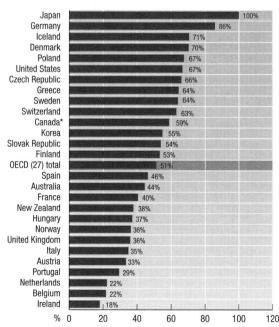

Japan	100%
Germany	86%
Iceland	71%
Denmark	70%
Poland	67%
United States	67%
Czech Republic	66%
Greece	64%
Sweden	64%
Switzerland	63%
Canada*	59%
Korea	55%
Slovak Republic	54%
Finland	53%
OECD (27) total	51%
Spain	46%
Australia	44%
France	40%
New Zealand	38%
Hungary	37%
Norway	36%
United Kingdom	36%
Italy	35%
Austria	33%
Portugal	29%
Netherlands	22%
Belgium	22%
Ireland	18%

6.4. 44% of employment reduction across the OECD occurred in only 10% of regions

Proportion of decline in national employment due to 10% of regions with the largest decline, 1998-2003 (TL3)

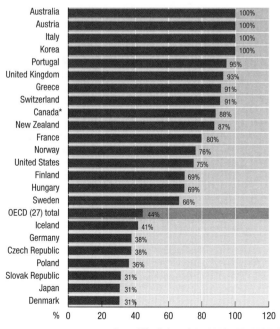

Australia	100%
Austria	100%
Italy	100%
Korea	100%
Portugal	95%
United Kingdom	93%
Greece	91%
Switzerland	91%
Canada*	88%
New Zealand	87%
France	80%
Norway	76%
United States	75%
Finland	69%
Hungary	69%
Sweden	66%
OECD (27) total	44%
Iceland	41%
Germany	38%
Czech Republic	38%
Poland	36%
Slovak Republic	31%
Japan	31%
Denmark	31%

StatLink http://dx.doi.org/10.1787/716512765568

6.5. **Regional employment growth: Asia and Oceania**

Average annual employment growth rate, 1998-2003

- ■ Higher than 3.5%
- ■ Between 1.5% and 3.5%
- ■ Between 0.5% and 1.5%
- ■ Between 0% and 0.5%
- ■ Between -1% and 0%
- □ Lower than -1%

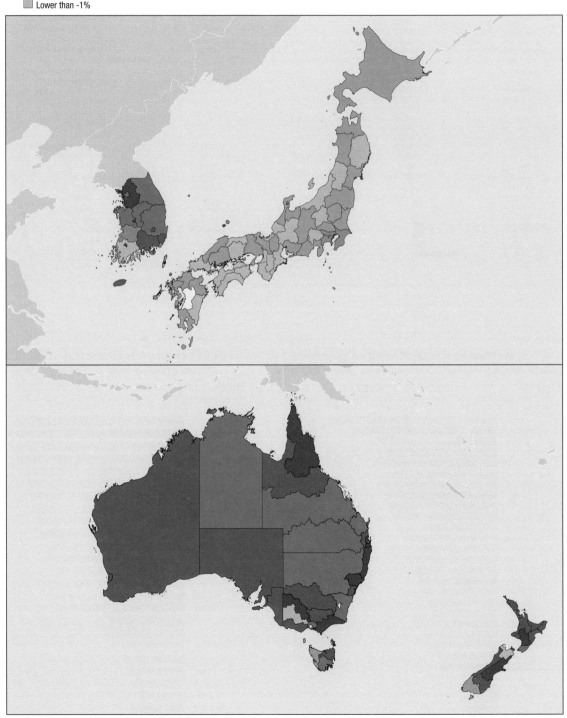

StatLink  http://dx.doi.org/10.1787/308803860387

6.6. **Regional employment growth: Europe**

Average annual employment growth rate, 1998-2003

- ■ Higher than 3.5%
- ■ Between 1.5% and 3.5%
- ■ Between 0.5% and 1.5%
- ■ Between 0% and 0.5%
- ■ Between -1% and 0%
- □ Lower than -1%

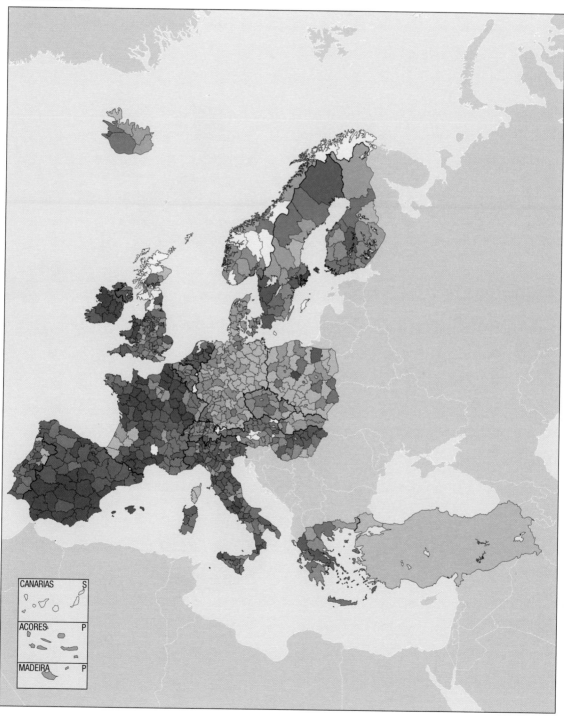

StatLink ‑‑‑‑‑‑ http://dx.doi.org/10.1787/308803860387

6.7. Regional employment growth: North America

Average annual employment growth rate, 1998-2003

- Higher than 3.5%
- Between 1.5% and 3.5%
- Between 0.5% and 1.5%
- Between 0% and 0.5%
- Between -1% and 0%
- Lower than -1%

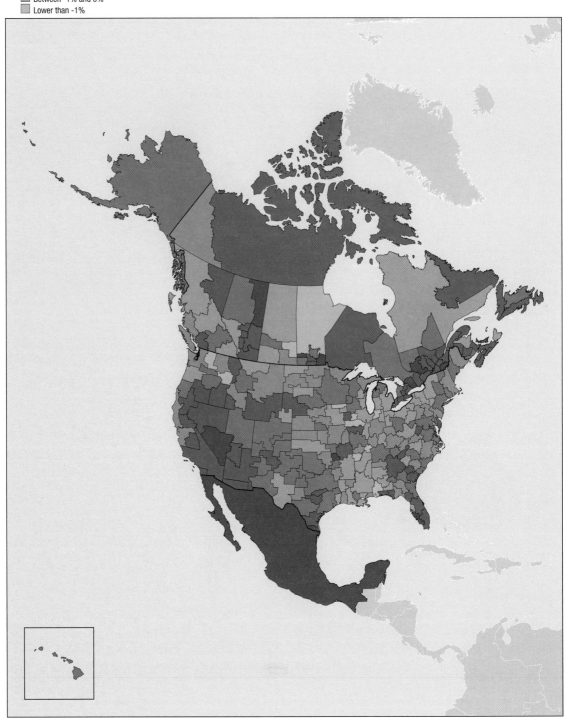

StatLink http://dx.doi.org/10.1787/308803860387

OECD REGIONS AT A GLANCE 2007 – ISBN 978-92-64-00987-5 – © OECD 2007

Fostering employment growth: a role for rural regions?

The structural change away from agriculture and manufacturing and towards services has produced uneven effects on regions. Traditionally specialised in primary activities, rural regions have been strongly affected by the secular decline in agricultural employment. As a result, economic activity during the last decades has shifted to urban and intermediate regions.

During 1998-2003, average employment growth rates were highest (Figure 6.8) in intermediate regions (0.93%) followed by urban (0.69%) and rural regions (0.64%).

Although average employment growth is lower in rural areas than in intermediate and urban ones, in Belgium, the Czech Republic, France, Hungary, Ireland, Portugal, the United Kingdom and the United States, the highest average employment rate occurred in rural regions (Figure 6.8), while in quite number of countries (12 out of 27), the region with the highest rate of growth in employment was a rural region (Figure 6.9).

This suggests that "successful" rural regions have been able to create employment at a faster rate than "successful" urban ones. Therefore, although rural regions may face difficulties in shifting their specialisation towards more dynamic activities, their potential in terms of employment creation remains significant.

6.8. **On average, employment in rural areas grew slower than in urban and intermediate areas,...**

Average yearly growth rate of employment by regional type, 1998-2003 (TL3)

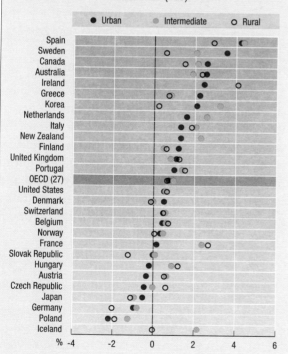

6.9. **... but in 9 countries, growth in employment was highest in a rural region**

Highest growth rate by regional type, 1998-2003 (TL3)

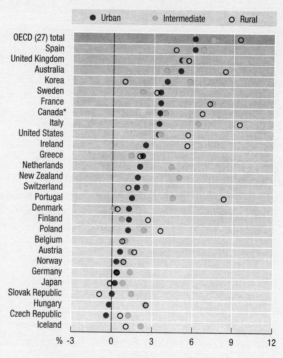

StatLink http://dx.doi.org/10.1787/716512765568

Patent statistics provide a measure of innovation, as they reflect the inventive performance of countries, regions and firms. The geographic distribution of patents therefore indicates the level of diffusion of technology and knowledge across regions.

Innovation is highly concentrated...

Figure 7.1 suggests that patents are concentrated in a small number of regions within countries. In 2003, 57% of all patents in OECD countries were recorded by 10% of regions.

The geographic concentration index reveals that Sweden and Korea (66), Japan and Greece (65), Turkey (63) and Hungary (60) had the highest concentration of patents in 2003 (Figure 8.2), followed closely by Spain (58), Mexico (56), Denmark and Finland (54), Norway and Portugal, (53), and Canada and Australia (52). The geographic concentration was lowest in Belgium (28), Austria and Poland (32), and the Czech Republic and Germany (35).

Over the period 1998-2003, the geographic concentration of patents increased most in the Slovak Republic (18) and Portugal (11), and it decreased most in Poland (–12) and Hungary (–8).

... particularly in urban areas

Predominantly urban regions appear to provide the most fertile ground for innovative activity. In 2003, the correlation between patents and population in urban regions was positive in all OECD countries (Figure 7.3). It was particularly pronounced in the Netherlands (0.92), Denmark (0.86), and Portugal (0.81).

Although somewhat less so, intermediate regions also make a noteworthy contribution to patent activity. In 10 out of 21 OECD countries the correlation between patents and population in intermediate regions was positive.

Finally the correlation between patent activity and population in rural regions was negative in all OECD countries except Korea (0.77), the Czech Republic (0.37) and Poland (0.01). The negative correlation was particularly pronounced in Canada (–0.90), the United Kingdom (–0.76) and Sweden (–0.74).

Innovation does not always mirror skill levels...

As patent activity is very skill-intensive, one might expect the regional distribution of patents to mirror that of skilled workers. In fact, a comparison of the geographic concentration indexes of patents and skilled workers (population with tertiary education) reveals that, in most countries, patents are more concentrated than the highly skilled population (Figure 7.4). Only in Australia is the skilled population more concentrated than patents.

... as it also requires physical capital

Thus, the geographic pattern of knowledge creation, as proxied by patent registrations, and of the skilled population, as proxied by the share of the workforce with a post-secondary degree or diploma, is not necessarily the same. The generation of patents requires inputs (e.g. physical capital) and infrastructure (e.g. laboratories) which tend to be geographically more concentrated than human capital.

Definition

A patent is defined as a right granted by a government to an inventor in exchange for the publication of the invention. It entitles the inventor to prevent any third party from using the invention in any way, for an agreed period.

Patant data refere to priority data which corresponds to the first filing of the invention.

The regional distribution of patent applications is assigned according to the inventor's region of residence. If an application has more than one inventor, the application is divided equally among all inventors and subsequently among their regions of residence, thus avoiding double counting.

7.1. In 2003, 57% of total patents were concentrated in only 10% of regions

Per cent of national patent applications in the 10% of regions with the highest concentration of patents (TL2)

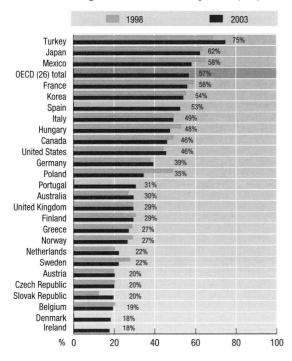

7.2. Sweden, Korea, Japan and Greece have the highest geographic concentration of patents

Index of geographic concentration of patents (TL2)

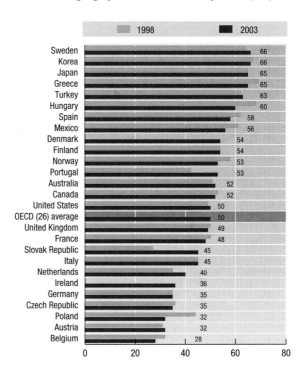

7.3. Predominantly urban regions provide the most fertile ground for innovative activity

Spearman correlation between patent applications and population share by regional type, 1998-2003 (TL2)

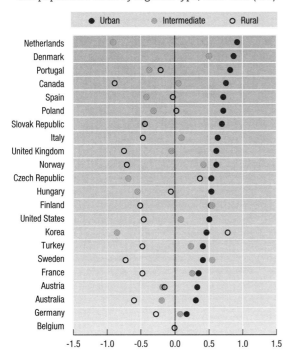

7.4. Patents are more concentrated than the highly skilled population

Concentration index, 2003 (TL2)

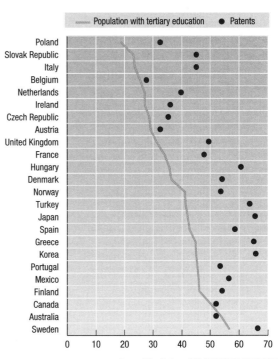

StatLink http://dx.doi.org/10.1787/632442377332

7.5. Patent applications by region: Asia and Oceania
2003

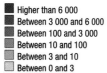

- Higher than 6 000
- Between 3 000 and 6 000
- Between 100 and 3 000
- Between 10 and 100
- Between 3 and 10
- Between 0 and 3

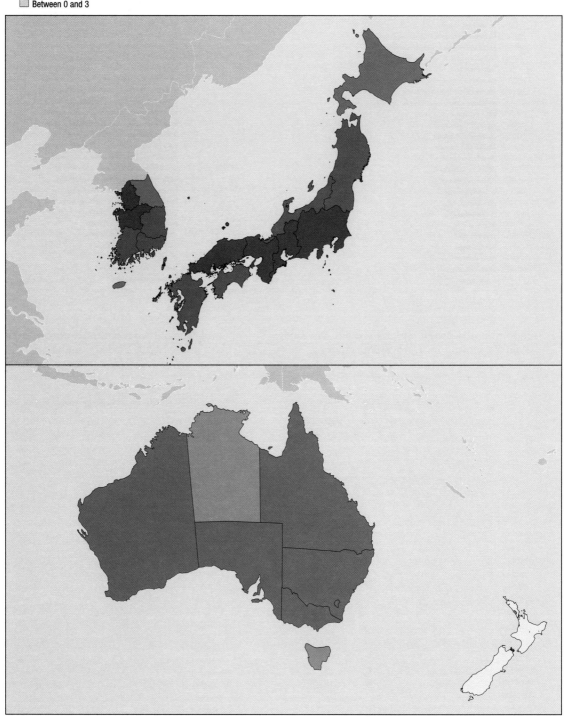

StatLink ⬛ㅍ⅃ http://dx.doi.org/10.1787/356300221452

7.6. **Patent applications by region: Europe**
2003

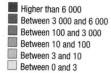

Higher than 6 000
Between 3 000 and 6 000
Between 100 and 3 000
Between 10 and 100
Between 3 and 10
Between 0 and 3

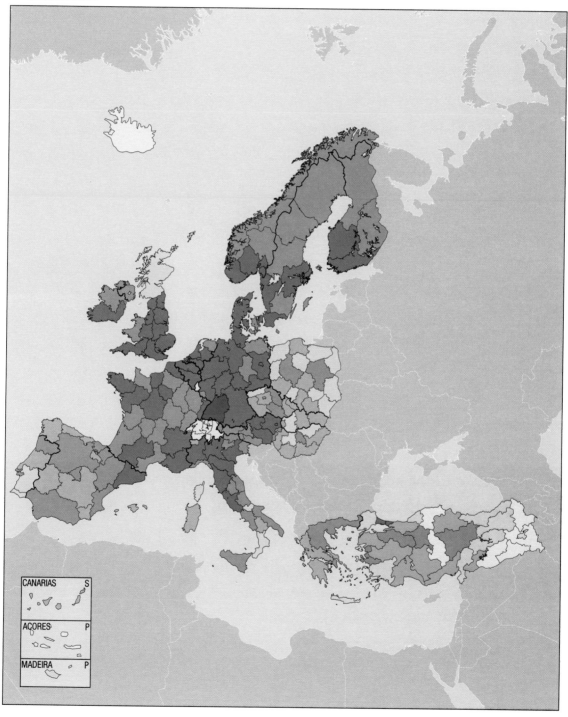

StatLink 🔗 http://dx.doi.org/10.1787/356300221452

7.7. Patent applications by region: North America

2003

Higher than 6 000
Between 3 000 and 6 000
Between 100 and 3 000
Between 10 and 100
Between 3 and 10
Between 0 and 3

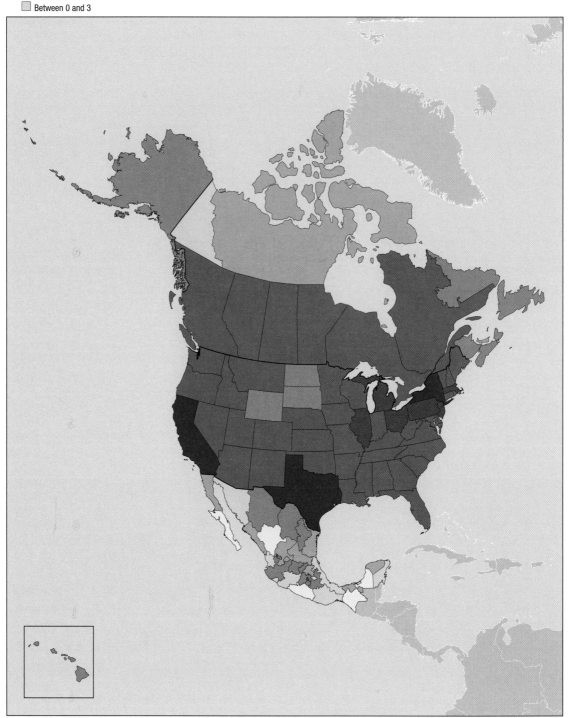

StatLink ⫿⫿⫿ http://dx.doi.org/10.1787/356300221452

OECD REGIONS AT A GLANCE 2007 – ISBN 978-92-64-00987-5 – © OECD 2007

Is higher labour productivity associated with more patents?

Innovation is expected to increase the productivity of firms. In fact the correlation between patent applications and labour productivity within regions during 1998-2003 is positive in 19 out of 22 OECD countries (Figure 7.8). Only in Belgium and Greece is the correlation negative and statistically significant.

The positive correlation was particularly pronounced in Japan (0.82), Norway (0.79) and Finland (0.64), followed by France (0.59), the United Kingdom (0.56), the Slovak Republic (0.54), the United States (0.49), Germany, Turkey and Poland (0.47), and Sweden (0.45). In all these countries it was statistically significant.

The ability to innovate may affect the competitiveness of different types of regions.

The correlation between patent applications and population was positive in rural regions in 14 OECD countries (Figure 7.9). In contrast, the correlation between patent applications and population was positive in urban and intermediate regions in seven and nine OECD countries, respectively.

This indicates that during 1998-2003 patent activity in rural regions was catching up relative to urban and intermediate regions. Nonetheless in Austria, Italy, Japan, the Netherlands, Portugal, the Slovak Republic and Turkey, predominantly urban regions provided the most fertile ground for innovative activity over the period.

7.8. In 19 out of 22 OECD countries the correlation between labour productivity and patent applications is positive

Spearman rank correlation of regional labour productivity and regional patent applications, 1998-2003 (TL2)

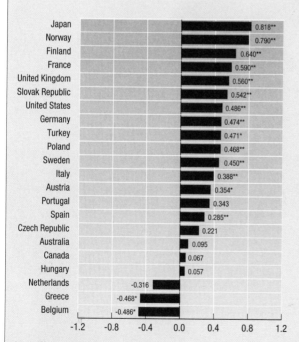

7.9. During 1998-2003 the share of patents filed in urban regions increased the most in the Netherlands and the Slovak Republic

Spearman correlation between patent growth and population share by regional type, 1998-2003 (TL2)

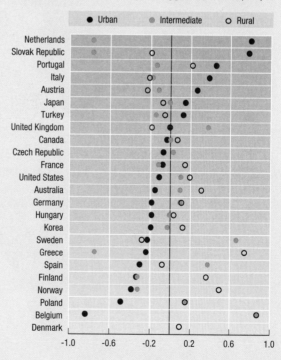

* Indicates significant at 95%.
** Indicates significant at 99%.

StatLink ⬛⬛⬛ http://dx.doi.org/10.1787/632442377332

II. MAKING THE BEST OF LOCAL ASSETS

THE KEY DRIVERS OF REGIONAL GROWTH

GDP per capita varies significantly among OECD countries (Figure 8.1). In 2003, GDP per capita in Luxembourg (USD 53 390) was more than double the OECD average (USD 24 824) and more than seven times that of Turkey (USD 6 910).

Regional disparities are larger than national ones

Although substantial, international disparities in GDP per capita are often smaller than differences among regions of the same country (Figure 8.2). In the United Kingdom, for instance, GDP per capita in Inner London-West was five times the national average but it was just above half the national average in the Isle of Anglesey. In Turkey, regional GDP per capita ranged between 3.5 times the national average (Koaceli) and less than one-third of that average (Agri).

These are by no means isolated examples. Significant territorial disparities are also observed in the United States, France, Poland and Mexico. In all these countries in 2003, GDP per capita in the "richest" region was at least four times higher than in the "poorest".

Commuting may distort the figures

Some of this variation may be due to commuting. By working in one area and living in another, commuters tend to increase GDP per capita in the region where they are employed and decrease it in the region where they reside. In several urban regions (e.g. Inner London-West, District of Columbia, Paris), GDP per capita appears significantly "oversize" if the impact of commuting is not taken into account.

While the range shows the difference between the region with the lowest and the highest GDP per capita, the Gini index measures disparities among all regions of a given country. The index ranges between 0 and 1: the higher its value, the larger the inequality among regions in terms of GDP per capita.

Between 1998 and 2003, disparities among countries remained stable (Figure 8.3) but regional disparities increased in 11 out of 26. Canada, Turkey, Ireland and Hungary showed the largest increase in the Gini index (0.02). The increase in regional disparities was more limited in Australia, Belgium, Denmark, Korea, the Slovak Republic, Poland and the United States (0.01). Austria, Finland, France, Greece, Italy, Norway, Portugal were the only countries with a modest reduction in regional disparities (–0.01). Sweden remained the country with lowest regional disparities in GDP per capita.

To appreciate the economic implications of this pattern, Figure 8.4 shows the percentage of national population living in regions where GDP per capita is below the national average. While the Gini index measures the size of regional disparities, this indicator shows how many people are affected by them.

More people are affected by regional variations

In 2003, more than half of the OECD population (52%) lived in a region where the level of GDP per capita was below the national average, a 1 percentage point increase from 1998. The increase was particularly large in Greece and Canada (15), Ireland (10), Germany (9) and Portugal (8). Hungary (–9) and the Czech Republic (–5) showed significant reductions in the proportion of people affected by regional disparities.

A comparison of Figures 8.3 and 8.4 shows that regional disparities in GDP per capita may increase while the number of people living in regions with low GDP per capita may decrease. This seems to have been the case between 1998 and 2003 for Hungary and Poland: highly populated regions improved their position compared to less populated ones. As a result, disparities increased but were a concern for fewer people. Portugal, Greece and Finland are the only countries in which GDP per capita grew more slowly in highly populated regions so that while disparities decreased, more people were affected.

Definition

GDP per capita is calculated by dividing the GDP of a country or a region – measured at constant Purchasing Power Parity (PPP) (2000) – by its population.

8.1. GDP per capita varies across OECD countries...

GDP per capita (USD constant PPP year 2000)

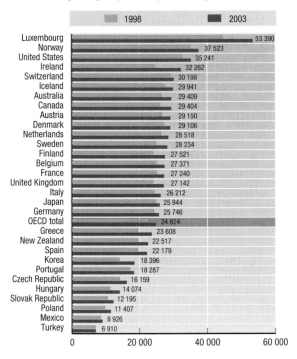

8.2. ... but the variation is even greater among regions of the same country

Range in GDP per capita across regions as a per cent of the national average, 2003 (TL3)

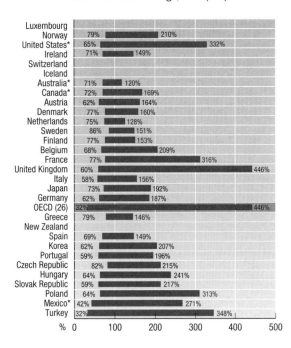

8.3. Between 1998 and 2003 regional disparities increased in 10 countries

Gini index of inequality of GDP per capita across regions within each country (TL3)

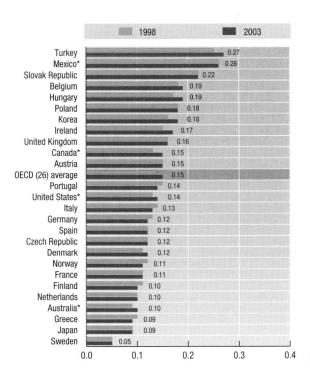

8.4. Disparities have become a concern for fewer people in Hungary, the Czech Republic, France and Norway

Percentage of population in regions with GDP per capita below the national average (TL3)

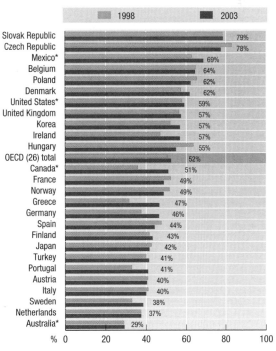

StatLink ᆲᇹᆲ http://dx.doi.org/10.1787/747881755121

8.5. **Regional GDP per capita: Asia and Oceania**
Constant 2000 USD (PPP), 2003

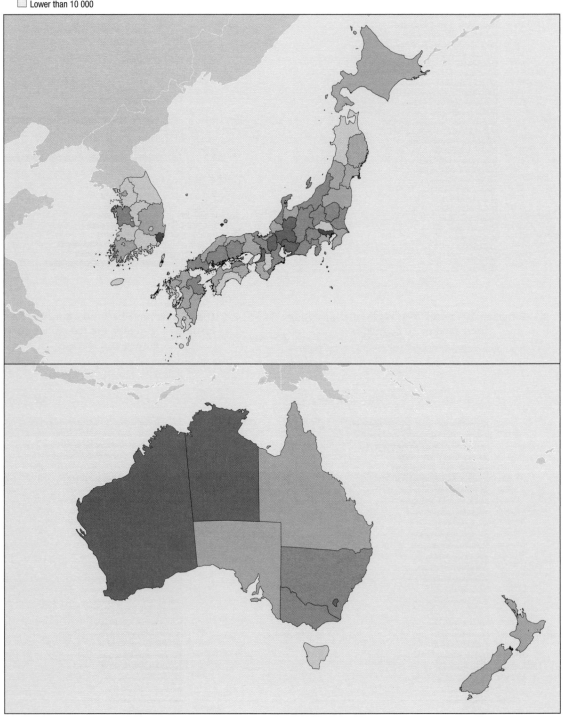

Legend:
- ■ Higher than 33 000
- ■ Between 28 000 and 33 000
- ■ Between 24 000 and 28 000
- ■ Between 20 000 and 24 000
- ■ Between 10 000 and 20 000
- □ Lower than 10 000

StatLink 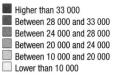 http://dx.doi.org/10.1787/370787736616

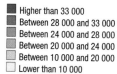

8.6. Regional GDP per capita: Europe

Constant 2000 USD (PPP), 2003

■ Higher than 33 000
■ Between 28 000 and 33 000
■ Between 24 000 and 28 000
■ Between 20 000 and 24 000
□ Between 10 000 and 20 000
□ Lower than 10 000

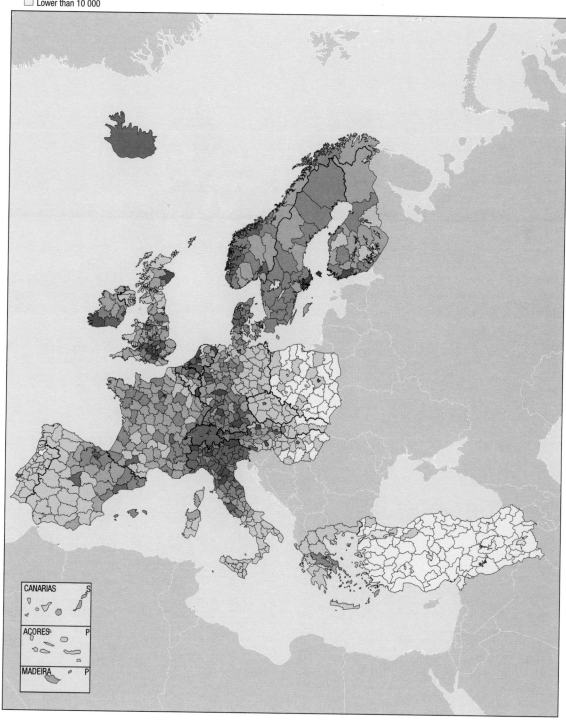

StatLink ⬛⬛⬛ http://dx.doi.org/10.1787/370787736616

8.7. **Regional GDP per capita: North America**

Constant 2000 USD (PPP), 2003

■ Higher than 33 000
■ Between 28 000 and 33 000
■ Between 24 000 and 28 000
■ Between 20 000 and 24 000
■ Between 10 000 and 20 000
□ Lower than 10 000

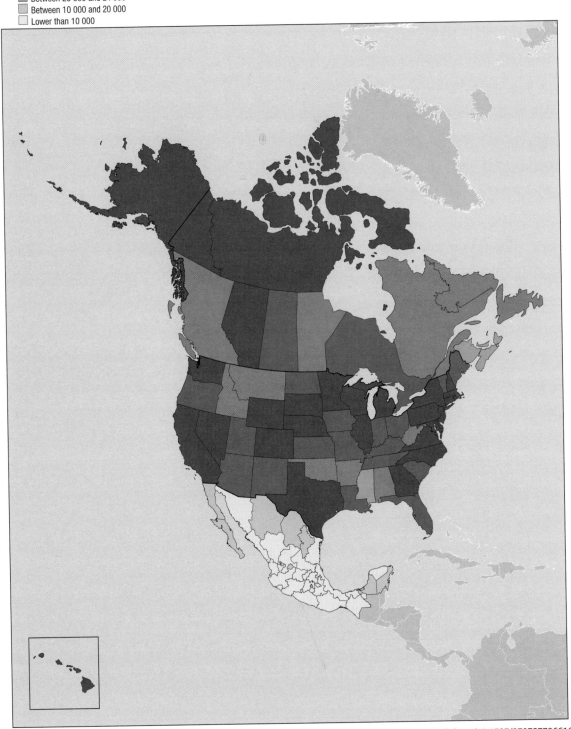

StatLink ⧉ http://dx.doi.org/10.1787/370787736616

OECD REGIONS AT A GLANCE 2007 – ISBN 978-92-64-00987-5 – © OECD 2007

Urban and rural regions: an increasing gap

GDP per capita tends to be higher in urban regions than in rural and intermediate ones. In 2003, GDP per capita in OECD urban regions was 51% higher than each country's average; in intermediate and rural regions it was only 77% and 64%, respectively, of the national average (Figure 8.8).

This gap widened during 1998-2003. Urban regions increased their advantage over intermediate and rural regions in 9 out of 22 OECD countries, while rural regions saw the gap increase in 5. The increase in urban regions was particularly large in Hungary (19 percentage points), the Slovak Republic (5), Greece (4) and Denmark (3). Norway (–13), Portugal (–4), Sweden and the Czech Republic (–2) were the only countries showing a significant reduction in the GDP gap in favour of urban regions.

The relative decrease in GDP per capita was particularly strong in the intermediate regions of Finland (–5 percentage points), Korea and Greece (–4), and Belgium (–3). A significant improvement in the relative position of intermediate regions was instead apparent in Norway, Hungary, Portugal, Sweden and Turkey (3).

Hungary and Turkey were the two countries with the largest decrease in the relative GDP per capita of rural regions (–7 and –4 percentage points, respectively), whereas the Czech Republic (9) and Korea (6) showed a significant improvement for rural regions.

8.8. Between 1998 and 2003, urban regions increased their advantage over intermediate and rural regions in 9 out of 22 OECD countries

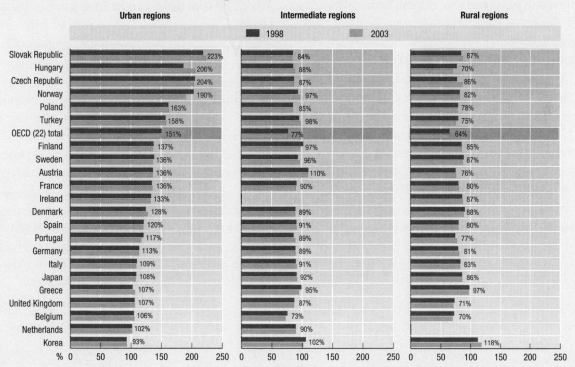

StatLink ᴍᴤᴧ http://dx.doi.org/10.1787/747881755121

Labour productivity, one of the main indicators of economic performance, varies significantly among OECD countries. In 2003, Luxembourg displayed the highest GDP per worker (measured at PPP in constant prices), about 47% higher than the OECD average. Turkey's productivity in 2003 was the lowest, at about 39% (Figure 9.1).

Productivity varies widely among regions

Regional differences within countries are even larger (Figure 9.2). In the United States, for instance, GDP per worker in the District of Columbia was 2.8 times higher than the national average while it was about half the national average in Montana. In Turkey, labour productivity in the region of Mus was approximately one-third of the national average, while in the region of Kocaeli it was over three times higher than the national average. A similar pattern can be observed in Japan, Mexico, Poland, France, Canada and Korea. In Denmark, Sweden, Finland and Belgium the range between the regions with the highest and lowest GDP per worker is narrower.

During 1998-2003 the gap between the region with the lowest and the highest labour productivity widened most in the United States (0.21 percentage points), Mexico and Australia (0.17), and Ireland (0.16). It decreased most in Poland (–0.40), Hungary (–0.35), Spain (–0.18), the Slovak Republic and Greece (–0.17).

While the range shows the difference between the regions with the lowest and the highest labour productivity, the Gini index measures disparities among all regions of a given country. The index ranges from 0 to 1: the higher the value, the larger the inequality among regions in terms of GDP per worker.

Gini indexes are highest in Mexico, Turkey and the United States

The largest regional disparities in labour productivity in 2003 were found in Mexico, Turkey and the United States with a Gini index of 0.26, 0.26 and 0.20, respectively (Figure 9.3). Regional disparities above the OECD average (0.11) occurred in Japan (0.18), Korea and Canada (0.16), Poland (0.14), Ireland (0.13), Hungary and Portugal (0.12). According to this index, the countries with the smallest disparities were Sweden and Denmark (0.04), Spain and Italy (0.05), and Norway, the Netherlands and Finland (0.06).

During 1998-2003, the Gini index increased the most in Australia, Ireland and Canada (0.03), and in Korea (0.02); it decreased the most in Poland (–0.05), the Slovak Republic and Spain (–0.02).

A half of workers are in low productivity areas

To appreciate the economic implications of this pattern, Figure 9.4 depicts the percentage of workers employed in regions where productivity is below the national average. This reveals the share of the national workforce that is affected by regional disparities in labour productivity. In 2003, 50% of all OECD workers were employed in regions where productivity is below the national average.

The percentage was particularly high in Greece (89%), Canada (88%), Korea (82%), Mexico (68%), the Czech Republic (63%) and Denmark (62%). In contrast, in Finland, Austria, Portugal, Australia, Sweden and Ireland, less than 35% of the workforce was employed in regions of low productivity

---

Definition

Labour productivity is defined as the ratio of constant GDP, measured in 2000 prices, to employment, where the latter is measured at the place of work.

9.1. Labour productivity varies significantly among OECD countries...

GDP per worker (USD constant PPP year 2000)

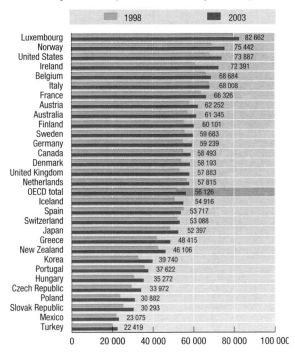

9.2. ... but disparities in productivity are even larger among regions

Range in GDP per worker across regions, as a per cent of national GDP per worker, 2003 (TL3)

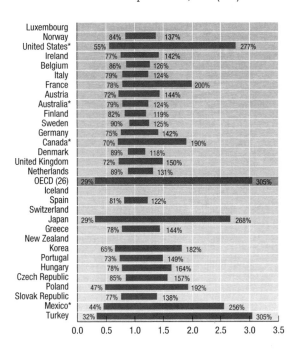

9.3. In 2003 the largest regional disparities in GDP per worker were in Mexico, Turkey and the United States

Gini index of inequality of GDP per worker (TL3)

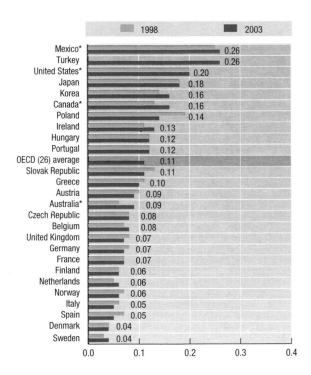

9.4. 50% of all OECD workers are employed in regions where GDP per worker is below the national average

Per cent of workers in regions with GDP per worker below the national average (TL3)

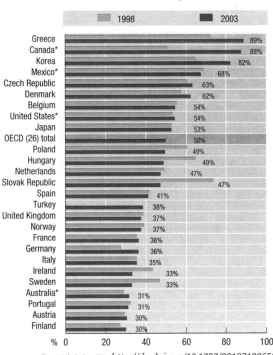

StatLink 🔗 http://dx.doi.org/10.1787/301371836530

9.5. Regional productivity: Asia and Oceania

Regional GDP per worker in constant 2000 USD (PPP), 2003

- ■ Higher than 85 000
- ■ Between 65 000 and 85 000
- ■ Between 55 000 and 65 000
- ■ Between 45 000 and 55 000
- □ Between 20 000 and 45 000
- □ Lower than 20 000

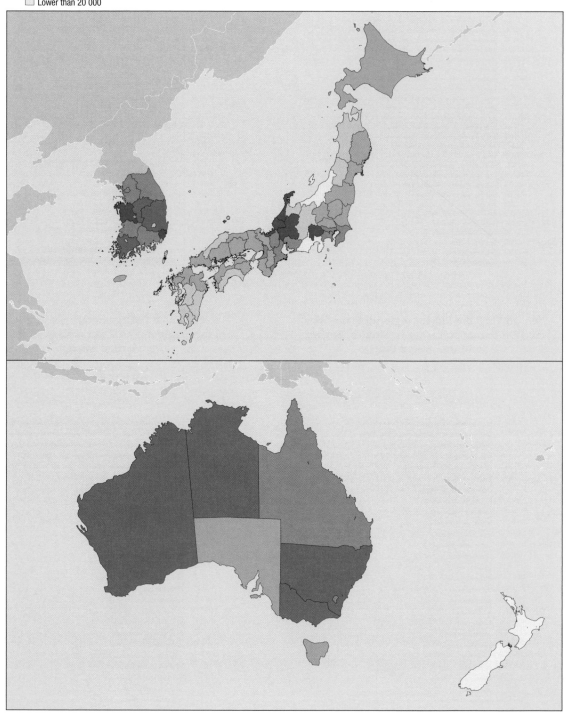

StatLink ᛗᚢ᛫ http://dx.doi.org/10.1787/800723772272

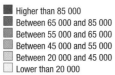

9.6. **Regional productivity: Europe**
Regional GDP per worker in constant 2000 USD (PPP), 2003

■ Higher than 85 000
■ Between 65 000 and 85 000
■ Between 55 000 and 65 000
■ Between 45 000 and 55 000
□ Between 20 000 and 45 000
□ Lower than 20 000

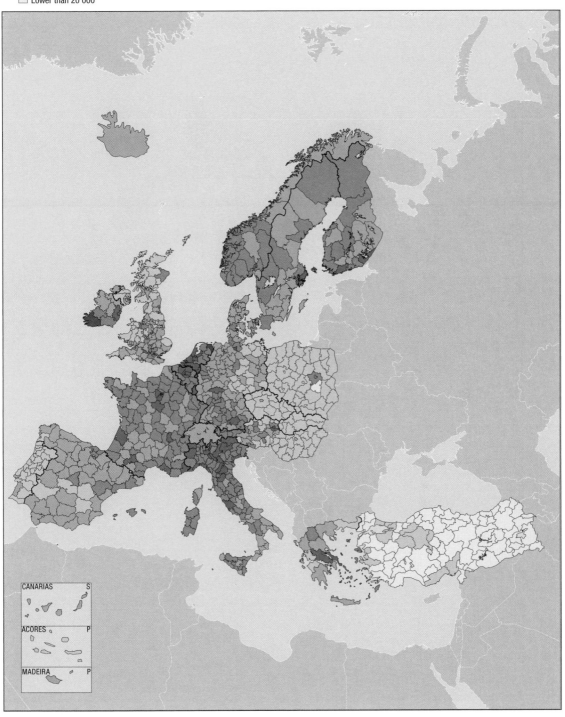

StatLink ⚌ http://dx.doi.org/10.1787/800723772272

9.7. **Regional productivity: North America**

Regional GDP per worker in constant 2000 USD (PPP), 2003

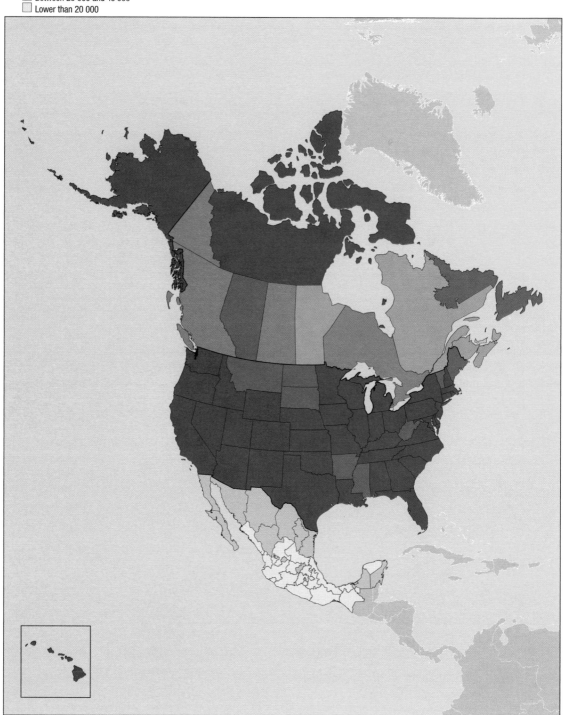

Legend:
- Higher than 85 000
- Between 65 000 and 85 000
- Between 55 000 and 65 000
- Between 45 000 and 55 000
- Between 20 000 and 45 000
- Lower than 20 000

StatLink 🔗 http://dx.doi.org/10.1787/800723772272

OECD REGIONS AT A GLANCE 2007 – ISBN 978-92-64-00987-5 – © OECD 2007

Regional labour productivity growth is the key to raising living standards

Growth in GDP per worker is often used as the key indicator to assess regional competitiveness. The growth potential in the long run depends on the ability to raise output per worker over prolonged periods of time.

During 1998-2003, labour productivity in OECD regions increased at an average annual rate of 1.9% (Figure 9.8), ranging from a 5.3% annual decline in the Norwegian region of Vest-Agder to an increase of 16.4% in the Hungarian region of Pest. Except in Norway, regional labour productivity growth increased on average in all countries during the period.

Increases in labour productivity are most desirable when they occur through a simultaneous increase in the rate of employment and in GDP. If, on the other hand, they occur through a reduction in the rate of employment, they will not be sustainable in the long run since tax revenue will fall and demand for income support (such as unemployment benefits) will rise.

Figure 9.9 displays the correlation between growth in the rate of employment and in labour productivity. When growth in productivity is accompanied by an increase in the employment rate the correlation is positive; when productivity growth is spurred by reductions in employment, the correlation is negative.

The correlation coefficient is negative and statistically significant only in Australia, the Czech Republic, Greece, Hungary, Korea and Italy. In these countries, regions seem to have achieved higher productivity at the cost of lower employment. In all other countries, the correlation is not statistically significant, suggesting that some regions have been able to raise both productivity and employment while others have only increased productivity through employment reduction. This pattern raises questions about the capacity of such regions to sustain productivity growth over a prolonged period of time.

9.8. Productivity growth varies significantly among OECD regions

Annual growth in GDP per worker, 1998-2003 (TL3)

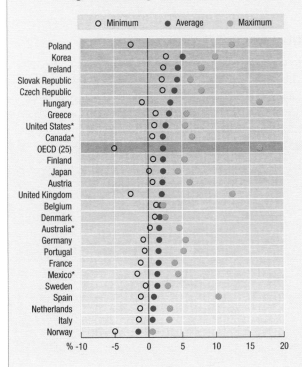

9.9. The correlation between growth in GDP and in employment is significantly negative in six OECD countries

Spearman correlation between employment rate growth and labour productivity growth, 1998-2003 (TL3)

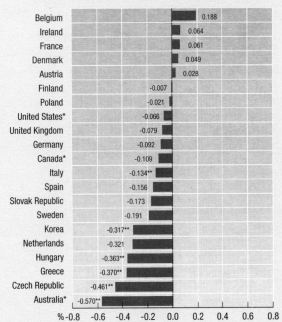

* Significant at 95%.
** Significant at 99%.

StatLink ᴍꜱ⅃ http://dx.doi.org/10.1787/301371836530

Regional specialisation varies considerably among OECD countries. Specialisation is commonly measured by the Balassa-Hoover index: the ratio between an industry's weight in a region and its weight in the country overall. A region is specialised in an industry when the index is above 1 and it is not specialised when the index is below 1. A region's degree of specialisation, therefore, can be measured as the weighted average of its degrees of specialisation in each industry. The higher this value, the more specialised the region.

In 2003, international differences in regional specialisation – the average degree of specialisation for all regions of a given country – ranged from 0.21 in Denmark to 0.62 in Korea (Figure 10.1).

Significant regional differences

These aggregate figures hide even larger differences among regions within countries. In 2003, the lowest degree of regional specialisation was observed in the Swedish region of Sydsverige (0.08), while the Mexican region of Campeche (1.87) recorded the highest (Figure 10.2). In Korea, Mexico, the United States and Sweden, the difference between the regions with the lowest and highest degree of specialisation was no less than 1. The differences were smaller but still considerable in Spain, Italy, Belgium and the Czech Republic (between 0.37 and 0.55). The differences were the smallest in Greece (0.11), Denmark (0.12), Iceland and Hungary (0.13).

While the range reveals the difference between the region with the lowest and the highest degree of specialisation, the Gini index measures disparities among all regions of a given country. The index ranges between 0 and 1: the higher its value, the larger the regional differences.

In 2003, the Gini index (Figure 10.3) demonstrated that the countries with the greatest differences in degrees of regional specialisation were Korea (0.60), Sweden (0.48), Ireland (0.44) and Belgium (0.38). Those with the least difference were Greece and Hungary (0.11), Portugal (0.17), France (0.18) and Denmark (0.19).

Definition

Specialisation in an industry is measured as the ratio of an industry's share of employment in a region to its share in the country as a whole (Balassa-Hoover index). A value of the index above 1 shows greater specialisation than in the country as a whole and a value below 1 shows less specialisation. A region's average degree of specialisation is the average of the sum of the absolute deviations from 1 of the Balassa-Hoover index over all industries (International Standard Industrial Classification [ISIC] Rev. 3.1 one digit).

10.1. In 2003 Korea, Mexico and Sweden had, on average, the highest degree of specialisation within regions

Average regional specialisation, 2003 (TL2)
(across one-digit ISIC industries)

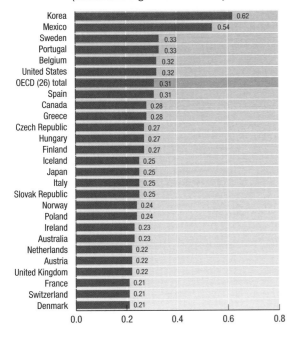

10.2. The degree of specialisation varies significantly across regions within countries

Range in the degree of industry specialisation across regions within a country, 2003 (TL2)

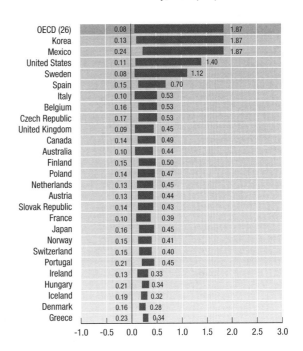

10.3. Korea, Sweden and Ireland showed the largest differences in the degree of regional specialisation

Gini index of inequality of industry specialisation across regions, 2003 (TL2)

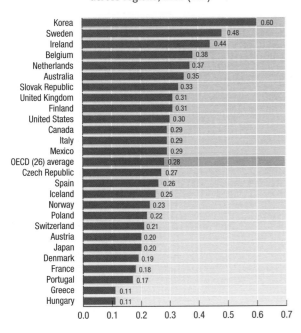

StatLink http://dx.doi.org/10.1787/168744331407

10.4. **Regional specialisation: Asia and Oceania**

Average degree of specialisation across industries, 2003

- Higher than 0.45
- Between 0.30 and 0.45
- Between 0.25 and 0.30
- Between 0.20 and 0.25
- Between 0.15 and 0.20
- Lower than 0.15

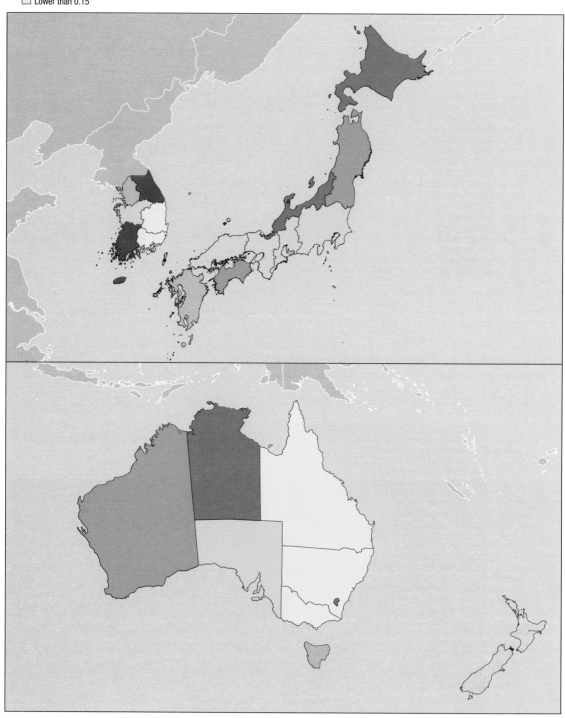

StatLink ᵐ𝓼ᵖ http://dx.doi.org/10.1787/573302327337

10.5. Regional specialisation: Europe
Average degree of specialisation across industries, 2003

- Higher than 0.45
- Between 0.30 and 0.45
- Between 0.25 and 0.30
- Between 0.20 and 0.25
- Between 0.15 and 0.20
- Lower than 0.15

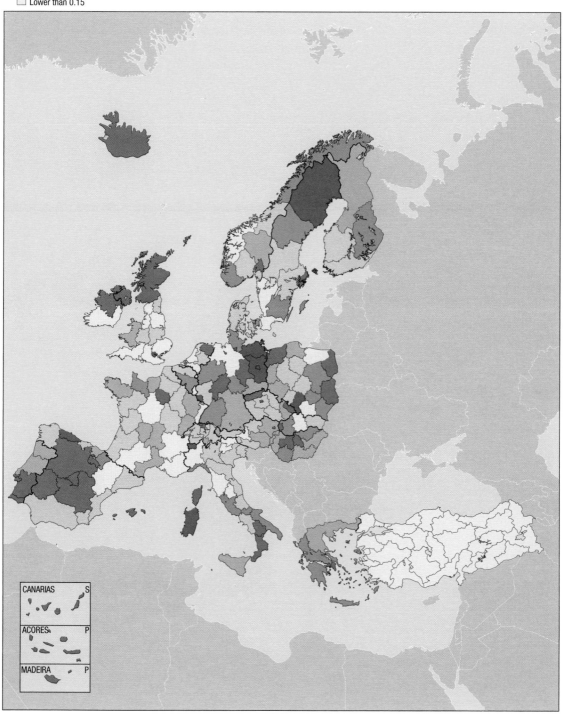

StatLink http://dx.doi.org/10.1787/573302327337

10.6. Regional degree of specialisation: North America

Average degree of specialisation across industries, 2003

- ■ Higher than 0.45
- ■ Between 0.30 and 0.45
- ■ Between 0.25 and 0.30
- ■ Between 0.20 and 0.25
- □ Between 0.15 and 0.20
- □ Lower than 0.15

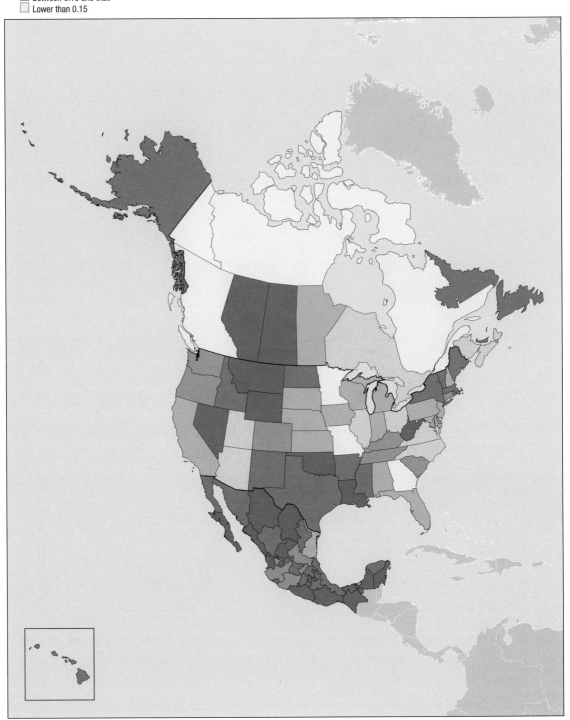

StatLink ▄▄▄ http://dx.doi.org/10.1787/573302327337

Construction and financial intermediation are the industries with the highest specialisation indexes

A region's degree of specialisation in an industry can be measured as the difference between the Balassa-Hoover index and 1. Higher values of the index above 1 reflect greater specialisation, and lower values below 1 indicate less specialisation than the national average. A region's average degree of specialisation, therefore, is obtained by averaging the absolute deviations from 1 of the Balassa-Hoover indexes of all industries within the region.

Table 10.7 displays the region with the greatest degree of specialisation in each OECD country and the corresponding Balassa-Hoover index of all industries for 2003. In a large number of these regions, the greatest degree of specialisation was recorded in financial intermediation (j) and construction (c). The financial intermediation industry displayed the highest specialisation index in Belgium, the Czech Republic, Denmark, Greece, Norway, Portugal, the Slovak Republic and the United Kingdom, while construction was the highest in Mexico, the Netherlands, Poland, Spain, Sweden, Switzerland and the United States.

The regions with the highest degree of specialisation in Canada, Iceland, Japan and Korea are specialised in agriculture, hunting, forestry and fishing (a+b); while the most specialised regions in Ireland and Italy are specialised in hotels and restaurants (h), and in Austria and Hungary they are specialised in real estate and business activities (k).

Finally the most specialised regions in France, Finland and Australia are specialised in electricity, gas and water supply (e), transport, storage and communication (i) and health and social work (o+p), respectively.

10.7. Regions with the highest degree of specialisation

	Region (TL2)	Average degree of regional specialisation	a + b	c	d	e	f	g	h	i	j	k	m	n	o + p
								Standard Industrial Classification (ISIC) Rev. 3.1							
Australia	Australian Cap. Territory	0.44	0.10	0.06	0.40	1.16	0.91	0.88	1.33	0.85	0.50	1.53	1.50	1.14	**1.80**
Austria	Wien	0.44	0.05	0.07	0.57	1.15	0.88	1.11	0.87	1.30	1.72	**1.82**	1.19	1.33	1.53
Belgium	Bruxelles	0.53	0.04	0.20	0.44	1.42	0.52	0.92	1.17	1.30	**3.25**	1.21	0.98	0.83	1.47
Canada	Saskatchewan	0.49	**3.64**	2.90	0.39	1.04	0.86	1.06	1.09	0.96	1.06	0.64	1.25	1.13	0.96
Czech Republic	Praha	0.53	0.09	0.04	0.36	0.87	1.02	1.19	1.25	1.37	**2.50**	2.14	0.93	1.05	1.71
Denmark	Hovedstadsregionen	0.28	0.21	0.46	0.63	1.01	0.87	1.05	1.14	1.20	**1.58**	1.47	1.02	1.01	.
Finland	Aland	0.50	1.10	.	0.44	0.95	0.87	0.75	1.39	**4.05**	1.51	0.43	0.93	0.79	0.94
France	Corse	0.39	1.19	0.70	0.34	**1.72**	1.69	1.27	1.69	1.33	0.64	0.57	1.28	1.11	0.95
Greece	Attiki	0.34	0.07	0.24	1.15	0.94	1.07	1.19	0.82	1.39	**1.63**	1.49	1.01	1.21	1.38
Hungary	Kosep-Magyarorszag	0.34	0.27	0.18	0.75	0.60	1.10	1.19	0.94	1.18	1.48	**1.70**	0.90	0.96	1.39
Iceland	Other Regions	0.32	**2.22**	.	1.33	1.12	1.13	0.75	0.89	0.78	0.63	0.55	0.90	0.82	.
Ireland	Border, Midlands and Western	0.33	1.38	1.48	0.91	0.85	1.00	0.87	**2.60**	0.71	0.52	0.54	0.89	0.95	0.88
Italy	Valle D'aosta	0.53	1.22	2.41	0.55	2.37	1.73	0.79	**2.44**	1.18	0.80	0.74	1.13	1.20	0.95
Japan	Hokkaido	0.45	**3.30**	2.31	0.55	1.20	1.37	1.08	1.10	1.14	1.01	0.97	0.79	1.17	.
Korea	Jeju	1.87	**19.80**	0.95	0.23	1.25	1.21	1.17	1.80	1.28	1.30	0.61	1.14	1.23	.
Mexico	Campeche	1.87	5.43	**15.37**	0.43	0.89	1.69	0.89	1.34	0.95	0.13	1.18	0.62	0.68	.
Netherlands	Noord-Nederland	0.45	1.50	**4.43**	1.14	1.16	1.05	0.91	1.01	0.80	0.83	0.74	1.16	1.18	.
Norway	Oslo	0.41	0.02	0.24	0.62	0.46	0.73	1.16	1.05	1.21	**1.67**	1.66	0.91	0.91	1.44
Poland	Slaskie	0.47	0.34	**5.24**	1.04	1.31	1.21	1.09	1.10	1.06	0.80	1.09	0.95	1.07	1.02
Portugal	Lisboa	0.45	0.11	0.33	0.58	1.29	0.89	1.20	1.29	1.45	**2.10**	2.00	1.01	1.08	1.33
Slovak Republic	Bratislav Kraj	0.43	0.29	0.29	0.60	0.66	0.95	1.03	1.05	1.15	**2.45**	1.86	0.73	0.75	1.38
Spain	Asturias	0.70	0.83	**8.81**	0.95	1.27	1.07	1.06	0.91	0.94	0.85	0.86	1.13	1.02	0.98
Sweden	Oevre Norrland	1.12	1.14	**13.23**	0.79	1.24	1.08	0.76	0.94	0.98	0.62	0.73	1.33	1.28	0.95
Switzerland	Nordwestschweiz	0.40	0.68	**4.96**	1.14	1.20	0.99	1.04	0.72	1.05	0.99	1.04	0.93	1.03	0.92
United Kingdom	London	0.45	0.12	0.25	0.48	0.42	0.73	0.85	1.04	1.29	**1.95**	1.60	0.78	0.76	1.38
United States	Wyoming	1.40	1.51	**14.41**	0.38	2.00	1.49	1.07	1.48	1.19	0.73	1.11	0.45	0.82	0.72

In today's knowledge-based economy a region's growth prospects depend to a large extent on its ability to generate and use innovation. This capability, in turn, depends, among other factors, on the skills level of the regional labour force. The proportion of the adult population with tertiary education is a common proxy for a region's skills level. It includes university-level education, from courses of short and medium duration to advanced research qualifications.

Figure 11.1 shows large differences in tertiary education attainment in OECD countries. In 2001, the proportion of the adult population with tertiary education was highest in Canada (42%) and the United States (37%). In Italy, Portugal and Turkey, it was less than 11%.

Regional differences are substantial

Significant differences among countries hide even larger differences among regions. In France, Australia, the United Kingdom and Canada, differences in tertiary attainments in 2001 exceeded 30 percentage points (Figure 11.2). These differences were also considerable (between 20 and 30 percentage points) in New Zealand, Japan, the United States, Mexico, Hungary, Norway, Korea, Poland, Spain and Denmark. Only in Switzerland and Austria did tertiary attainment reveal a more balanced regional pattern.

While the range concerns the difference between the regions with the lowest and the highest attainment in tertiary education, the Gini index measures disparities among all regions of a given country. The index ranges between 0 and 1: the higher its value, the larger the regional disparities.

Mexico shows the largest variations

In 2001 the country with the highest Gini index was Mexico (0.33), followed by New Zealand, Poland and the Czech Republic (0.20). For most countries the Gini index ranged between 0.10 and 0.20. Only Finland (0.07), Switzerland (0.08) and Sweden (0.09) had a value below 0.10 (Figure 11.3).

On average, 57% of the OECD adult population possessing tertiary education lives in urban regions, 19% in intermediate regions and 24% in rural ones (Figure 11.4). Poland and Denmark show the most balanced distribution of skills among the three types of region: respectively 37% and 38% in urban regions, 34% and 32% in intermediate regions and 29% and 30% in rural ones. Most other countries show significantly higher shares in urban regions, with the Netherlands and Belgium reaching 88% and 85%, respectively. In only a few countries is the share of the population with advanced qualifications higher in rural or intermediate regions. The ratio is higher in rural regions in Ireland (59%), Finland (55%), Austria (46%) and Sweden (42%) and in intermediate regions in the Czech Republic (70%), Switzerland (66%), the Slovak Republic (55%), Turkey (51%) and Spain (46%).

Migration increases the variations

Concentration of tertiary-level attainment in urban regions is often the result of migration away from rural areas. The existence of significant differentials in the return to education between rural and urban areas is a major incentive for individuals with advanced educational levels to migrate to urban regions.

Definition

The tertiary-level attainment rate is defined as the number of persons in the 25-64 age group who have completed tertiary educational programmes as a percentage of all persons of the same age. Tertiary education includes both university studies and advanced professional programmes.

OECD REGIONS AT A GLANCE 2007 – ISBN 978-92-64-00987-5 – © OECD 2007

11.1. Tertiary attainment rates vary significantly among OECD countries

National tertiary attainment rate, 2001

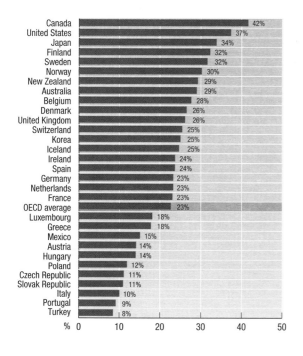

11.2. ... but disparities in tertiary attainments are even larger among regions

Range of tertiary attainment rates across regions within each country, 2001 (TL3)

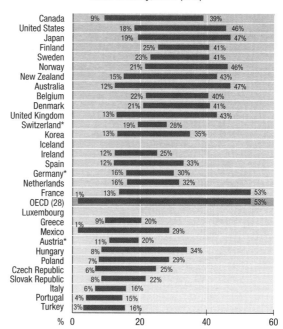

11.3. The largest regional disparities in tertiary attainments in 2001 occurred in Mexico

Gini index of inequality of regional tertiary attainment rates, 2001 (TL3)

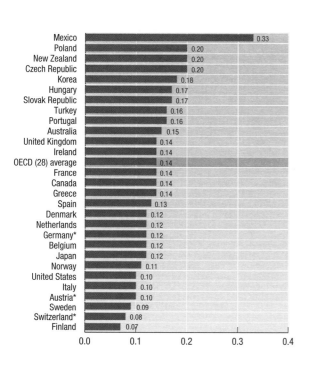

11.4. 57% of the population with tertiary attainments was concentrated in urban regions in 2001

Tertiary education attainment rate by regional type, 2001 (TL3)

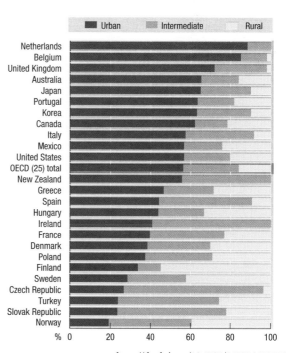

StatLink ⬛ᴍˢᴸ http://dx.doi.org/10.1787/317856428656

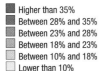

11.5. Tertiary educational attainment: Asia and Oceania
As a percentage of the population aged 25-64, 2001

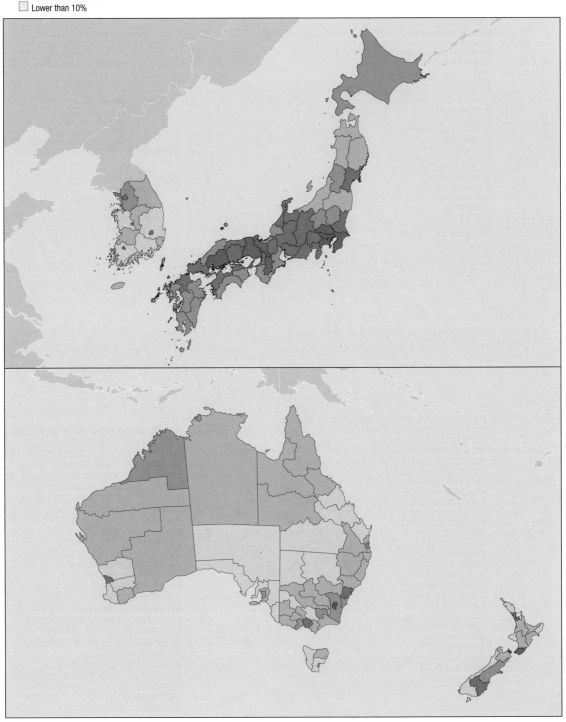

■ Higher than 35%
■ Between 28% and 35%
■ Between 23% and 28%
■ Between 18% and 23%
□ Between 10% and 18%
□ Lower than 10%

StatLink ⬛⬛⬛ http://dx.doi.org/10.1787/134460624616

OECD REGIONS AT A GLANCE 2007 – ISBN 978-92-64-00987-5 – © OECD 2007

11.6. Tertiary educational attainment: Europe

As a percentage of the population aged 25-64, 2001

- Higher than 35%
- Between 28% and 35%
- Between 23% and 28%
- Between 18% and 23%
- Between 10% and 18%
- Lower than 10%

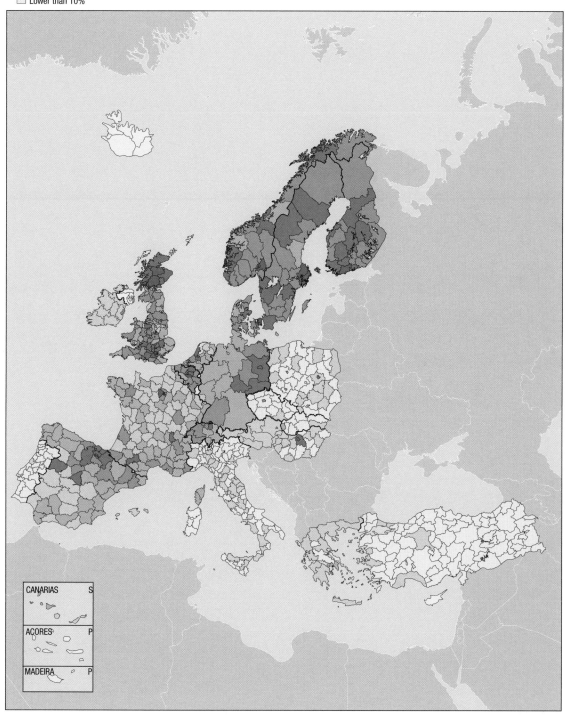

StatLink ⊟₅ http://dx.doi.org/10.1787/134460624616

11.7. **Tertiary educational attainment: North America**

As a percentage of the population aged 25-64, 2001

Higher than 35%
Between 28% and 35%
Between 22% and 28%
Between 18% and 22%
Between 8% and 18%
Lower than 8%

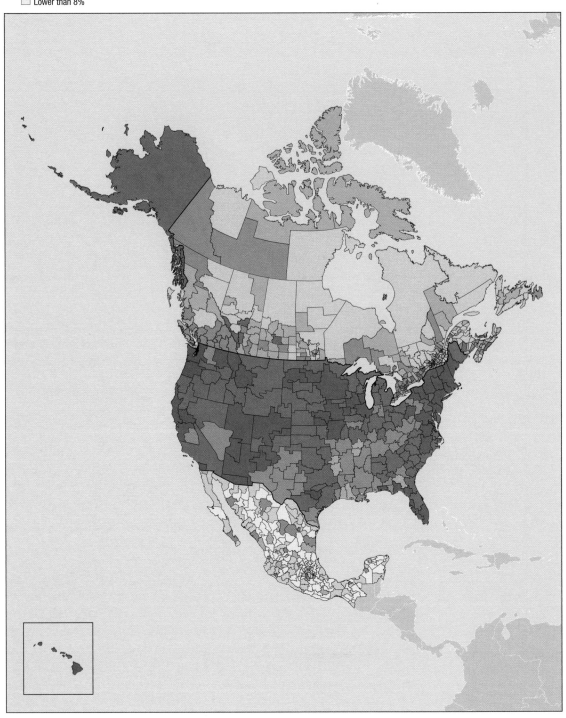

StatLink ᵐⁱˢ⁻ http://dx.doi.org/10.1787/134460624616

Participation in tertiary education and tertiary education attainment: what relationship?

A well-educated and well-trained population is central to the social and economic well-being of regions and individuals. Education plays a key role in providing individuals with the knowledge, skills and competencies needed to participate effectively in society. Tertiary educational attainment and participation in tertiary education are indicators respectively of the current and of the future stock of a region's "human capital".

The distribution of the highly skilled population depends mainly on the wage returns to education. People with advanced qualifications have a strong incentive to migrate towards places where people with similar skills are highly concentrated. On the other hand, participation in tertiary education depends on the location of universities. In some countries these tend to be concentrated in a few main cities, while in others they tend to be more decentralised.

In many countries students participating in tertiary education are less evenly distributed than the population with advanced qualifications (Figure 11.8). However, in most countries differences in the coefficient of variation are not large. Only Austria, Belgium, the Czech Republic, Denmark, the Slovak Republic and Turkey display very large differences in variation coefficients. As mentioned, this may indicate that universities are concentrated in a few regions.

In general there seems to be some positive correlation between tertiary attainment and the number of students participating in advanced education (Figure 11.9), suggesting a connection between students in university and the highly skilled labour market. However the correlation is only significant for the Czech Republic, France, Japan, the Netherlands, Poland, Portugal, Sweden, Turkey and the United Kingdom.

11.8. Students in tertiary education are less evenly distributed than the population with advanced qualifications

Coefficient of variation, regional tertiary education attainment and regional student enrolment rate, 2003 (TL2)

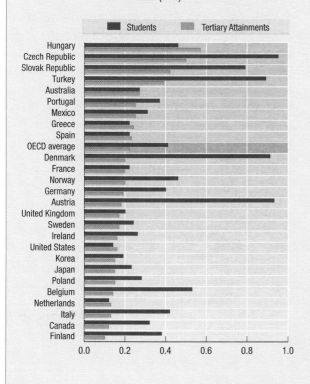

11.9. The correlation between tertiary attainments and students participation in advanced education is positive for most countries

Spearman correlation between regional tertiary attainment rates and regional enrolment rate in tertiary education, 2003 (TL2)

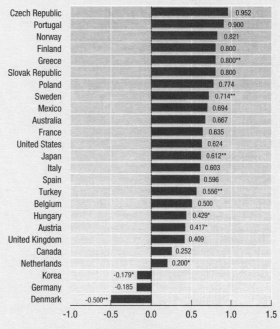

* Significant at 95%. ** Significant at 99%.

StatLink 🔗 http://dx.doi.org/10.1787/317856428656

Unemployment rates vary significantly among OECD countries. In 2003, international differences in unemployment rates were as large as 17 percentage points, ranging from 2.5% in Mexico to 19.6% in Poland (Figure 12.1).

Regional unemployment is a significant issue

Significant international differences in unemployment rates hide even larger differences among regions. In Italy, Poland, Spain and Germany, differences in regional unemployment rates in 2003 were over 19 percentage points (Figure 12.2). Only in Mexico, the Netherlands, Korea and Ireland did unemployment rates reflect a more balanced regional pattern (below 3 percentage points).

While the range shows the difference between the region with the lowest and the highest unemployment rates, the Gini index measures disparities among all regions of a given country. The index ranges between 0 and 1: the higher its value, the larger the regional disparities.

In 2003 the countries with the highest Gini index were Italy (.43), Iceland (.34), Germany (.28), Portugal (.25), Canada, Belgium, and Spain (.24), while the Netherlands (.09), Ireland and Japan (0.11), Sweden, the United States and Greece (.12) had the lowest (Figure 12.3).

Almost half of the OECD workforce lives in areas of high unemployment

In 2003, 49% of the OECD labour force was located in regions with unemployment rates above the national average. The percentage was particularly high in Iceland (75%), Switzerland (74%), Korea (66%), Mexico (65%), Portugal (64%), Turkey (60%), Austria, France and the United States (58%), the Netherlands (57%), and Denmark (56%). Canada and Australia were the countries with the largest share of the labour force living in regions with low unemployment rates (78% and 76%, respectively).

During 1998-2003, the share of the labour force living in regions of high unemployment increased the most in the Netherlands (41 percentage points), the United States (23), Switzerland (16), the Slovak Republic (14), Norway (12), France (11), the Czech Republic and Poland (10). The share declined the most in Greece (–28) and Japan (–18).

Long-term unemployment also varies widely

There are also significant differences in long-term unemployment rates among regions within countries.

In 2003 the country with the highest Gini index for long-term unemployment rates (Figure 12.4) was Italy (0.55), followed by Austria (0.43), Belgium (0.38) and the Czech Republic (0.35). Those with the lowest Gini index were Poland and the Netherlands (0.12), Sweden (0.14) and Ireland (0.15).

In 2003, 57% of the OECD labour force was based in regions with long-term unemployment rates above the national average. The percentage was particularly high in Greece (90%), the Slovak Republic (87%), Canada (79%), Portugal (68%) and Spain (61%). The Netherlands (10%), Germany (22%) and Ireland (25%) had smallest shares of their labour forces living in regions with high long-term unemployment rates.

Definitions

The unemployment rate is the ratio of unemployed people to the total labour force, *i.e.* unemployed plus employed people. A person is defined as unemployed when he or she is without work, available for work and actively looking for it.

The long-term unemployment rate is the ratio of long-term unemployment to the total labour force. It includes all those who have been unemployed and looking for work for 12 months or more.

OECD REGIONS AT A GLANCE 2007 – ISBN 978-92-64-00987-5 – © OECD 2007

12.1. Unemployment rates vary significantly among OECD countries...

National unemployment rate

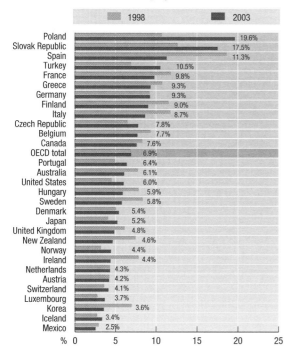

12.2. ... but disparities in unemployment rates are even larger among regions

Range of unemployment rates across regions within each country, 2003 (TL3)

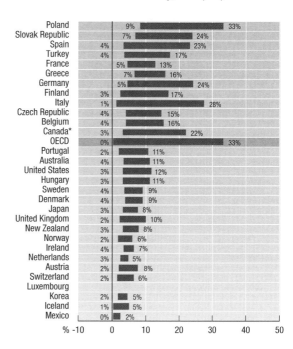

12.3. The largest regional disparities in unemployment rates in 2003 occurred in Italy and Iceland

Gini index of inequality of regional unemployment rates (TL3)

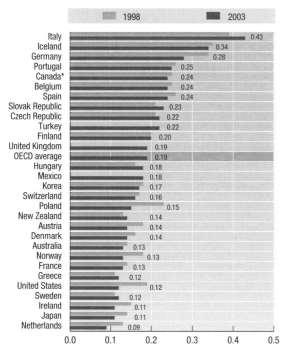

12.4. In 2003, Italy displayed the largest regional disparities in long-term unemployment rates

Gini index of inequality in long term unemployment rates (TL2)

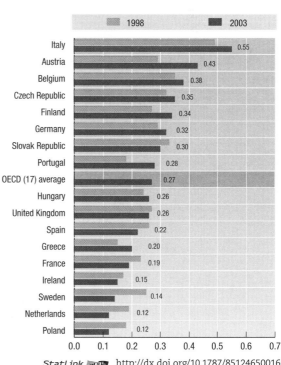

StatLink http://dx.doi.org/10.1787/851246500166

12.5. **Regional unemployment rate: Asia and Oceania**
2003

- Higher than 19%
- Between 14% and 19%
- Between 9% and 14%
- Between 6% and 9%
- Between 4% and 6%
- Lower than 4%

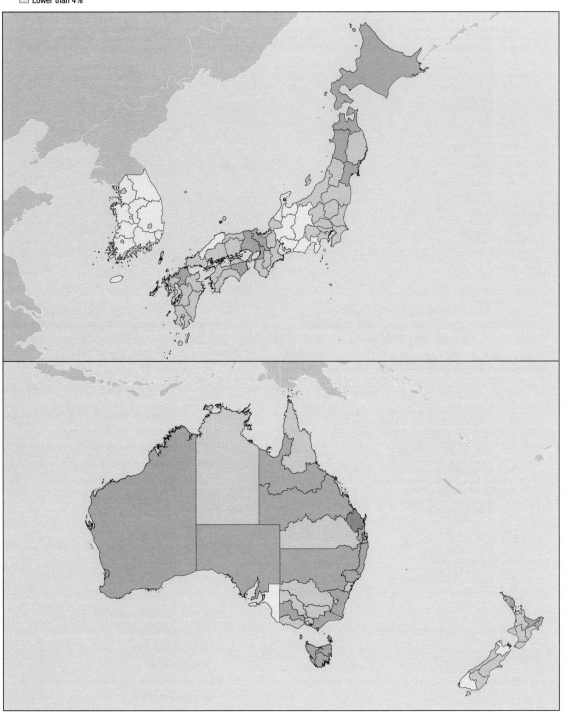

StatLink ⏷ http://dx.doi.org/10.1787/845177763644

OECD REGIONS AT A GLANCE 2007 – ISBN 978-92-64-00987-5 – © OECD 2007

12.6. Regional unemployment rate: Europe
2003

- ■ Higher than 19%
- ■ Between 14% and 19%
- ■ Between 9% and 14%
- ■ Between 6% and 9%
- ■ Between 4% and 6%
- □ Lower than 4%

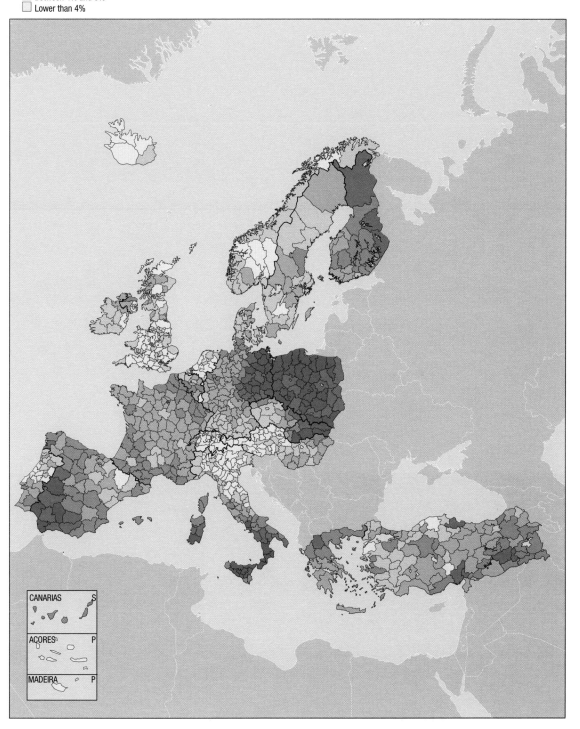

StatLink ⟨⟩ http://dx.doi.org/10.1787/845177763644

12.7. **Regional unemployment rate: North America**
2003

- Higher than 19%
- Between 14% and 19%
- Between 9% and 14%
- Between 6% and 9%
- Between 4% and 6%
- Lower than 4%

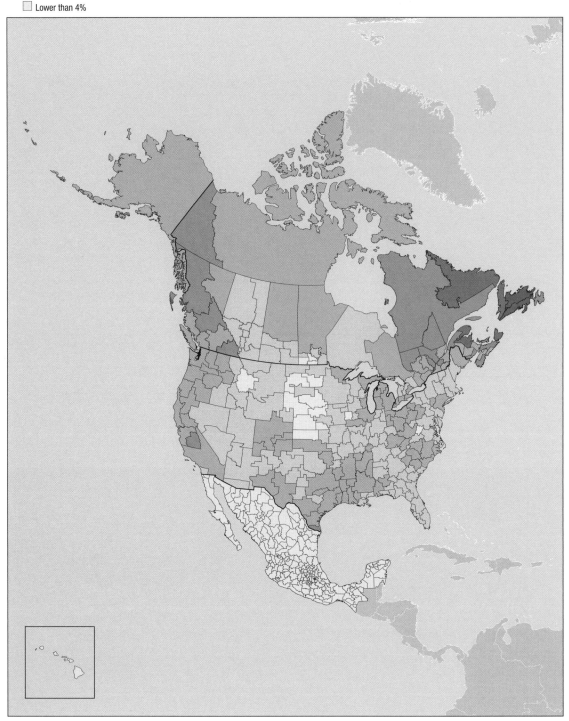

StatLink ⟲ http://dx.doi.org/10.1787/845177763644

OECD REGIONS AT A GLANCE 2007 – ISBN 978-92-64-00987-5 – © OECD 2007

Regional unemployment: market failure or wage inflexibility?

Unemployment rates vary significantly among regions, and, in many countries, regional disparities have persisted over long periods of time. Persistent disparities in unemployment should provide individuals with the incentive to move from regions with high unemployment to regions with low unemployment. Mobility, however, is not without cost, and even if in the long run the monetary return to moving to another region would exceed the monetary costs, imperfect capital markets, risk aversion or social ties may make the net economic plus social returns to mobility insufficient to induce geographic mobility from regions of high unemployment to those with low unemployment.

If some "market failure" prevents adjustment between regions, wage flexibility should ensure labour market clearing within regions. In theory, as long as wages are set according to marginal labour productivity, the demand for labour will always adjust to supply across industrial sectors within regions. This is why wage inflexibility is often considered the main cause of regional disparities in unemployment rates. If wages are set at the national level, regional differences in productivity (Figure 12.8) will translate into higher unemployment rates in regions with low productivity.

Figure 12.9 shows the correlation coefficients between countries' unemployment rates and productivity. A negative coefficient – indicating that unemployment is high in regions with low productivity – would be consistent with the hypothesis that wage inflexibility or labour immobility between regions is a significant explanation of regional disparities. In 17 out of 25 countries, the correlation is negative; in 11 of these 17 countries, the coefficient is also statistically significant. These results should be interpreted with caution for at least two reasons. First, there are considerable regional differences in price levels but, owing to lack of data, regional productivity is measured at national prices. Second, economic theory predicts a relationship between marginal productivity and wages whereas the correlation is based on average productivity. However, the observed patterns of regional unemployment are still roughly consistent with the hypothesis that unemployment disparities result from wage inflexibility.

12.8. There are significant differences in labour productivity among regions

Range in labour productivity across regions, as a per cent of the national average, 2003 (TL3)

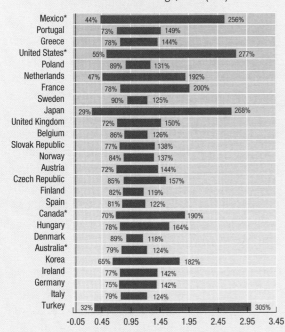

12.9. In several countries, low-productivity regions tend to have higher unemployment rates

Spearman correlation between regional unemployment rates and regional GDP per worker, 1998-2003 (TL3)

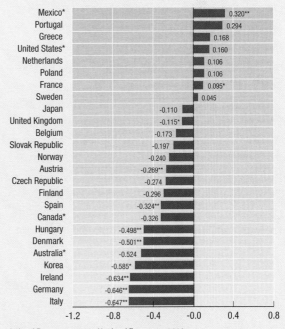

*Significant at 95%. ** Significant at 99%

StatLink ⟶ http://dx.doi.org/10.1787/851246500166

Labour force participation rates vary significantly among OECD countries. In 2003, international differences in participation rates ranged from 51% in Turkey to 87% in Iceland (Figure 13.1).

Large variations in France, Australia and Germany

Differences between regions were even greater. In 2003 differences in regional participation rates were above 40 percentage points in France (49), Turkey (44), and Australia (42) (Figure 13.2). The Netherlands and Norway (6), Denmark (7), Sweden, the Czech Republic, the Slovak Republic (8), Iceland (10) and Belgium (9) displayed a more balanced regional pattern.

While the range shows the difference between the region with the lowest and the highest participation rates, the Gini index measures disparities among all regions of a given country. The index ranges between 0 and 1: the higher its value, the larger the disparities between regions.

In 2003, the countries with the highest Gini index for participation rates were Poland and Ireland (0.07), and Turkey, Italy and Mexico (0.06) (Figure 13.3). The countries with the lowest regional dispersion were Norway, the Czech Republic, Sweden, and the Netherlands (0.01).

Low participation affects over half of the population

In 2003, 53% of the OECD population was located in regions with a participation rate below the national average. The percentage was particularly high in Iceland (85%), the Slovak Republic (78%), Korea (76%), Japan (72%), Greece (71%) and Turkey (68%). In contrast, a majority of the working-age population was based in regions with high participation rates in Australia (82%),

Austria (80%), Canada (77%), Mexico (74%), Portugal and Switzerland (69%).

During 1998-2003 the share of the working age population in regions with a participation rate below the national average increased the most in Korea (21 percentage points), Portugal (19), France (15) and the Slovak Republic (14). It decreased the most in Sweden (–18), Belgium (–16), Spain (–11) and Canada (–10).

Female participation varies even more

In 2003, the female participation rate in all OECD countries stood at 61% and ranged from 29% in Turkey to 87% in Iceland. According to the Gini index, the largest regional disparities in female participation rates were in Italy (0.12), Ireland (0.08), and Spain and Poland (0.07) (Figure 13.4). The countries with the smallest disparities in 2003 were the Czech Republic, Sweden, Denmark, Norway and the Netherlands, all with a Gini index of 0.02.

In 2003, more than half (59%) of the OECD female working age population was located in regions with a participation rate below the national average. The percentage was particularly high in Greece (83%), the United States (72%), Japan (71%), the Czech Republic (69%), the Slovak Republic (65%), New Zealand (64%) and Belgium (63%). In Australia, Canada, Austria, Norway, Finland, Spain, Hungary and Ireland, a majority of the female working age population was based in regions with high female participation rates.

During 1998-2003, the share of females living in regions with low participation rates increased the most in Greece (13 percentage points), Belgium (10) the Netherlands (6), the Czech Republic and Austria (5) and the United Kingdom (4). It decreased the most in Sweden (–29), Hungary (–8), Italy (–5), Finland (–4), the United States, Australia and Norway (–3).

Definition

The participation rate is the ratio of the labour force to the working age population (aged 15-64 years). The labour force is defined as the sum of employed and unemployed people. Similarly, the female participation rate is defined as the ratio of the female labour force to the female working age population.

OECD REGIONS AT A GLANCE 2007 – ISBN 978-92-64-00987-5 – © OECD 2007

13.1. Participation rates vary significantly among OECD countries...

National participation rates

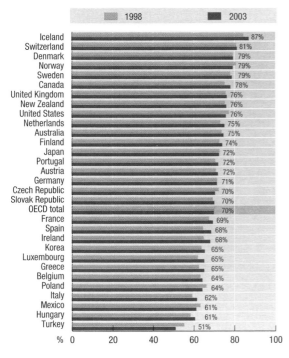

13.2. ... but disparities in participation rates are even larger among regions

Range in labour force participation rates across regions within each country, 2003 (TL3)

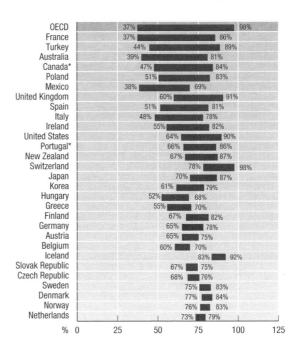

13.3. In 2003, the largest regional disparities in participation rates were in Poland and Ireland

Gini index of inequality of participation rates across regions (TL3)

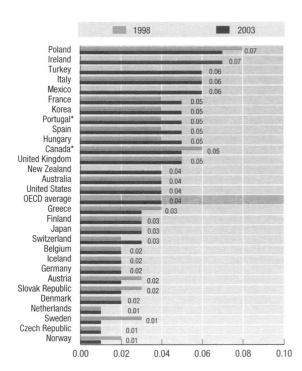

13.4. In 2003, the largest regional disparities in female participation rates were in Italy, Ireland, Spain and Poland

Gini index of inequality of female participation rates across regions (TL3)

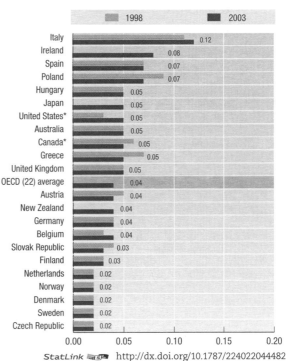

StatLink ᴍꜱᴾ http://dx.doi.org/10.1787/224022044482

13.5. Regional participation rates: Australia and Oceania

Males and females, 2003

- Higher than 85%
- Between 81% and 85%
- Between 70% and 81%
- Between 65% and 70%
- Between 55% and 65%
- Lower than 55%

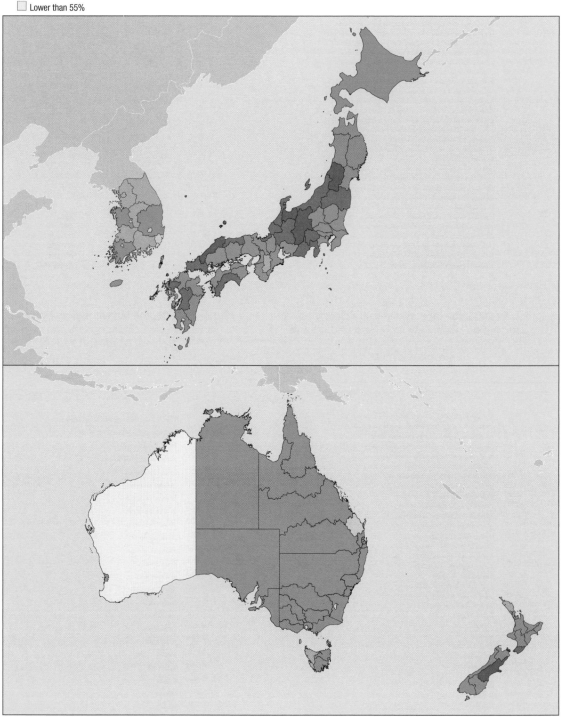

StatLink 🖳🖩 http://dx.doi.org/10.1787/134403004826

13.6. Regional participation rate: Europe
Males and females, 2003

- ■ Higher than 85%
- ■ Between 81% and 85%
- ■ Between 70% and 81%
- ■ Between 65% and 70%
- ■ Between 55% and 65%
- □ Lower than 55%

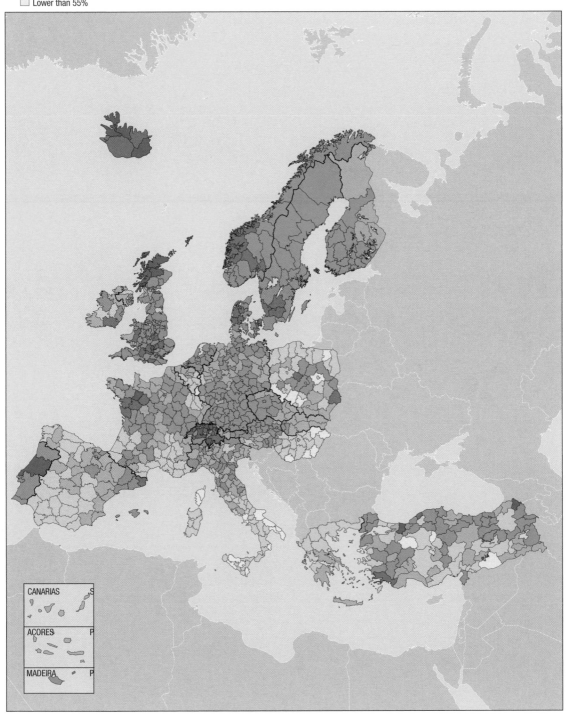

StatLink ⧉ http://dx.doi.org/10.1787/134403004826

13.7. **Regional participation rate: North America**

Males and females, 2003

- Higher than 85%
- Between 81% and 85%
- Between 70% and 81%
- Between 65% and 70%
- Between 55% and 65%
- Lower than 55%

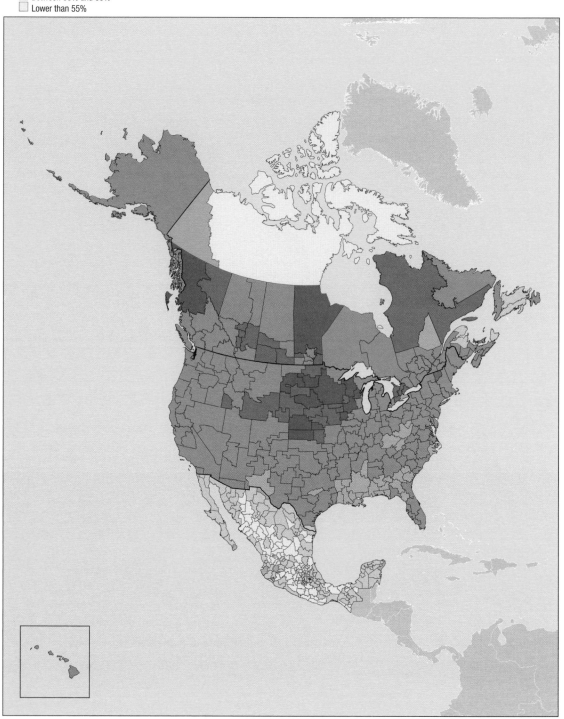

StatLink 🔗 http://dx.doi.org/10.1787/134403004826

OECD REGIONS AT A GLANCE 2007 – ISBN 978-92-64-00987-5 – © OECD 2007

Entering the job market: job opportunities and regional disparities

Participation rates, *i.e.* the ratio of the labour force to the working age population, vary significantly among regions, largely as a result of three factors: demographic structure, social norms (*e.g.* the role of women in society) and economic opportunities.

Age affects the propensity to participate in the labour market: participation is low for young people during education, it increases for adults and it decreases with age owing to retirement. Therefore, the larger the percentage of the young or old in a given population, the lower the participation rate.

The gender composition of the population also affects participation rates. Owing to social customs, labour market participation tends to be lower for women than for men so that the larger the share of women in a region, the lower its participation rate. However, female participation in the labour market increases when adequate social services (*i.e.* child care and day care facilities, parental leave, etc.) are available. Female participation rates also tend to be higher where more economic opportunities are available; therefore their participation rates are higher in urban and intermediate regions. In fact, in 2003 in 13 out of 19 OECD countries the participation of women was highest in predominantly urban regions.

The degree of economic opportunity is the third factor affecting participation rates. Marked regional disparities in unemployment rates (Figure 13.8) suggest that job opportunities vary significantly among regions: the higher the unemployment rate, the lower the probability that an individual will find a job and thus the incentive to enter the labour market. In fact (Figure 13.9) there is a significant negative correlation between regional participation rates and regional unemployment rates in all OECD countries except in Portugal, Iceland, Switzerland and Ireland (not statistically significant).

In the remaining 25 countries, the correlation is negative and statistically significant except for New Zealand, Mexico and the Netherlands, indicating that participation rates are low in regions of high unemployment. This general pattern suggests that regional differences in job opportunities are a major explanation for the observed differences in labour market participation.

13.8. **Unemployment rates vary significantly among regions**

Range in unemployment rates across regions within each country, 2003 (TL3)

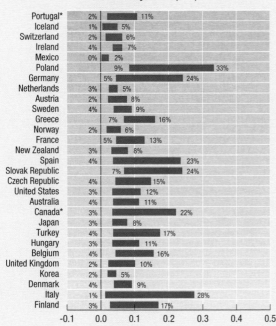

13.9. **Participation rates are low in high-unemployment regions**

Spearman correlation between regional participation rates and regional unemployment rates, 1998-2003 (TL3)

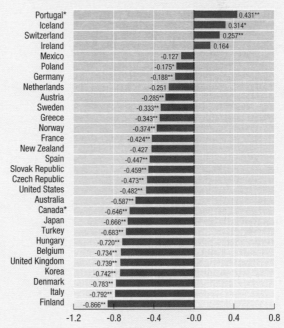

* Significant at 95%. ** Significant at 99%.

StatLink http://dx.doi.org/10.1787/224022044482

THE KEY DRIVERS OF REGIONAL GROWTH

Economic performance varies significantly among OECD regions. But why are some regions more competitive than others? Regional benchmarking makes it possible to identify the factors behind the success of certain regions and to perceive the existence of unused resources in others.

Regional benchmarking means comparing a region's growth rate to that of all other OECD regions. Successful regions grow faster than others and therefore raise their share of total GDP. GDP growth will be slower in less competitive regions and their share of total OECD GDP will decline.

National and regional sources of growth

Growth in regional GDP can be regarded as the joint result of several factors. First, regional performance is significantly affected by country-specific factors, such as national policies and the business cycle. Second, it depends on region-specific factors, such as demographic trends and natural resources. Finally, it depends on regional policies, *i.e.* on the region's ability to increase productivity, change industry specialisation to seize new market opportunities, increase the efficiency of the local labour market, and invest in skills and in innovation.

In order to account for the contribution of these different factors, changes in each region's share of GDP in total OECD GDP can be broken down into:

- *National factors:* Changes in the country's share of total OECD GDP.
- *Regional factors:* Changes in the region's share of the country's GDP.

If all of a country's regions grow faster than the regions in other OECD countries, this faster growth can be ascribed to that country's good performances (national factors).

If a region grows faster than all other OECD regions, including those in the same country, faster growth can be ascribed to the region's good performance (regional factors).

Six key drivers of growth

Regional factors, in turn, are the result of changes in six major components:

- *Productivity*
- *Industry specialisation*
- *Employment rates*
- *Participation rates*
- *Age activity rates*
- *Population*

A detailed explanation of this methodology is provided in the "Source and Methodology".

Each of these components can be viewed as an indicator of the determinants of economic performance at the regional level. Average labour productivity is a proxy for the productivity of the regional production system; industry specialisation captures the contribution of high value added industries; employment rates measure the efficiency of the local labour market; participation rates summarise the characteristics of the regional labour force; age activity rates and population control for region-specific developments in working-age and overall demographic growth.

Natural resources and regional assets

These six components are affected by two types of resources: natural endowments and regional assets. Natural endowments are the characteristics of a region that cannot be changed or can only be changed in the long run, such as geographic location, natural resources, urban or rural setting, and demographics. Regional assets indicate all the resources that could be more efficiently used and allocated so as to generate a higher level of GDP per capita, such as transport, general infrastructure, tourism-oriented facilities, labour market conditions, and human and social capital. The distinction has important implications for policy: while a region's natural endowments are a "given", regional assets can be mobilised through appropriate policies.

The role of specialisation

Changes in a region's share of GDP in the country's total GDP can be explained in terms of the methodology illustrated in Table 14.1. A rapid rise in GDP per worker – relative to the country's growth rate – may be due to specialisation or to a change in specialisation towards sectors with high productivity growth, better infrastructure, higher skill levels or more efficient production technology. As specialisation is driven by comparative advantage, the share of productivity growth that is due to irreproducible inputs (*e.g.* land, oil) can be seen as attributable to natural endowments. To the extent that infrastructure, technology and skills are reproducible resources, the rest of productivity growth can be regarded as a function of the region's policies.

Labour market efficiency can be improved

High growth in employment rates may be due to higher skill levels or to greater efficiency of the local labour market. Both can be regarded as resulting from regional assets: skills can be upgraded through training and education, and changes in employment regulations and labour institutions can increase the efficiency of the regional labour market.

A relative rise in activity rates may be the result of an increase in the working-age population or of an increase in participation rates across all age groups. As young and elderly individuals tend to have lower participation rates, the difference in activity rates due to the age profile of the population can be seen as resulting from natural endowments. In contrast, higher participation rates across all age groups are an indicator of regional assets. Finally, higher rates of population growth may either follow natural demographic trends or be due to policies to attract migrants from other regions and countries.

14.1. **The factors of regional competitiveness**

Changes in the regional share of GDP are due to changes in:	Natural endowments	Regional assets
Productivity		Technology, skills + Infrastructure
Industry specialisation	Irreproducible inputs (natural resources)	Reproducible inputs (skills, capital)
Employment rate		Skills of the labour force + Labour market efficiency
Participation rate		Labour market participation
Age activity rate	Changes in working age (15-64) population	
Population	Demographics	Migration

A region's economic performance can be measured as the difference between its growth rate and that of all OECD regions. Competitive regions will grow faster than others and will increase their share of total OECD GDP. By the same token, GDP growth will be slower in less competitive regions and their share in total GDP will fall.

Top-performing regions are widely spread...

Over 1998-2003, about half of OECD regions – 149 out of 297 – increased their share in total OECD GDP. The 20 fastest-growing regions were: **Canada**: Northwest Territories and Alberta; **Ireland**: Southern and Eastern and Border, Midlands and Western; **Korea**: Seoul region, Chungcheong, Gyeonbuk, Jeju, Gyeongnam and Gangwon; **Czech Republic**: Stredni Cechy; **Mexico**: Quintana Roo and Campeche; **United States**: Wyoming and Nevada; **Hungary**: Kosep-Magyarorszag; **Australia**: Northern Territory; **Spain**: Murcia and Canaries; and **Greece**: Athens region (Figure 15.1).

... as are weaker performers

Over the same period, the other half of regions reduced their share in total OECD GDP. The 20 worst-performing regions were: **Germany**: Berlin, Nordrhein-Westfalen, Mecklenburg-Vorpommern, Niedersachsen and Saarland; **Czech Republic**: Moravskoslezko; **Spain**: Ceuta and Melilla; **Poland**: Opolskie; **Norway**: Nord-Norge; **France**: Bourgogne and Champagne-Ardennes; **Japan**: Tohoku, Kinki, Hokuriku, Shikoku and Hokkaido; **Italy**: Basilicata; **Mexico**: The state of Mexico; and **United States**: Ohio (Figure 15.2).

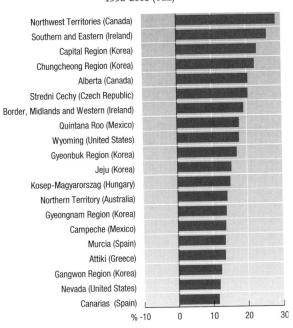

15.1. Increase in the GDP share of the 20 fastest-growing OECD regions

Change in the regional GDP share of the OECD, 1998-2003 (TL2)

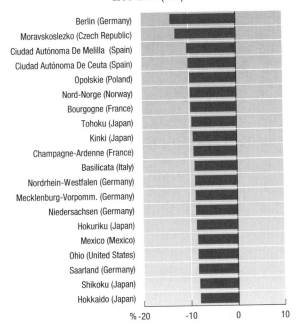

15.2. Decrease in the GDP share of the 20 slowest-growing OECD regions

Change in the regional GDP share of the OECD, 1998-2003 (TL2)

StatLink ᐧᔕᑊ http://dx.doi.org/10.1787/817581470547

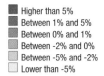

15.3. Change in the regional GDP share of the OECD: Asia and Oceania
1998-2003

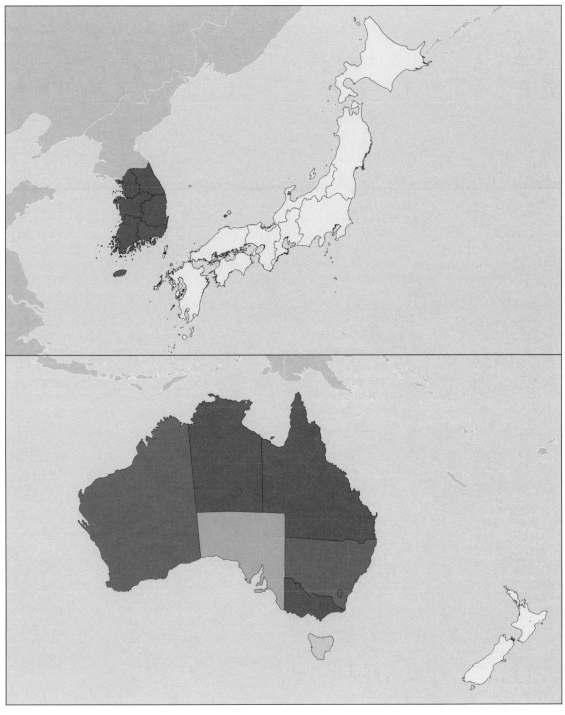

- ■ Higher than 5%
- ■ Between 1% and 5%
- ■ Between 0% and 1%
- ■ Between -2% and 0%
- ■ Between -5% and -2%
- □ Lower than -5%

StatLink http://dx.doi.org/10.1787/520742150613

15.4. Change in the regional GDP share of the OECD: Europe
1998-2003

- Higher than 5%
- Between 1% and 5%
- Between 0% and 1%
- Between -2% and 0%
- Between -5% and -2%
- Lower than -5%

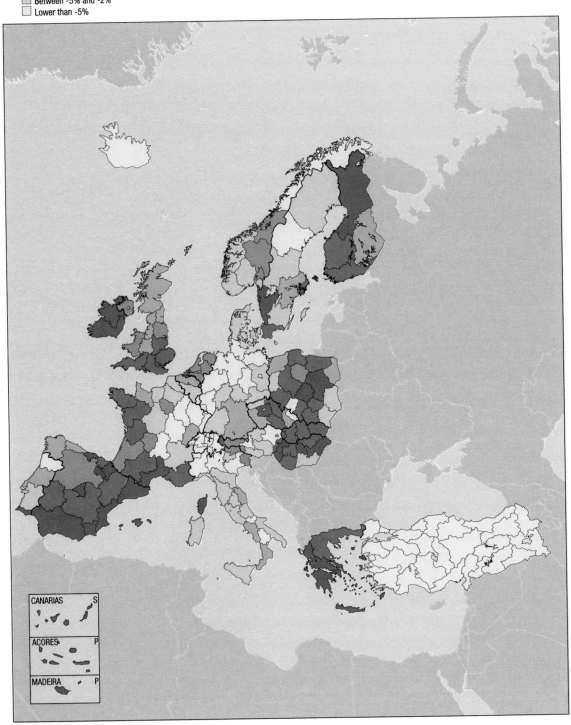

StatLink http://dx.doi.org/10.1787/520742150613

15.5. Change in the regional share of the OECD: North America
1998-2003

- ■ Higher than 5%
- ■ Between 1% and 5%
- ■ Between 0% and 1%
- ■ Between -2% and 0%
- □ Between -5% and -2%
- □ Lower than -5%

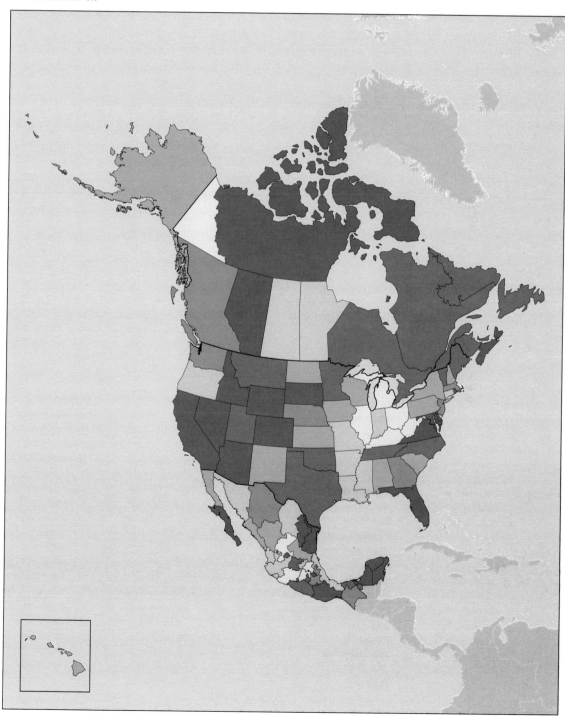

StatLink ⬛⬛⬛ http://dx.doi.org/10.1787/520742150613

Regional performance is a result both of national factors – such as national policies and the business cycle – and regional factors – such as demographic trends and regional policies. If all regions in a country grow faster than the regions in other OECD countries, their faster growth can be ascribed to national factors. On the other hand, to the extent that a region exhibits faster growth than all other OECD regions, including those in the same country, that growth can be ascribed to the region's good performance (regional factors).

Regional factors have a significant impact

Over 1998-2003, about half of OECD regions – 149 regions out of 297 – increased their share in total OECD GDP. In more than two-thirds of these regions – 68%, or 101 regions – regional factors explain more than 10% of the increase in their share of total GDP. In most cases, therefore, regions' good international performance seems to be driven by their own success rather than that of their country.

National factors dominate in Ireland and Korea

Among the 20 fastest-growing regions (Figure 15.1) the good performance of Irish regions seems to be largely due to good national performance; the same applies to four Korean regions: Gyeonbuk, Jeju, Gyeongnam and Gangwon (Figure 16.1).

In 76% of the 112 slow-growing regions, region-specific factors explained more than 10% of the reduction in their share of total OECD GDP. In particular, in none of the 20 slowest-growing regions (Figure 15.2) did national factors account for more than 90% of the decrease in their share of OECD GDP (Figure 16.2).

16.1. Factors explaining faster GDP growth in the top 20 OECD regions

Change in the regional GDP share of the OECD 1998-2003 (TL2) due to:

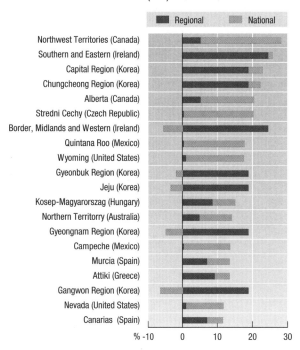

16.2. Factors explaining slower GDP growth in the bottom 20 OECD regions

Change in the regional GDP share of the OECD 1998-2003 (TL2) due to:

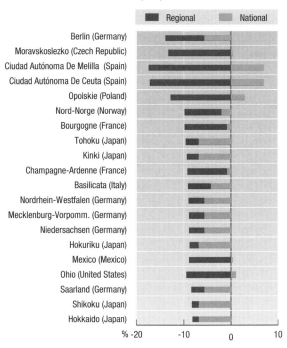

StatLink ⬛⬛ http://dx.doi.org/10.1787/014362733567

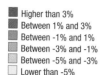
16.3. Change in the regional GDP share of the OECD due to regional factors: Asia and Oceania

1998-2003

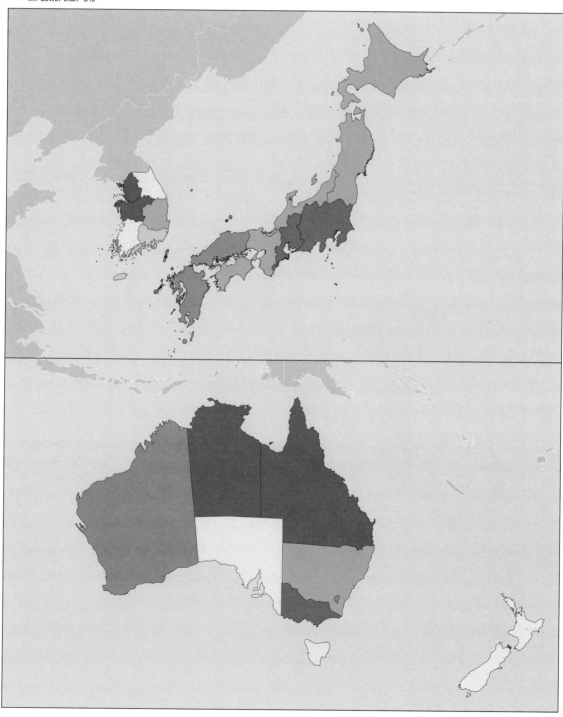

- Higher than 3%
- Between 1% and 3%
- Between -1% and 1%
- Between -3% and -1%
- Between -5% and -3%
- Lower than -5%

StatLink ⬛🖳 http://dx.doi.org/10.1787/354020600675

16.4. Change in the regional GDP share of the OECD due to regional factors: Europe

1998-2003

- ■ Higher than 3%
- ■ Between 1% and 3%
- ■ Between -1% and 1%
- ■ Between -3% and -1%
- ■ Between -5% and -3%
- □ Lower than -5%

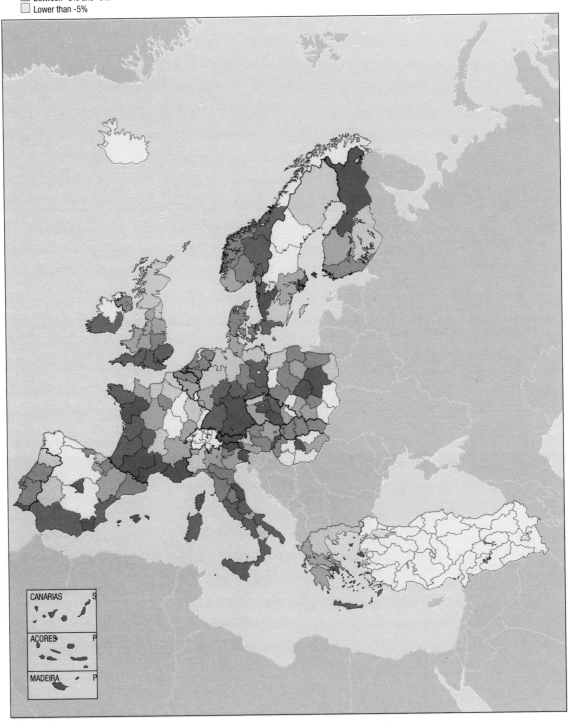

StatLink ⬛⬛🔊 http://dx.doi.org/10.1787/354020600675

16.5. Change in the regional GDP share of the OECD due to regional factors: North America

1998-2003

- Higher than 3%
- Between 1% and 3%
- Between -1% and 1%
- Between -3% and -1%
- Between -5% and -3%
- Lower than -5%

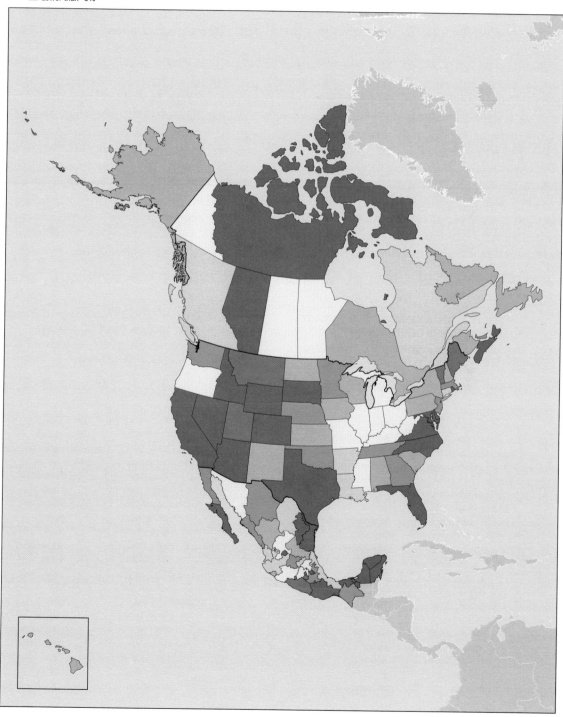

StatLink http://dx.doi.org/10.1787/354020600675

Over 1998-2003, about one-third of OECD regions – 34% or 101 regions – increased their share in total OECD GDP owing to region-specific factors. The increase was due to a relative increase in population in 37% of these regions, a relative rise in GDP per capita in 22% and relative growth in both components in the other 41%.

Population Growth is important

The relative increase in population was the main source of fast growth in a number of the 20 top-performing regions (Figure 17.1). This was the case of the Capital region (Korea), Quintana Roo and Baja California Sur (Mexico), Nevada (United States), Canaries, Baleares and Madrid (Spain), where the (relative) increase in population was large enough to offset the (relative) decrease in GDP per capita.

Despite population decline, some top-performing regions, particularly Chungcheong (Korea), Wyoming (United States), Kosep-Magyarorszag (Hungary), Northern Territory (Australia) and Madeira (Portugal), owe their success entirely to faster growth in GDP per capita.

During 1998-2003, 38% of regions (112 regions) decreased their share in total OECD GDP owing to specific factors. This was due to a relative decrease in population in 18%, a relative decrease in GDP per capita in 22%, and a relative increase in both components in the remaining 60%.

Poor performances are du to GDP per capita

In general, the regional decrease in the share of OECD GDP was small when it was due exclusively to population decline (Figure 17.2). This was the single cause of low GDP growth in just three of the 20 bottom performing regions: Mecklenburg-Vorpommern (Germany), Shikoku and Hokkaido (Japan).

The state of Mexico (Mexico), Niedersachsen and Schleswig-Holstein (Germany) were the only regions where faster population growth was associated with a significant decline in the share of OECD GDP (above –8%) because of a relative decrease in GDP per capita.

The large majority of low-performing regions, therefore, registered a relative decrease in both GDP per capita and population.

17.1. **Factors explaining faster GDP growth in the top 20 OECD regions**

Change in the regional GDP share of the OECD
1998-2003 (TL2) due to:

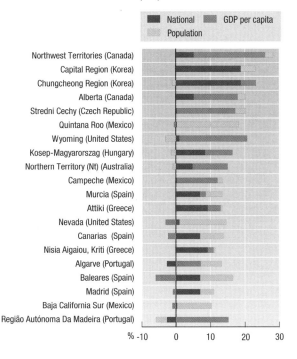

17.2. **Factors explaining slower GDP growth in bottom 20 OECD regions**

Change in the regional GDP share of the OECD
1998-2003 (TL2) due to:

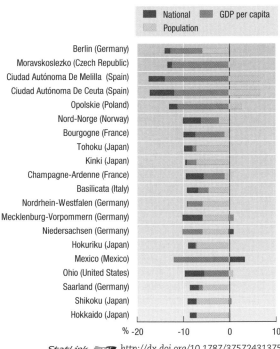

StatLink 🔗 http://dx.doi.org/10.1787/375724313753

OECD REGIONS AT A GLANCE 2007 – ISBN 978-92-64-00987-5 – © OECD 2007

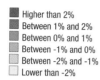

17.3. Change in the regional GDP share of the OECD due to change in population: Asia and Oceania

1998-2003

- ■ Higher than 2%
- ■ Between 1% and 2%
- ▨ Between 0% and 1%
- ▨ Between -1% and 0%
- ▨ Between -2% and -1%
- □ Lower than -2%

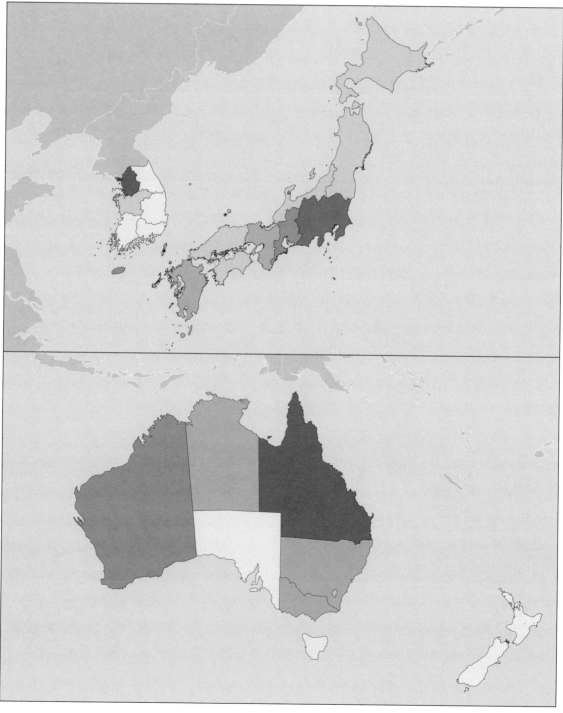

StatLink ⧉ http://dx.doi.org/10.1787/721173138253

17.4. Change in the regional GDP share of the OECD due to change in population: Europe

1998-2003

Higher than 2%
Between 1% and 2%
Between 0% and 1%
Between -1% and 0%
Between -2% and -1%
Lower than -2%

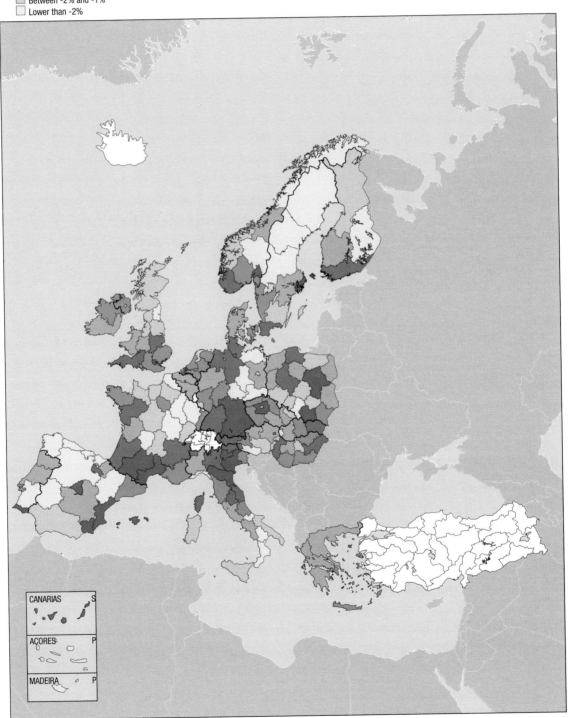

StatLink ᗧ᙮ http://dx.doi.org/10.1787/721173138253

OECD REGIONS AT A GLANCE 2007 – ISBN 978-92-64-00987-5 – © OECD 2007

17.5. Change in the regional GDP share of the OECD due to change in population: North America

1998-2003

- ■ Higher than 2%
- ■ Between 1% and 2%
- ■ Between 0% and 1%
- ■ Between -1% and 0%
- □ Between -2% and -1%
- □ Lower than -2%

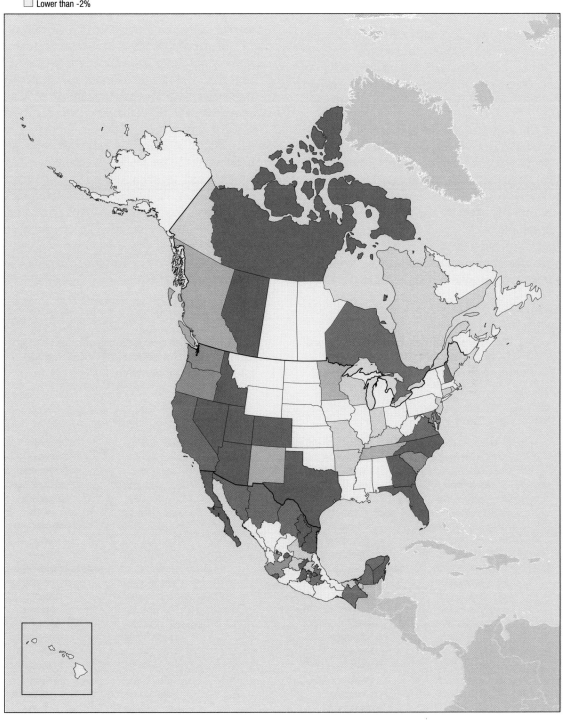

StatLink ⬛🖾▄ http://dx.doi.org/10.1787/721173138253

High growth in GDP per capita for 1998-2003 was a result of a relative increase in GDP per worker in a large majority of OECD regions (77%).

Productivity gains are boosted by specialisation

The rise in GDP per worker was due to a relative increase in average productivity in 53%, while specialisation was a factor in the remaining 47%. More specifically, specialisation in industries with high productivity growth contributed to the rise in GDP per worker in 17% of regions, a change in specialisation towards high productivity industries in 10% and both components in the remaining 20%.

Among the 20 fastest-growing regions (Figure 18.1), productivity growth had the largest impact on GDP per worker in the Northern Territories (19%), Madeira (16%), Stredni Cechy and Wyoming (12%). Specialisation in industries with high productivity growth had the biggest impact in Quintana Roo (12%) and Campeche (9%). Finally, a change in specialisation towards high productivity industries accounted for a 5% increase in GDP per worker in Campeche and 3% in Attiki.

The relative decrease in GDP per capita over 1998-2003 was a result of a relative decrease in GDP per worker in 80% of regions.

Sectors of low productivity undermine growth

The drop in GDP per worker was due to a relative decline in average productivity in 35% of these regions. Specialisation and changes in specialisation contributed to declines in GDP per worker in the remaining 65% of regions.

In particular, specialisation in industries with low productivity growth was a factor in 25% of regions, a change in specialisation towards industries with low productivity in 15% and both components in the remaining 25%.

Among the 20 slowest-growing regions (Figure 18.2) a decline in productivity had the largest impact on GDP per worker in Champagne-Ardennes (–24%) and Bourgogne (–16%). The effect of specialisation in industries with low productivity growth was the largest in Shikoku (–4%) and Kinki (–1.5%). Finally, a change in specialisation towards industries with low productivity accounted for a 3% decrease in GDP per worker in Berlin and 2% in Mexico and Shikoku.

18.1. Factors explaining faster GDP growth in the top 20 OECD regions

Change in the regional GDP share of the OECD 1998-2003 (TL2) due to:

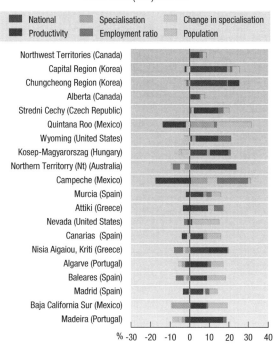

18.2. Factors explaining slower GDP growth in the bottom 20 OECD regions

Change in the regional GDP share of the OECD 1998-2003 (TL2) due to:

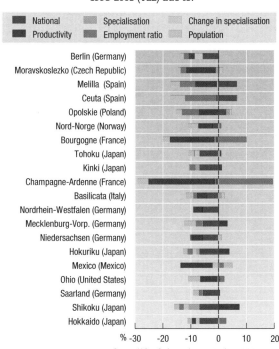

StatLink 🔗 http://dx.doi.org/10.1787/323232674827

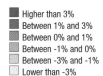
18.3. **Change in the regional GDP share of the OECD due to change in productivity: Asia and Oceania**

1998-2003

- ■ Higher than 3%
- ■ Between 1% and 3%
- ■ Between 0% and 1%
- ■ Between -1% and 0%
- □ Between -3% and -1%
- □ Lower than -3%

StatLink ⬛️📊⬛ http://dx.doi.org/10.1787/143233464433

18.4. Change in the regional GDP share of the OECD due to change in productivity: Europe

1998-2003

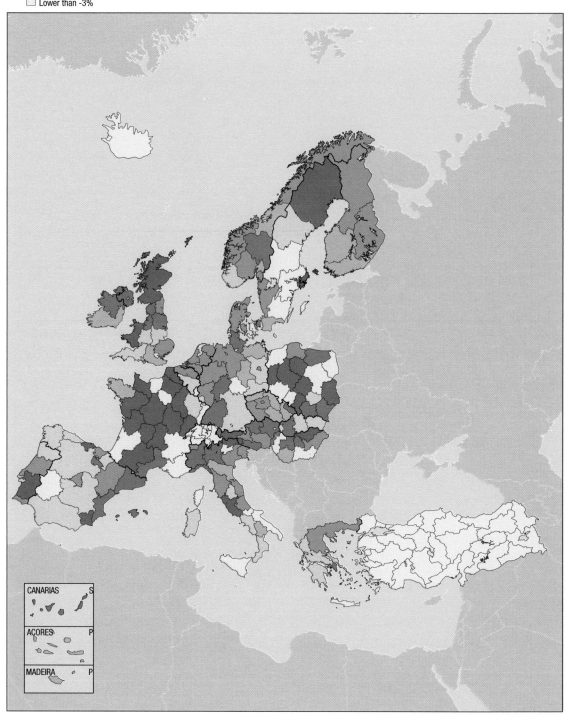

- ■ Higher than 3%
- ■ Between 1% and 3%
- ■ Between 0% and 1%
- ■ Between -1% and 0%
- ■ Between -3% and -1%
- □ Lower than -3%

CANARIAS S

AÇORES P

MADEIRA P

StatLink http://dx.doi.org/10.1787/143233464433

18.5. Change in the regional GDP share of the OECD due to change in productivity: North America

1998-2003

- ■ Higher than 3%
- ■ Between 1% and 3%
- ■ Between 0% and 1%
- ▨ Between -1% and 0%
- ▨ Between -3% and -1%
- □ Lower than -3%

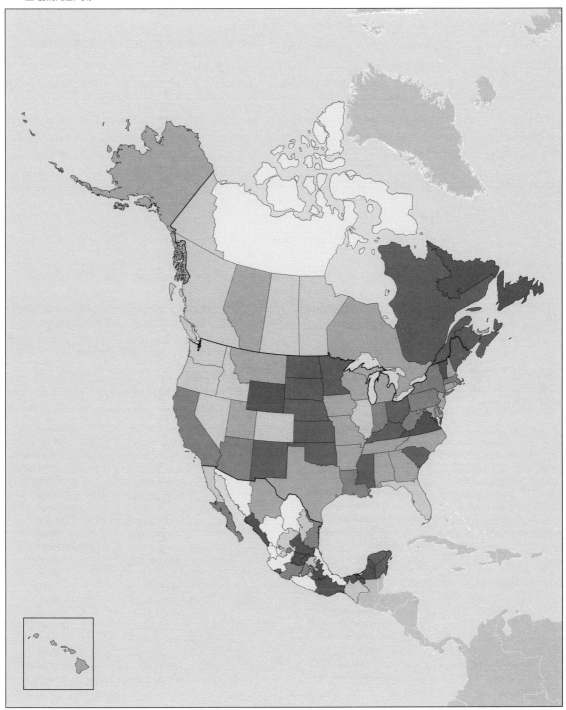

StatLink ⟋⟋⟋ http://dx.doi.org/10.1787/143233464433

Rapid growth in GDP per capita over 1998-2003 was due to a strong rise in productivity in 77% of regions. However, in 23%, the relative boost in GDP per capita was driven by a relative increase in one or more of the following variables: employment rates, participation rates and working age population.

Demographics and the labour force

Among the 20 fastest-growing regions (Figure 19.1) the increase in employment rates had the largest impact on GDP per capita in the Northwest Territories (4%) and Stredni Cechy (3%). The contribution of higher participation rates was the most significant in Campeche (14%), Murcia (4%) and Wyoming (4%). Finally, a rise in the working age population accounted for a 2% increase in GDP per capita in Baleares and Madeira.

The relative decrease in GDP per capita over 1998-2003 was due to a relative decline in productivity in 80% of regions, but in the remaining 20% it was driven by a relative drop in employment rates, participation rates and/or the working age population. In general, however, the regional decrease in GDP per capita was small when it was not due to productivity decline.

Participation rates are important

Among the 20 slowest-growing regions (Figure 19.2) the decrease in employment rates had the largest impact in Moravskoslezko (–4%), Mecklenburg-Vorpommern (–3%) and Berlin (–3%). The effect of lower participation rates was greatest in Ceuta (–24%), Melilla (–16%) and Opolskie (–9%). Finally, a reduction in the working age population was significant in Nord-Norge, Kinki, Niedersachsen, Opolskie and Ohio.

19.1. Factors explaining faster GDP growth in the top 20 OECD regions

Change in the regional GDP share of the OECD
1998-2003 (TL2) due to:

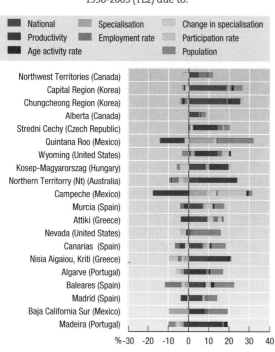

19.2. Factors explaining slower GDP growth in the bottom 20 OECD regions

Change in the regional GDP share of the OECD
1998-2003 (TL2) due to:

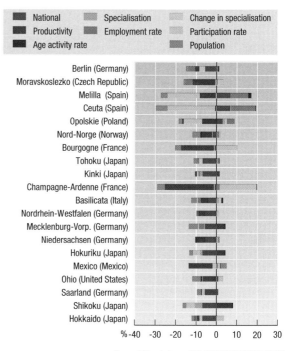

StatLink ᴹˢᴸ http://dx.doi.org/10.1787/661216747758

19.3. Change in the regional GDP share of the OECD due to change in employment rates: Asia and Oceania

1998-2003

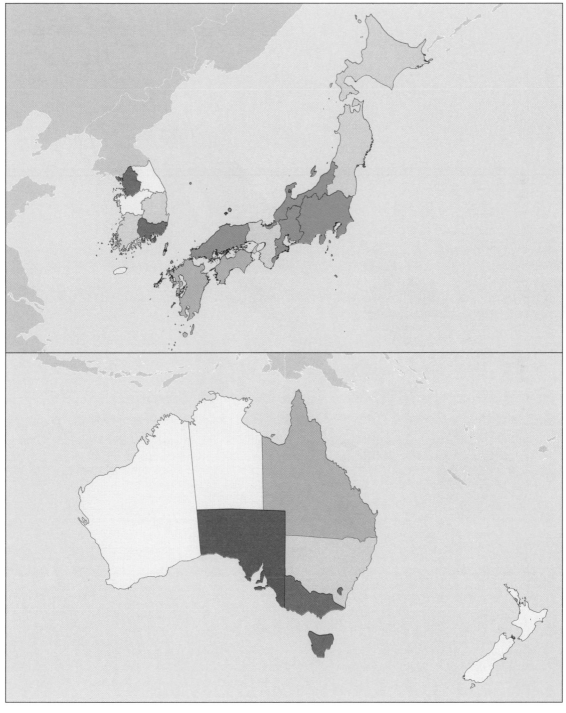

■ Higher than 1%
■ Between 0.5% and 1%
■ Between 0% and 0.5%
■ Between -0.4% and 0%
□ Between -1% and -0.4%
□ Lower than -1%

StatLink ᴍᴤᴸ http://dx.doi.org/10.1787/613518777232

19.4. **Change in the regional GDP share of the OECD due to change in employment rates:
Europe**
1998-2003

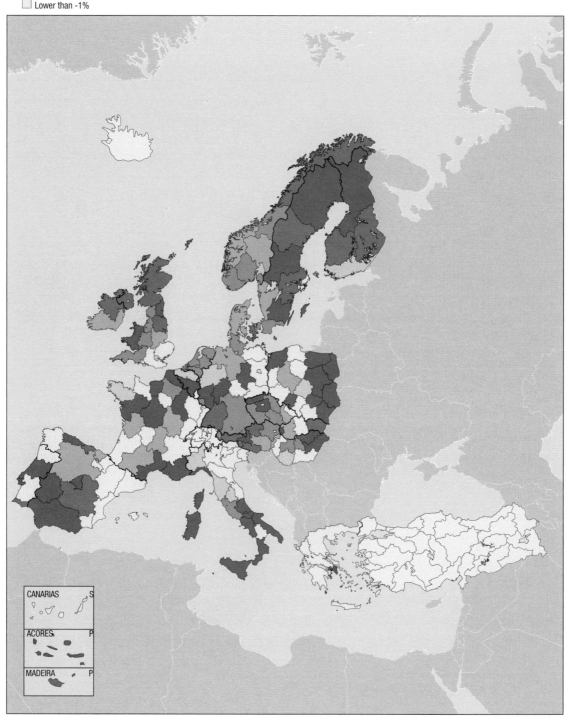

CANARIAS S

ACORES P

MADEIRA P

StatLink http://dx.doi.org/10.1787/613518777232

19.5. **Change in the regional GDP share of the OECD due to change in employment rates: North America**

1998-2003

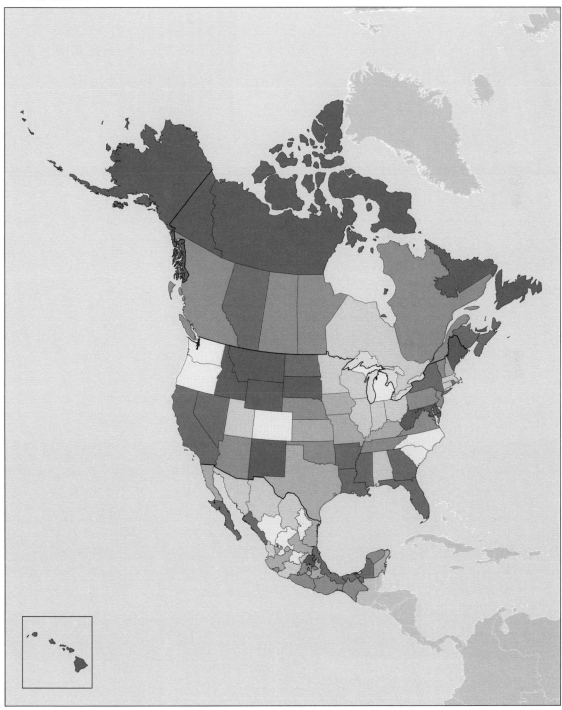

- Higher than 1%
- Between 0.5% and 1%
- Between 0% and 0.5%
- Between -0.4% and 0%
- Between -1% and -0.4%
- Lower than -1%

StatLink http://dx.doi.org/10.1787/613518777232

III. COMPETING ON THE BASIS OF REGIONAL WELL-BEING

The well-being of a region's inhabitants depends on their ability to access resources and services that are often available only in large urban centres. The travelling time necessary to reach the closest agglomeration gives a measure of a region's ability to quickly access resources and services.

Variations in accessibility are significant

Travelling times vary widely among regions (Figure 20.1). Sparsely populated countries, such as Australia, the United States and Canada, have the largest variations in travelling times (about 34, 30 and 25 hours, respectively). Regional variations are also significant in Greece (about 21 hours), Mexico and Norway (about 20 hours in both countries).

In most European countries differences in travelling times are narrower. In Belgium Switzerland and the Netherlands, all regions are located within 2 hours or less of the closest centre. Greece, Turkey and the United Kingdom are exceptions to this pattern, as travelling times from the most remote regions are much higher.

Rural populations face the longest journeys

Not surprisingly, accessibility tends to be lower for rural regions (Figure 20.2). On average, travelling times are more than 3.5 hours for rural regions, about 2 hours for intermediate regions, and just 37 minutes for urban regions. In Australia, even intermediate regions face limited accessibility: the average travelling time to the closest centre is longer (by about one hour) from intermediate regions than from rural ones.

20.1. Sparsely populated countries have the largest travelling times to reach the closest centre

Regional variation in travelling time (hours) to reach the closest centre, 2001 (TL3)

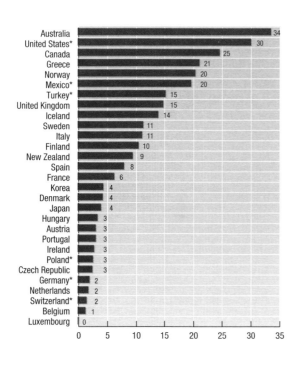

20.2. On average travelling times are more than 3.5 hours for rural regions across OECD countries

Average time (minutes) to be travelled to reach the closest centre, by type of region, 2001 (TL3)

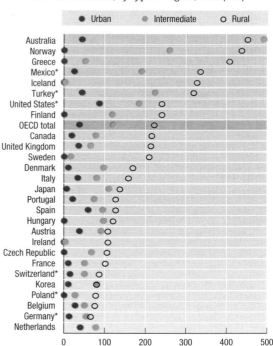

StatLink ⟨ᵐˢ⟩ http://dx.doi.org/10.1787/717381344782

Definition

Accessibility is defined as the travelling time to reach the closest urban centre. Centres are defined as either a city with no less than 300 000 inhabitants or an urban agglomeration with no less than 500 000. Cities and urban agglomerations are defined according to *UN Principles and recommendations for Population and Housing Census*.

20.3. Travelling time to the closest urban centre: Asia and Oceania

2001

- ■ Lower than 30 min.
- ■ Between 60 and 30 min.
- ■ Between 120 and 60 min.
- ■ Between 180 and 120 min.
- ■ Betwenn 240 and 180 min.
- □ Higher than 240 min.

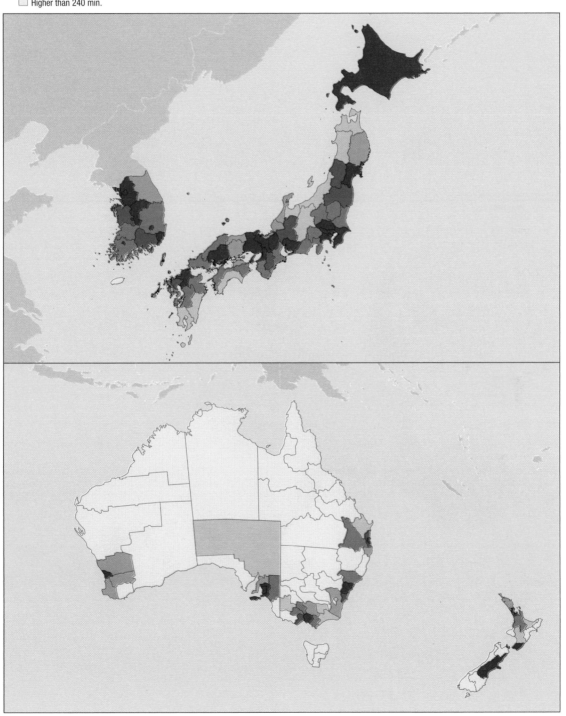

StatLink ⬛⬛⬛ http://dx.doi.org/10.1787/032250487377

20.4. Travelling time to the closest urban centre: Europe
2001

■ Lower than 30 min.
■ Between 60 and 30 min.
■ Between 120 and 60 min.
■ Between 180 and 120 min.
□ Betwenn 240 and 180 min.
□ Higher than 240 min.

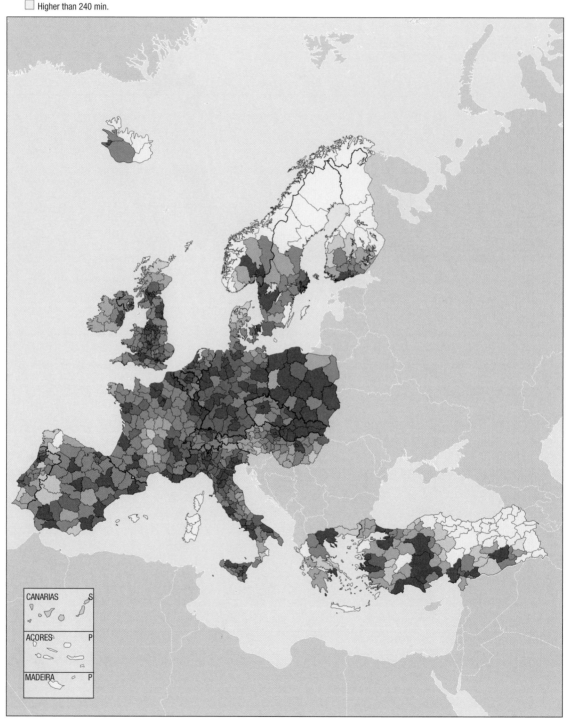

StatLink ⧉ http://dx.doi.org/10.1787/032250487377

20.5. **Travelling time to the closest urban centre: North America**
2001

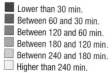

Lower than 30 min.
Between 60 and 30 min.
Between 120 and 60 min.
Between 180 and 120 min.
Betwenn 240 and 180 min.
Higher than 240 min.

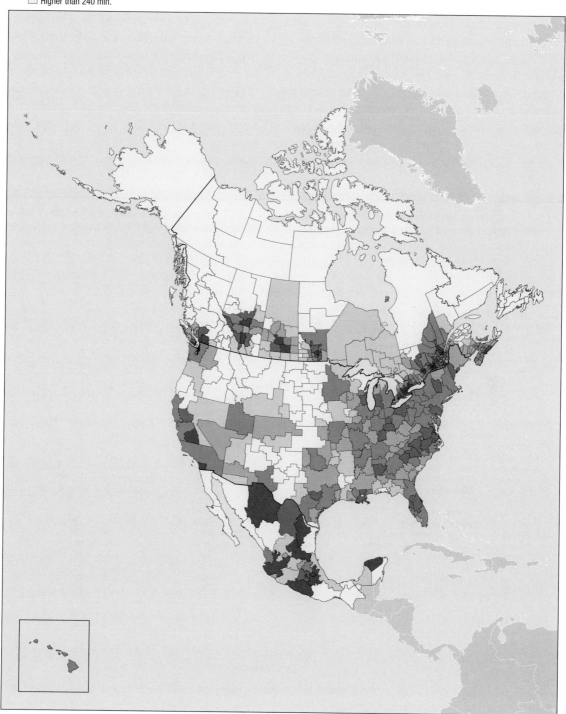

StatLink ᴴⁱˢ⅃ http://dx.doi.org/10.1787/032250487377

A highly educated labour force is a major factor in determining regional competitiveness. The enrolment ratio is a commonly used measure of the level of participation in tertiary level education.

Korea outperforms in terms of education

Figure 21.1 shows regional variations in tertiary education enrolment rates in 2003. The Czech Republic has the largest disparities in enrolment rates: the capital (Prague) has the highest rate (94) and the surrounding region (Stredni Cechy) has the lowest (3). The countries with the smallest disparities are the Netherlands and Japan. Korea has the region with the highest enrolment rate of all OECD regions (96 per 1 000 in Chungcheong). Moreover, the lowest regional enrolment rate in Korea (52) is above the highest regional rate in several OECD countries.

Urban regions enjoy the highest enrolment rates

In most OECD countries the correlation between student enrolment rates in tertiary education and the share of population by type of region (urban, intermediate and rural) (Figure 21.2) is positive for urban regions, as universities tend to be concentrated in large urban centres. In rural regions the correlation is negative for most countries (except for the Slovak Republic, the Czech Republic, the United Kingdom, Korea, Spain and Mexico). For intermediate regions the coefficient is positive in 12 countries out of the 27 considered.

21.1. **The Czech Republic is the country with the highest disparities in enrolment rates**

Range of variation in the number of students enrolled in tertiary education per 1 000 population, 2003 (TL2)

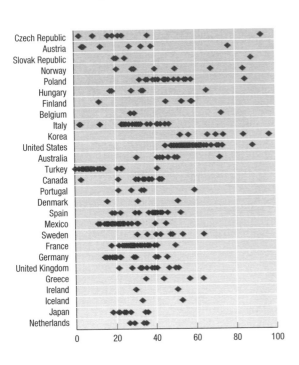

21.2. **In most OECD countries tertiary education institutions tend to be concentrated in urban regions**

Spearman correlation between student enrollment rate and share of population by regional type, 2003 (TL2)

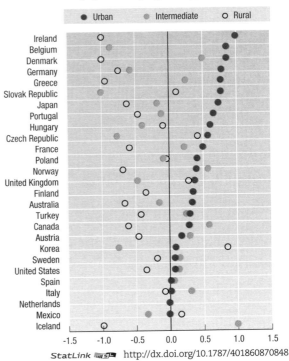

StatLink 🔗 http://dx.doi.org/10.1787/401860870848

Definition

Total enrolment is defined as the number of students, regardless of age, enrolled in all types of schools and educational institutions in the region, including public, private and all other institutions that provide organised tertiary level (ISCED 5-6) educational programmes.

21.3. Student enrolments in tertiary education: Asia and Oceania

Number of students per 1 000 population, 2003

- Higher than 53
- Between 43 and 53
- Between 33 and 43
- Between 23 and 33
- Between 10 and 23
- Lower than 10

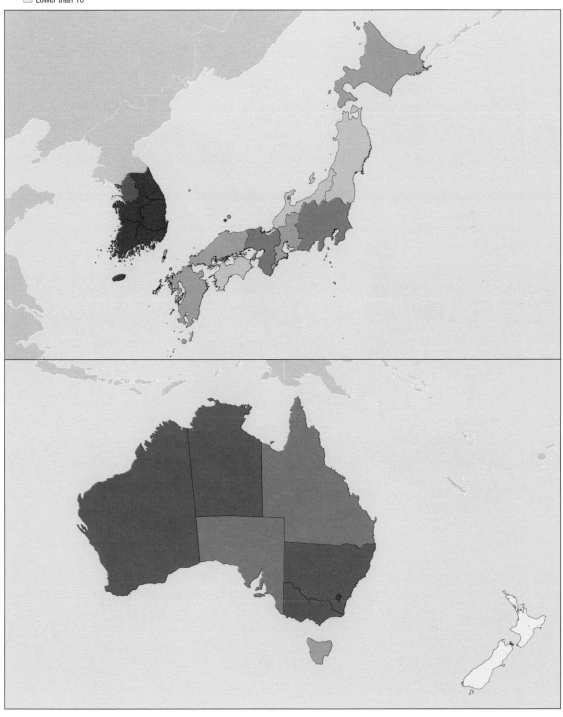

StatLink ⌐ㅍ⑤ http://dx.doi.org/10.1787/165846477157

21.4. Student enrolments in tertiary education: Europe

Number of students per 1 000 population, 2003

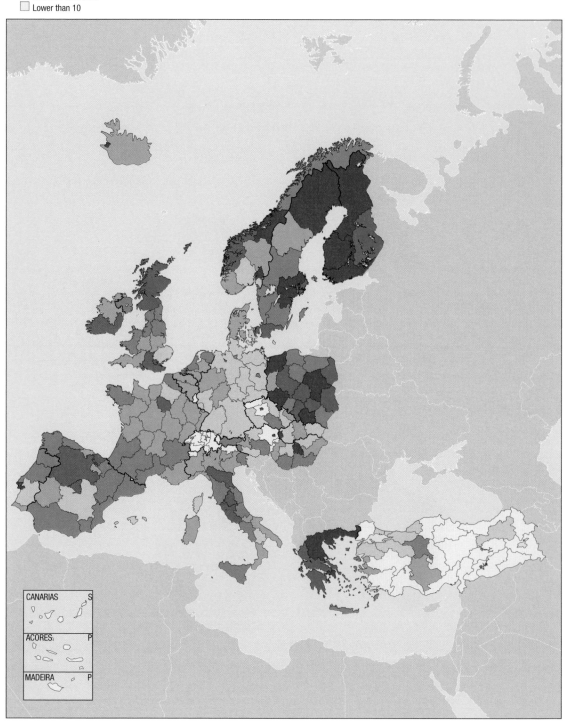

Higher than 53
Between 43 and 53
Between 33 and 43
Between 23 and 33
Between 10 and 23
Lower than 10

StatLink   http://dx.doi.org/10.1787/165846477157

OECD REGIONS AT A GLANCE 2007 – ISBN 978-92-64-00987-5 – © OECD 2007

21.5. Student enrolments in tertiary education: North America

Number of students per 1 000 population, 2003

- Higher than 53
- Between 43 and 53
- Between 33 and 43
- Between 23 and 33
- Between 10 and 23
- Lower than 10

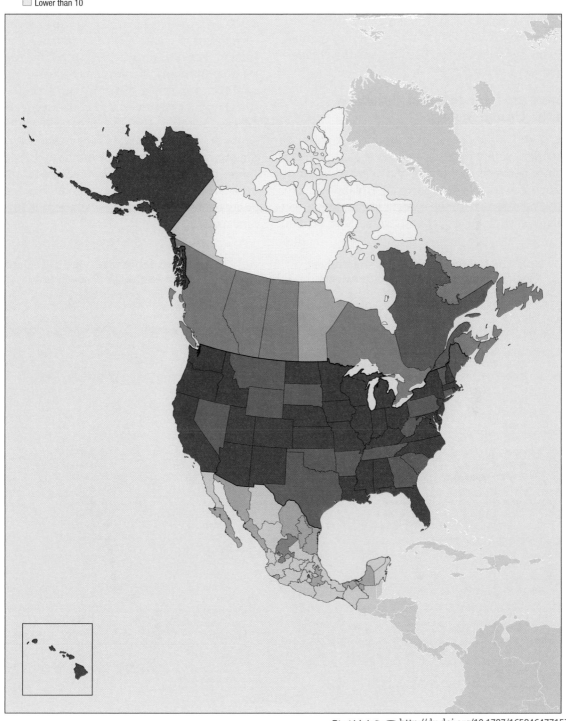

StatLink http://dx.doi.org/10.1787/165846477157

Voter turnout provides an indication of the degree of public trust in government and of citizens' involvement in the political process.

Figure 22.1 shows the variation in voter turnout across regions in OECD countries in the last national election. In Australia, where voting is mandatory, Tasmania records the highest OECD-area turnout rate (96%). Belgium, Austria, Italy and Turkey also record very high turnout rates in some regions. Among these countries, Belgium has the smallest regional variation (87%-93%).

There are large regional variations in the United States

The United States has the largest regional variation, with a difference of about 31 percentage points between the lowest and the highest rate, followed by Spain (24), Mexico (22), Finland and Italy (20). The regions with the lowest turnout rates are in Poland (34% in Opolskie) and Switzerland (43% in Ostschweiz). New Zealand, Sweden and Ireland show the lowest regional variation in turnout rates.

Turnout rates vary across regional types

The correlation between voter turnout rates and share of population by type of region (urban, intermediate and rural) reveals no clear trend across OECD countries (Figure 22.2). In urban regions the correlation is positive for 11 countries (Portugal, Finland, Poland, Hungary, Norway, Italy, Australia, Mexico, Germany, Turkey and Sweden), and it is negative for the others. In rural regions the correlation is positive in 12 countries (Australia, Turkey, Sweden, Canada, Japan, Spain, Slovak Republic, United States, France, Austria, United Kingdom and Ireland). In Australia, Sweden and Turkey the correlation of the voter turnout rate with the share of population in rural and urban regions is positive, but in Sweden the coefficient is higher for rural regions.

22.1. The United States shows the highest regional variation in voter turnout rate

Range of variation in voter turnout at the latest national elections (TL2)

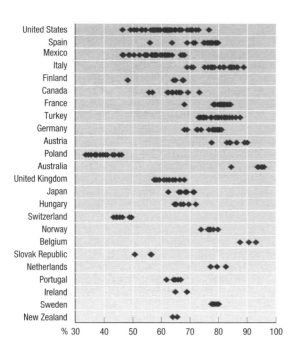

22.2. Voter turnout rates vary by regional type across OECD countries

Spearmank correlation between voter turnout rate and share of population by regional type, latest national elections (TL2)

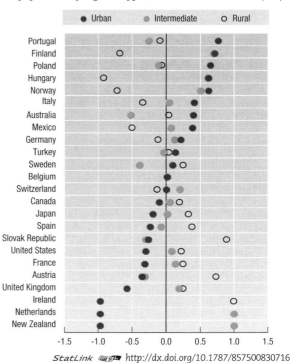

StatLink ⌦ http://dx.doi.org/10.1787/857500830716

Definition

Voter turnout is the ratio of the number of voters to the number of persons with voting rights at the last national election.

22.3. Regional voter turnout: Asia and Oceania

As a percentage of the country average in the last national/federal elections

- Higher than 106%
- Between 102% and 106%
- Between 100% and 102%
- Between 97% and 102%
- Between 93% and 97%
- Lower than 93%

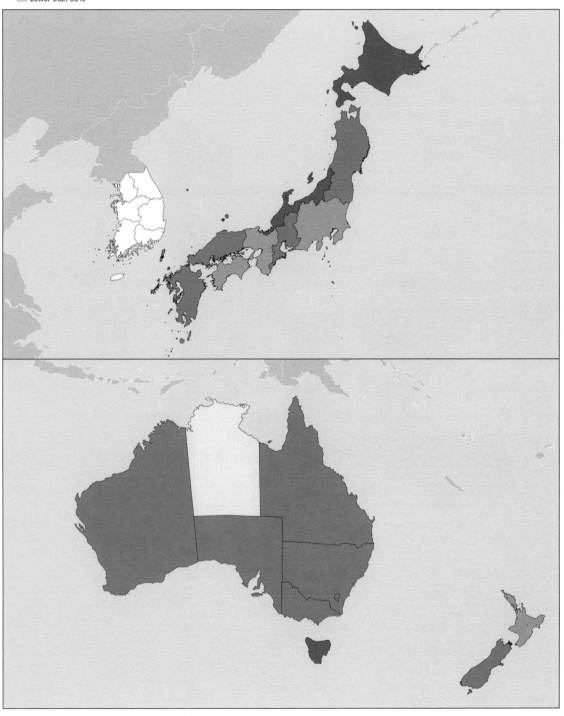

StatLink ᴍ⬛ http://dx.doi.org/10.1787/154080857367

22.4. Regional voter turnout: Europe

As a percentage of the country average in the last national/federal election

- ■ Higher than 106%
- ■ Between 102% and 106%
- ■ Between 100% and 102%
- ■ Between 97% and 102%
- ■ Between 93% and 97%
- □ Lower than 93%

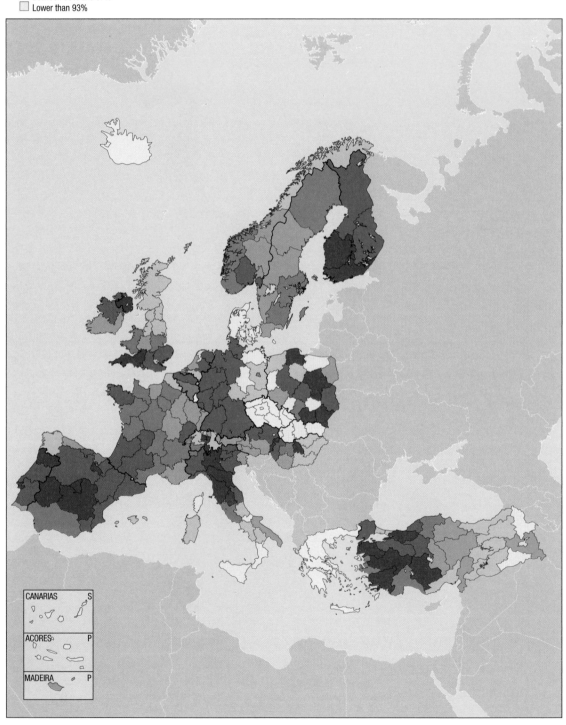

StatLink ⌨️ http://dx.doi.org/10.1787/154080857367

22.5. **Regional voter turnout: North America**

As a percentage of the country average in the last national/federal elections

Higher than 106%
Between 102% and 106%
Between 100% and 102%
Between 97% and 102%
Between 93% and 97%
Lower than 93%

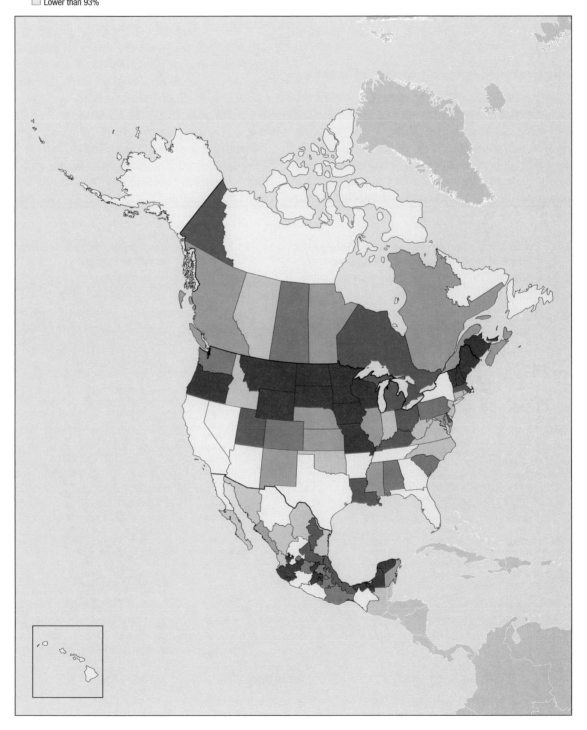

StatLink http://dx.doi.org/10.1787/154080857367

Safety is an important factor in the attractiveness of regions, but the lack of international standards for crime statistics makes international comparisons difficult. Statistics on reported crime are affected by how crime is defined in the national legislation and by the statistical criteria used in recording offences. In addition, public propensity to report offences varies greatly, not only among countries, but also among regions in the same country.

Crime rates vary for a number of reasons

Figure 23.1 shows the variation of the rate of crime against property with respect to the national average. Spain, Mexico and Turkey show the largest regional variation, and New Zealand, Greece and Denmark the lowest. The large variation in Spain is mainly due to two regions (Melilla and Aragon) with a crime rate three times the national average. Several

countries have regions with a crime rate double the national average: Austria (Wien), Belgium (Brussels), Mexico (Baja California Norte, Baja California Sur, Colima), Portugal (Algarve), Spain (Ceuta) and Turkey (Istanbul).

Crime rates are lower in rural areas

The correlation between the rate of crime against property and the share of population by type of region (urban, intermediate and rural) is positive for urban regions in all countries considered except Switzerland and the United States (Figure 23.2). The correlation coefficient is negative for rural regions in most countries; exceptions are Australia, Canada, Japan, Mexico, and the United Kingdom. For Mexico and Canada the correlation coefficient is positive for both rural and urban regions; but is higher in rural regions.

23.1. Spain shows the largest regional differences in the rate of reported crime against property

Variation around the national average of the rate of crime against property, 2003 (TL2)

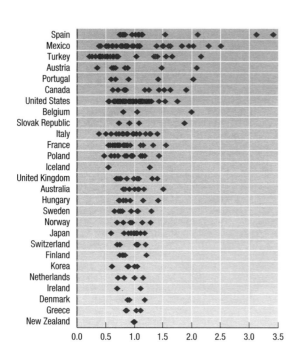

23.2. Crime against property is more frequent in urban regions

Spearman correlation between crime rate against property and share of population by regional type, 2003 (TL2)

StatLink http://dx.doi.org/10.1787/773310211202

Definition

The rate of crime against proprety is the number of reported crimes per 100 population.

Reported crimes against property are the number of crimes reported to the police. Crimes against property include: forgery, arson, burglary, theft, fraud, robbery and malicious damage to property.

OECD REGIONS AT A GLANCE 2007 – ISBN 978-92-64-00987-5 – © OECD 2007

23.3. **Regional crime against the property: Asia and Oceania**

Per inhabitant, as a percentage of the national average – 2003

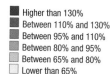

■ Higher than 130%
■ Between 110% and 130%
■ Between 95% and 110%
■ Between 80% and 95%
□ Between 65% and 80%
□ Lower than 65%

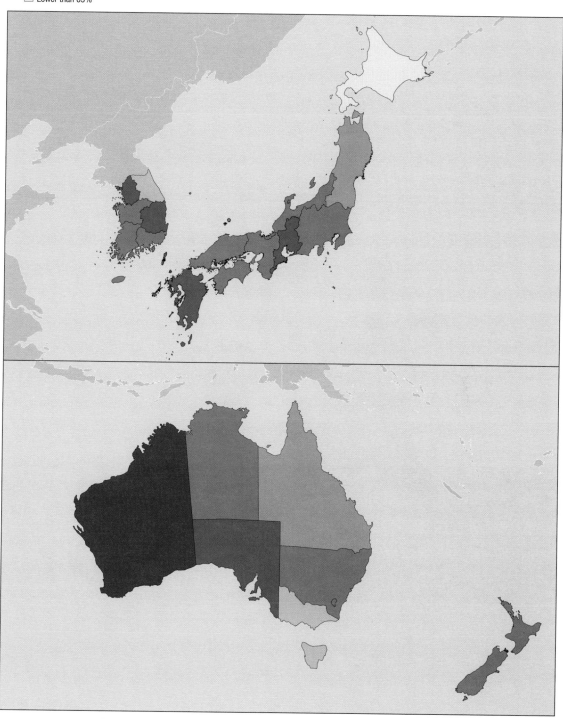

StatLink ▄▄▆▙▅ http://dx.doi.org/10.1787/838840005320

23.4. **Regional crime against the property: Europe**

Per inhabitant, as a percentage of the national average – 2003

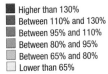

- Higher than 130%
- Between 110% and 130%
- Between 95% and 110%
- Between 80% and 95%
- Between 65% and 80%
- Lower than 65%

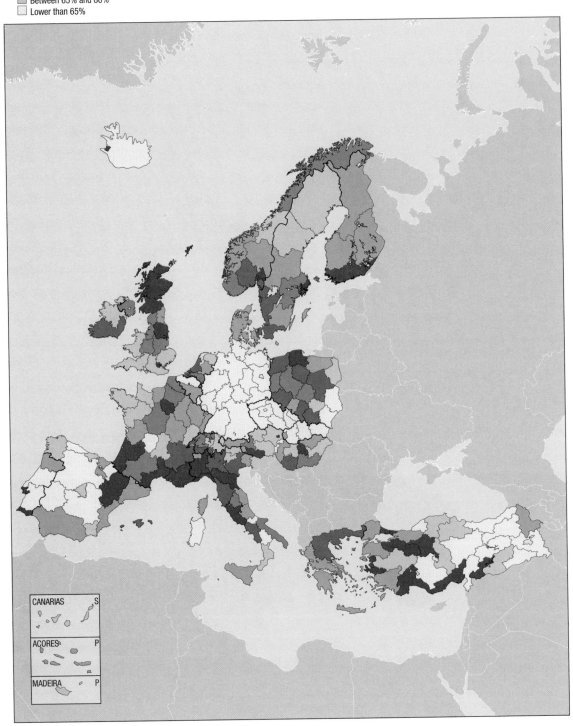

StatLink ⬛⬛ http://dx.doi.org/10.1787/838840005320

23.5. **Regional crime against the property: North America**

Per inhabitant, as a percentage of the national average – 2003

- ■ Higher than 130%
- ■ Between 110% and 130%
- ■ Between 95% and 110%
- ■ Between 80% and 95%
- ▢ Between 65% and 80%
- ▢ Lower than 65%

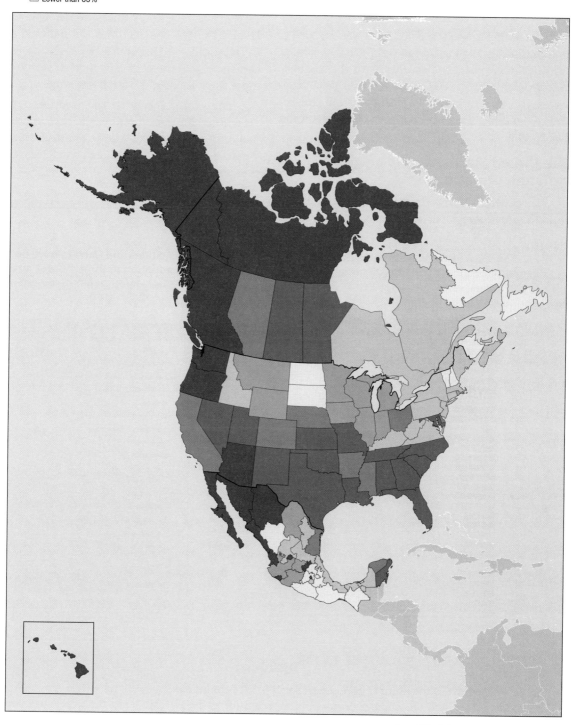

StatLink ⬛⬛⬛ http://dx.doi.org/10.1787/838840005320

The number of murders per inhabitant is a main indicator of a region's safety level. Unlike other safety indicators, such as reported crime against property, the number of reported murders is less affected by the public propensity to report an offence. It is therefore more suitable for international comparison.

Mexico has the highest murder rate

According to the UN *Eight United Nations Survey on Crime Trends and the Operations of Criminal Justice Systems*, Mexico was the country with the highest murder rate (13) in 2002, followed by the United States (5.6) and Turkey (3.8). Japan, Austria, Greece and Luxembourg were the countries with the lowest (Figure 24.1).

The United States has the biggest variation across regions

Murder rates in the United States and Canada show the greatest regional variation from the national

average (Figure 24.2). In both, the variation is due to an outlier region with a very high rate. In the United States, it is the District of Columbia with 7.9 times the national average, and in Canada it is the Northwest Territories (5.7). Australia, France and Italy also show large regional variations from the national average. In Australia, the Northern Territory has 3.6 times the national average and in France, Corsica has 3.3 times the national average. In Italy and the United States, Calabria (2.7) and Louisiana (2.3), respectively, register a murder rate more than double the national average.

The countries with the smallest regional variation in murder rates are the Netherlands, New Zealand and Sweden. Maine (United States) and Yucatan (Mexico), have values up to 80% lower than their country average.

24.1. **Mexico displays the highest number of reported murders per 100 000 population**

Murder rates by country, 2003

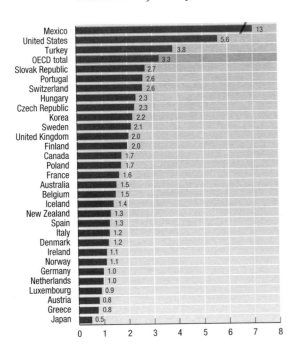

24.2. **The United States and Canada have the largest regional variation in their murder rates**

Variation around the national average of the murder rate, 2003 (TL2)

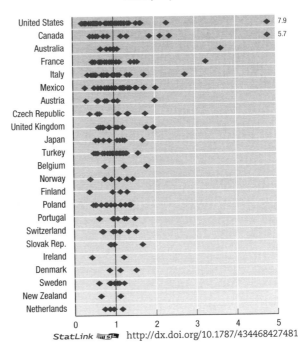

StatLink ᴹˢᴸ http://dx.doi.org/10.1787/434468427481

Definition

The rate of murdes is the number of murders per 100 000 population.

Reported murders are the number of murders reported to the police. Murder is the unlawful killing of a human being with malice aforethought, more explicitly wilful murder.

OECD REGIONS AT A GLANCE 2007 – ISBN 978-92-64-00987-5 – © OECD 2007

24.3. **Regional murders per inhabitant: Asia and Oceania**

As a percentage of the national average, 2003

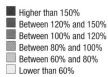

- Higher than 150%
- Between 120% and 150%
- Between 100% and 120%
- Between 80% and 100%
- Between 60% and 80%
- Lower than 60%

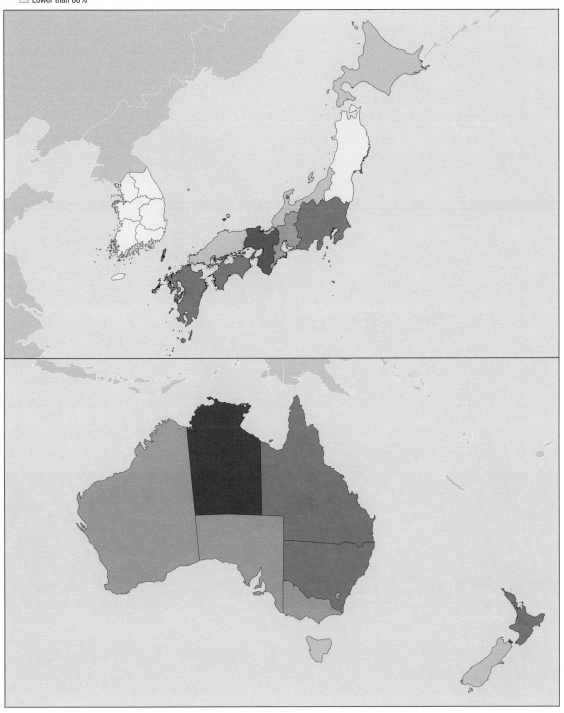

StatLink http://dx.doi.org/10.1787/100216724512

24.4. **Regional murders per inhabitant: Europe**
As a percentage of the national average, 2003

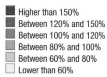

- ■ Higher than 150%
- ■ Between 120% and 150%
- ■ Between 100% and 120%
- ■ Between 80% and 100%
- ■ Between 60% and 80%
- □ Lower than 60%

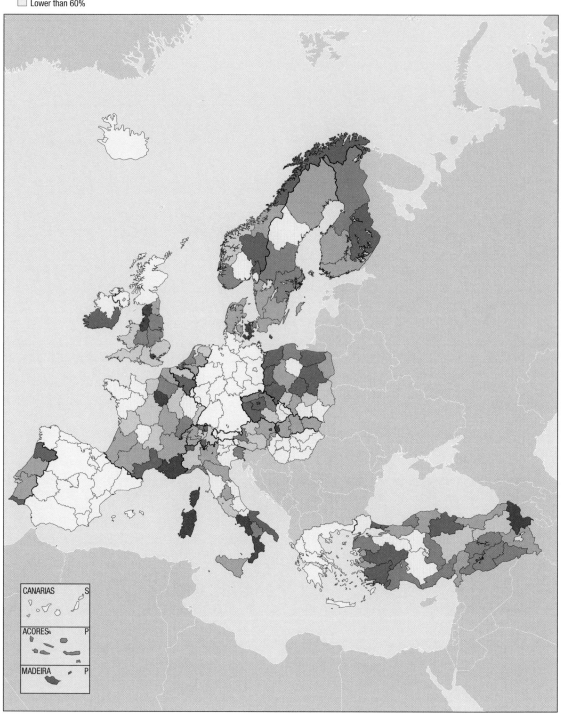

StatLink ⬛⬛ http://dx.doi.org/10.1787/100216724512

OECD REGIONS AT A GLANCE 2007 – ISBN 978-92-64-00987-5 – © OECD 2007

24.5. **Regional murders per inhabitant: North America**

As a percentage of the national average, 2003

- Higher than 150%
- Between 120% and 150%
- Between 100% and 120%
- Between 80% and 100%
- Between 60% and 80%
- Lower than 60%

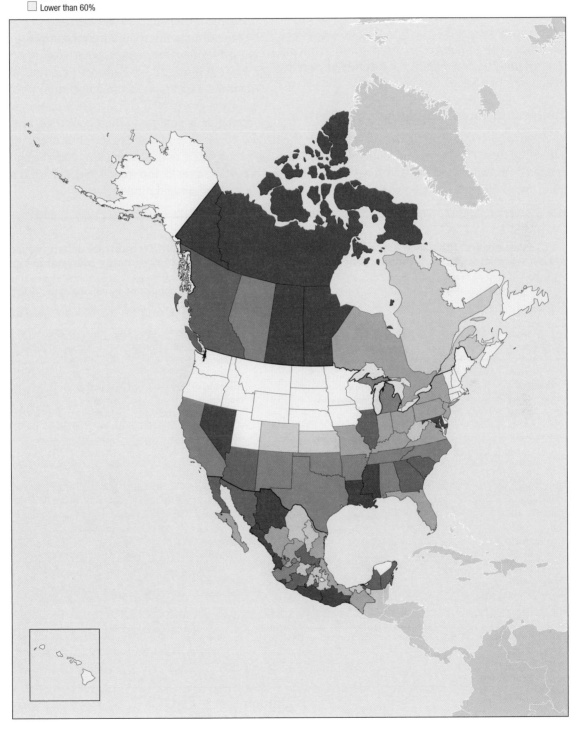

StatLink ᗒᗕᔕ᙮ http://dx.doi.org/10.1787/100216724512

In many OECD countries home ownership is an important dimension of well-being. It protects owners from fluctuations in rents and ensures families a stable and secure shelter. In addition, the value of a property represents a major source of wealth for households. Differences in the rate of home ownership across OECD countries depend significantly on several factors, including rental subsidies, the existence of high-quality social housing and the deductibility of interest payments on loans from taxable income.

Ownership rates vary greatly in Austria

Figure 25.1 shows regional variations in the ownership rate. The largest regional variations are registered in Austria and the Czech Republic, where home ownership rates vary between 17 and 76% and

27 and 67%, respectively. In both countries the capital region has the lowest rate of home ownership, probably owing to higher property prices.

Home ownership is higher in rural areas

In most OECD countries the correlation between the home ownership rate and the share of population by type of region (urban, intermediate and rural) is negative for urban regions, where estate prices are higher (Figure 25.2). Only in Portugal, Greece, Australia and Spain is the correlation positive for urban regions. For rural regions, instead, the correlation is positive in most countries. In Australia the correlation is positive for both urban and rural regions, while in the United Kingdom the correlation is positive only for intermediate regions; it is negative for both urban and rural regions.

25.1. **Austria and the Czech Republic show the highest regional variation in home ownership rates**

Range of regional variation in home ownership rate, 2001 (TL2)

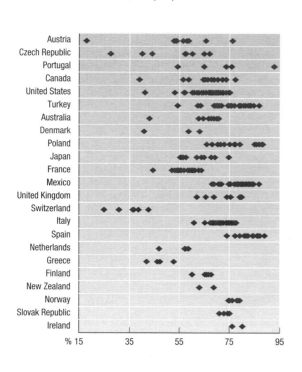

25.2. **In most OECD countries urban regions tend to have a lower home ownership rate**

Spearman correlation between home ownership rate and share of population by regional type, 2001 (TL2)

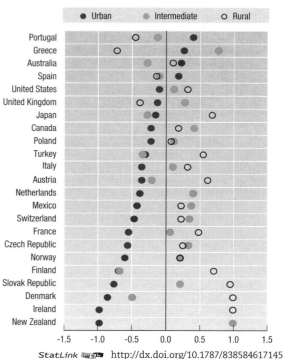

StatLink ⌘⌐⍔ http://dx.doi.org/10.1787/838584617145

Definition

The home ownership rate is defined as the number of dwellings inhabited by the owner as a percentage of total occupied dwellings.

OECD REGIONS AT A GLANCE 2007 – ISBN 978-92-64-00987-5 – © OECD 2007

25.3. **Home ownership rate: Asia and Oceania**
2001

Higher than 83
Between 73 and 83
Between 68 and 73
Between 63 and 68
Between 53 and 63
Lower than 53

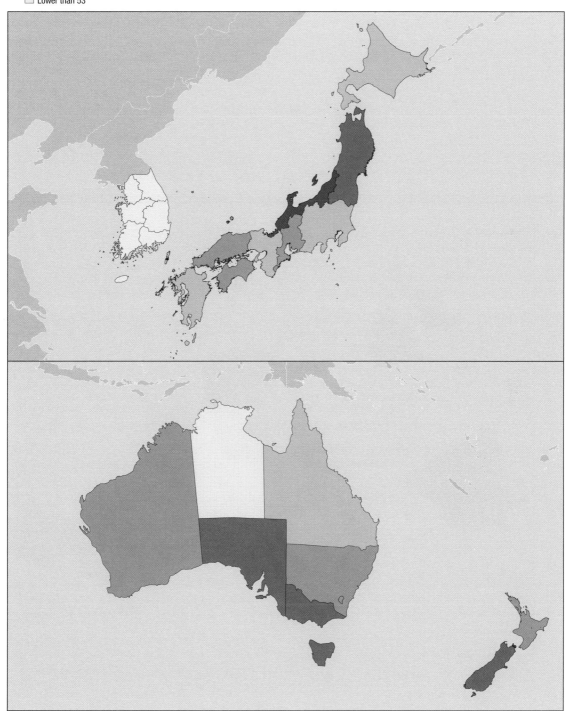

StatLink ⟨ ⟩ http://dx.doi.org/10.1787/860207754414

25.4. **Home ownership rate: Europe**
2001

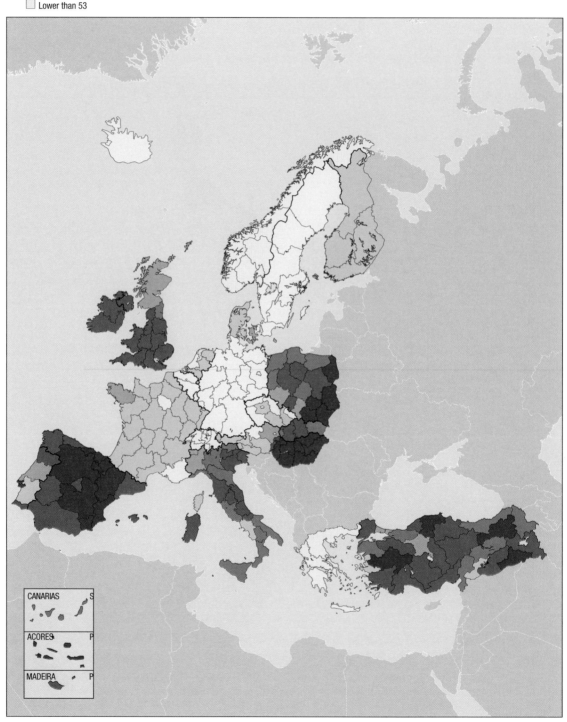

Legend:
- Higher than 83
- Between 73 and 83
- Between 68 and 73
- Between 63 and 68
- Between 53 and 63
- Lower than 53

CANARIAS S

AÇORES P

MADEIRA P

StatLink ᴍꜱᴸ http://dx.doi.org/10.1787/860207754414

OECD REGIONS AT A GLANCE 2007 – ISBN 978-92-64-00987-5 – © OECD 2007

25.5. **Home ownership rate: North America**
2001

- Higher than 83
- Between 73 and 83
- Between 68 and 73
- Between 63 and 68
- Between 53 and 63
- Lower than 53

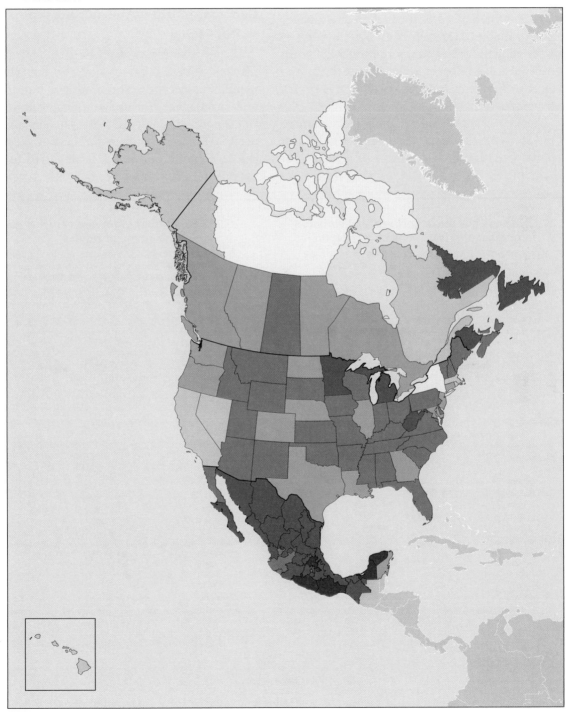

StatLink ⟨⟩ http://dx.doi.org/10.1787/860207754414

Reducing vehicle pollution is a policy objective

Motor vehicles emit millions of tons of pollutants into the air. In many urban areas, motor vehicles are the single largest contributor to ground-level ozone, a major component of smog. The reduction of motorised traffic is therefore a policy target in many OECD countries. The number of private vehicles per capita is the indicator most commonly used to set policy targets for the integration of environmental objectives with transport policies.

Figure 26.1 shows the variation in the number of private vehicles per 100 inhabitants. The largest regional variation in the number of vehicles per inhabitant occurs in Canada (ranging from 32 to

78 per 100 inhabitants), the United States (20 to 64), Greece (20 to 52), and Japan (29 to 59). At the other end of the scale, Ireland, Iceland, the Netherlands and Belgium display the lowest regional variation in the number of cars per capita.

Car ownership varies across types of regions

The correlation between the number of private vehicles per capita and the share of population by type of region (urban, intermediate and rural) does not show a clear trend across OECD countries, (Figure 26.2). The correlation is positive for urban regions for 15 countries out of the 26 considered, and it is negative for rural regions in 14 countries.

26.1. **Canada has the largest regional variation in number of private vehicles per capita**

Range of regional variation in the number of private vehicles per 100 inhabitants, 2003 (TL2)

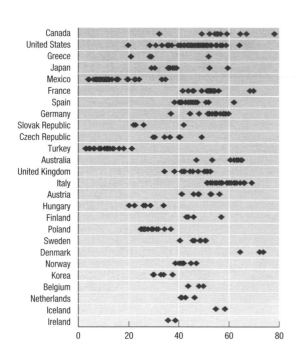

26.2. **The number of private vehicles varies by type of region**

Spearmank correlation between number of private vehicles per 100 population and share of population by regional type, 2003 (TL2)

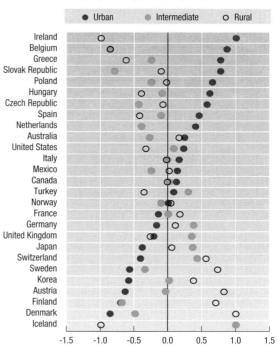

StatLink 🔗 http://dx.doi.org/10.1787/248421278185

Definition

Private vehicles are defined as the number of road motor vehicles, other than motorcycles, intended for the carriage of passengers and designed to seat no more than nine persons including the driver.

OECD REGIONS AT A GLANCE 2007 – ISBN 978-92-64-00987-5 – © OECD 2007

26.3. Number of private vehicles per 100 inhabitants: Asia and Oceania
2003

- Higher than 65
- Between 53 and 65
- Between 45 and 53
- Between 35 and 45
- Between 13 and 35
- Lower than 13

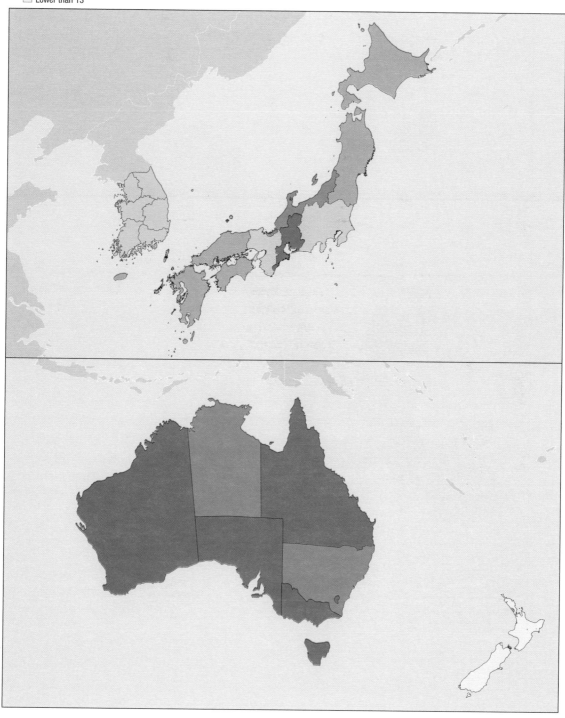

StatLink 🔗 http://dx.doi.org/10.1787/356536818280

26.4. **Number of private vehicles per 100 inhabitants: Europe**
2003

- Higher than 65
- Between 53 and 65
- Between 45 and 53
- Between 35 and 45
- Between 13 and 45
- Lower than 13

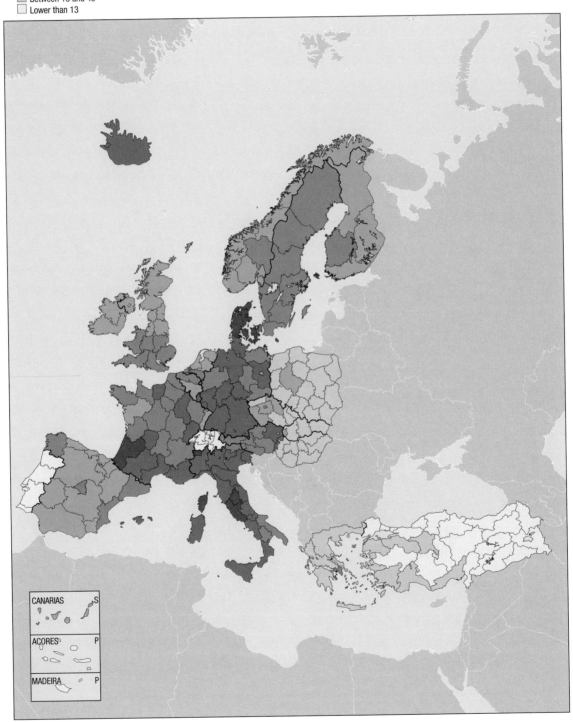

StatLink ⫘ http://dx.doi.org/10.1787/356536818280

OECD REGIONS AT A GLANCE 2007 – ISBN 978-92-64-00987-5 – © OECD 2007

26.5. **Number of private vehicles per 100 inhabitants: North America**
2003

- Higher than 65
- Between 53 and 65
- Between 45 and 53
- Between 35 and 45
- Between 13 and 35
- Lower than 13

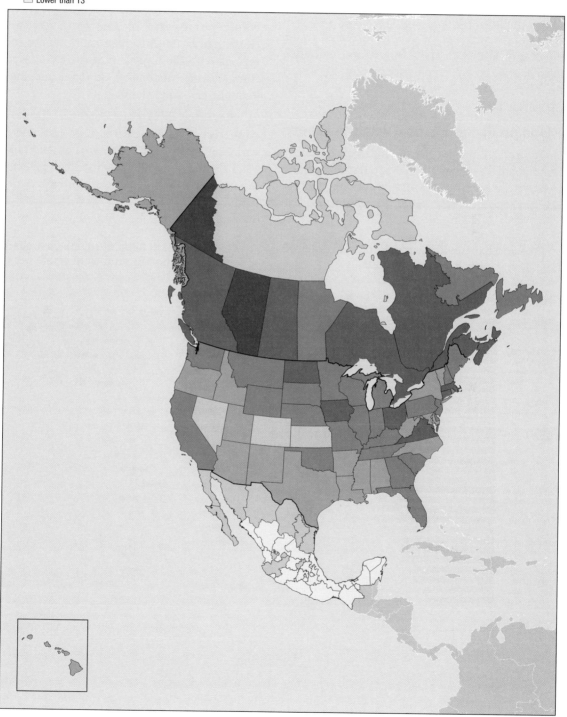

StatLink 🔗 http://dx.doi.org/10.1787/356536818280

Waste has an economic impact because waste disposal represents a significant cost for local authorities. It also has an environmental impact because waste is usually buried in landfills or burned in incinerators, often resulting in groundwater pollution, poor air quality and other forms of environmental degradation. Waste also has a social impact related to the location of waste disposal facilities. Concerns include odours, increased traffic and potential health risks. Anecdotal evidence indicates that poor and minority communities may be burdened with more than their fair share of waste disposal facilities.

Iceland produces the most waste per capita

Figure 27.1 shows average national amounts of municipal waste per 100 000 population. Iceland produces the most waste (73 kilo-tonnes [Kt]) per inhabitant, while the Czech Republic and the Slovak Republic produce the least (28 and 32 Kt, respectively). The OECD average is 54 Kt.

Regional variations are substantial

The volume of municipal waste per inhabitant varies significantly among regions across countries (Figure 27.2). The regions with the lowest volume of waste per capita in Australia (64) and the Netherlands (59) produce more waste than the regions with the highest in Austria (56), Japan (48), Hungary and Sweden (46), Germany (44), the Slovak Republic (39) and Poland (33).

Regional differences are also large within countries. The Czech Republic has the largest variation (19 to 100 Kt), followed by Australia (64 to 138 Kt) and France (26 to 89 Kt). Regional variations are very small in Ireland, the United Kingdom and Japan.

27.1. Iceland has the highest volume of municipal waste per inhabitants

Municipal waste per 100 000 population in Ktonnes, 2002

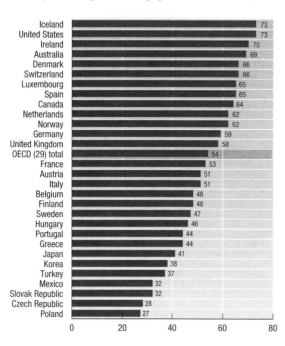

Iceland	73
United States	73
Ireland	70
Australia	69
Denmark	66
Switzerland	66
Luxembourg	65
Spain	65
Canada	64
Netherlands	62
Norway	62
Germany	59
United Kingdom	58
OECD (29) total	54
France	53
Austria	51
Italy	51
Belgium	48
Finland	48
Sweden	47
Hungary	46
Portugal	44
Greece	44
Japan	41
Korea	38
Turkey	37
Mexico	32
Slovak Republic	32
Czech Republic	28
Poland	27

27.2. The Czech Republic displays the largest regional variation in municipal waste per capita

Range variation in volume of municipal waste per 100 000 population, Ktonnes (TL2)

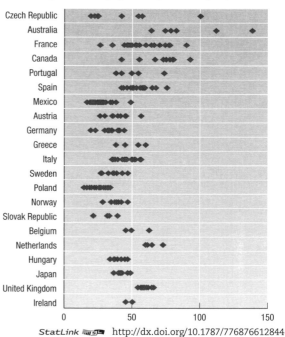

Czech Republic, Australia, France, Canada, Portugal, Spain, Mexico, Austria, Germany, Greece, Italy, Sweden, Poland, Norway, Slovak Republic, Belgium, Netherlands, Hungary, Japan, United Kingdom, Ireland

StatLink ⚙ http://dx.doi.org/10.1787/776876612844

Definition

Total amount of municipal waste collected by or on behalf of municipalities. Waste refers to materials that are not prime products (i.e. products produced for the market), for which the generator has no further use for own purpose of production, transformation or consumption, and which he or she discards, or intends or is required to discard.

27.3. Municipal waste per 100 000 inhabitants: Asia and Oceania
Kilo-tonnes, latest available year

- ■ Higher than 75
- ■ Between 57 and 75
- ■ Between 45 and 57
- ■ Between 30 and 45
- ■ Between 23 and 30
- □ Lower than 23

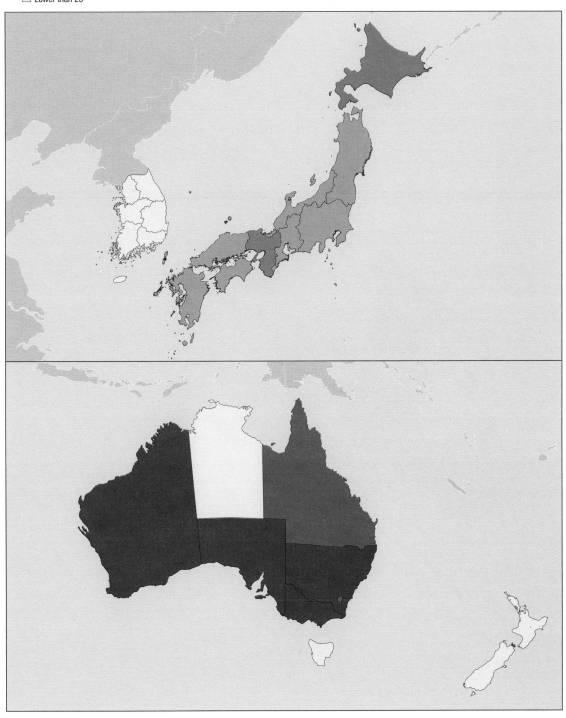

StatLink 🔗 http://dx.doi.org/10.1787/106157461070

27.4. **Municipal waste per 100 000 inhabitants: Europe**
Kilo-tonnes, latest available year

- Higher than 75
- Between 57 and 75
- Between 45 and 57
- Between 30 and 45
- Between 23 and 30
- Lower than 23

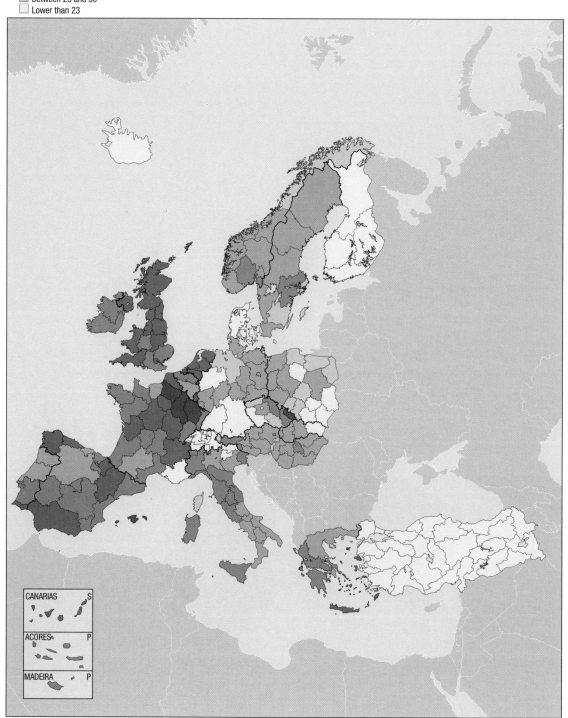

StatLink ᗊᔿᔊ http://dx.doi.org/10.1787/106157461070

27.5. **Municipal waste per 100 000 inhabitants: North America**
Kilo-tonnes, latest available year

- Higher than 75
- Between 57 and 75
- Between 45 and 57
- Between 30 and 45
- Between 23 and 30
- Lower than 23

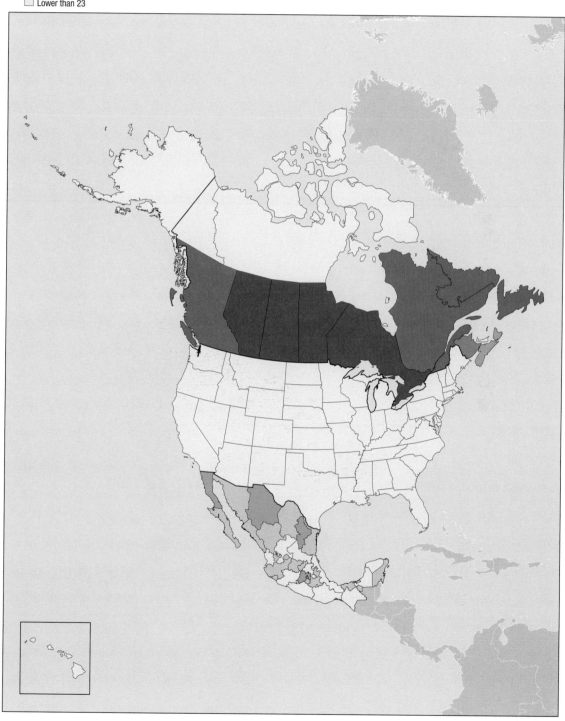

StatLink ⬛🗐🔗 http://dx.doi.org/10.1787/106157461070

IV. REGIONAL FOCUS ON HEALTH

The age-adjusted mortality rate is a basic indicator of the population's health status. At the national level, it is the death rate that would occur in a country if its population's age profile was the same as the OECD average. Therefore, a value higher than the OECD average indicates that, after accounting for differences in age, that country's mortality rate is higher than the OECD average.

Mortality rates for males are considerably higher than for females

Age-adjusted mortality rates of men and women vary significantly among OECD countries (Figure 28.1). In 2003, mortality rates for males were, on average, much higher (847 per 100 000 population) than for females (516).

The difference between the country with the lowest age-adjusted mortality rate (Japan) and the highest (Hungary) was considerably greater for males (684 deaths) than for females (463 deaths). Japan recorded the lowest female mortality rate and Mexico the highest.

Regional variations are high in North America, Australia and Portugal

At the regional level, the age-adjusted mortality rate is expressed as the ratio of the observed number of deaths to expected number, i.e. the number of deaths that would occur in a given region if age-specific mortality rates in that region were the same as in the country overall. A value higher than the national average indicates that, after accounting for differences in age, mortality rates in that region are higher than in the other regions of that country.

Considerable international differences in mortality rates hide even larger differences among regions. In 2003, the gap between the region with the lowest and the highest age-adjusted mortality rate for males was widest in Australia (75 percentage points), Canada (74), Denmark (72) and Portugal (53). For females the gap was widest in Canada (108), Denmark (76), Australia (62) and the United States (49).

In Canada and Australia the gap was driven by the high mortality rate of a single region: the Northwest Territories for the former and the Northern Territory for the latter. In Portugal the large gap was driven by the high mortality rates of two regions: Açores and Madeira (Figure 28.2).

In contrast, for males the regional pattern in age-adjusted mortality rates was more balanced in New Zealand, the Netherlands, Greece, Japan, Sweden and Iceland, and for females it was more balanced in the Netherlands, Greece, New Zealand, the Slovak Republic, Japan, Switzerland, Iceland, Hungary, Finland and Sweden, where the gap between the region with the lowest and the highest age-adjusted mortality rate was no larger than 9 percentage points.

Definition

Crude mortality rates are adjusted for age, which is a primary factor of mortality. Age-adjusted mortality rates eliminate differences due to a population's age profile and are comparable across countries and regions.

28.1. Age-adjusted mortality rates in OECD countries (per 100 000 population), 2003

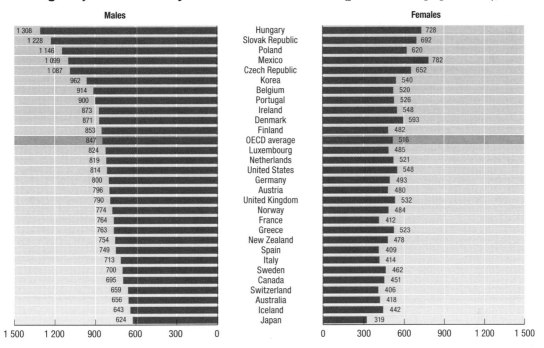

28.2. Regional disparities in age-adjusted mortality rates

Regional age-adjusted mortality rates, 2003 (TL2)

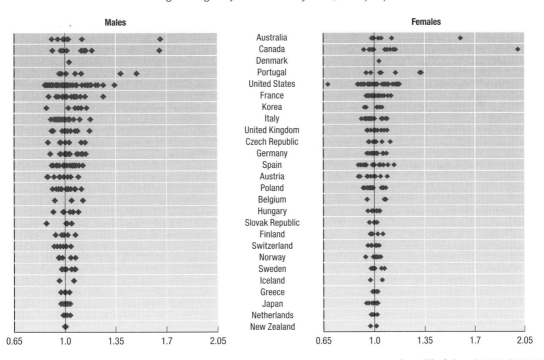

StatLink 🖥 http://dx.doi.org/10.1787/520004880758

28.3. Age-adjusted mortality rate for females: Asia and Oceania
Percentage of national average 2003

- ■ Higher than 105%
- ■ Between 102% and 105%
- ■ Between 100% and 102%
- ■ Between 98% and 100%
- ■ Between 95% and 98%
- □ Lower than 95%

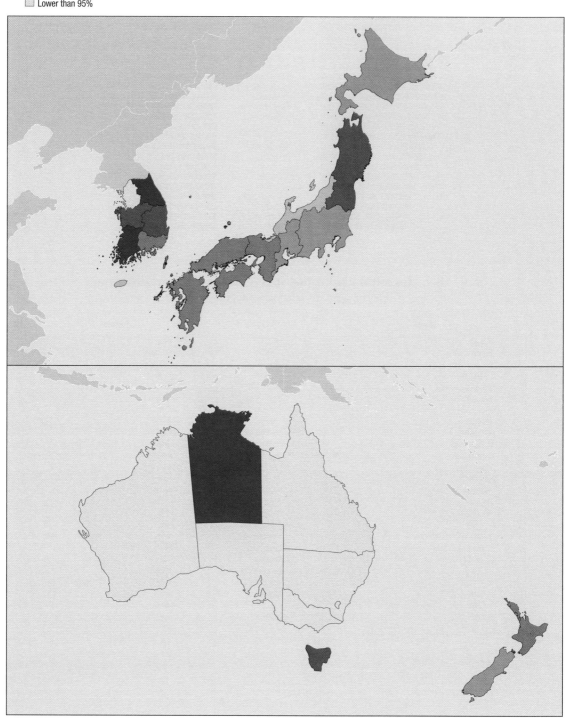

StatLink ᵃ₁₅₱ http://dx.doi.org/10.1787/087413716410

28.4. Age-adjusted mortality rate for females: Europe
Percentage of national average 2003

- ■ Higher than 105%
- ■ Between 102% and 105%
- ■ Between 100% and 102%
- ■ Between 98% and 100%
- ■ Between 95% and 98%
- □ Lower than 95%

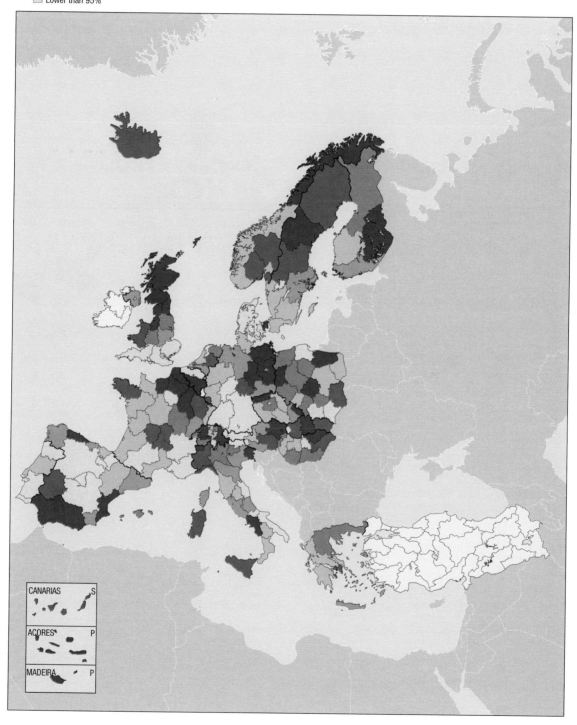

StatLink ⬛⬛⬛ http://dx.doi.org/10.1787/087413716410

28.5. **Age-adjusted mortality rate for females: North America**

Percentage of national average 2003

- Higher than 105%
- Between 102% and 105%
- Between 100% and 102%
- Between 98% and 100%
- Between 95% and 98%
- Lower than 95%

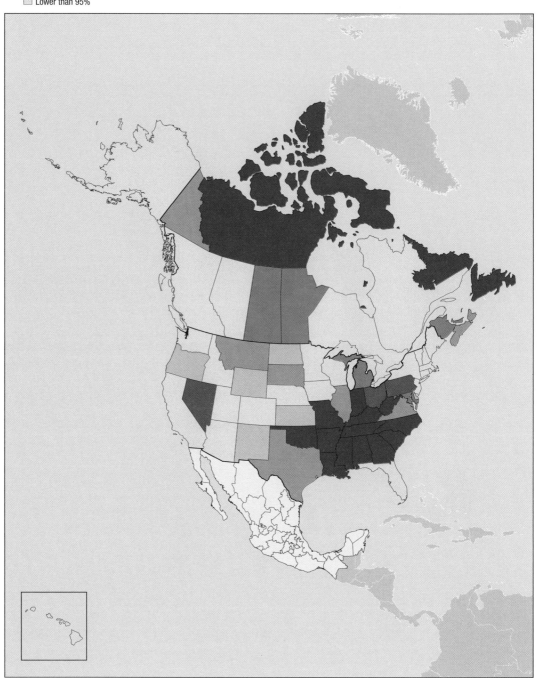

StatLink ᠊᠊᠊᠊ http://dx.doi.org/10.1787/087413716410

OECD REGIONS AT A GLANCE 2007 – ISBN 978-92-64-00987-5 – © OECD 2007

Age-adjusted mortality rates are significantly higher for males in rural regions and for females in urban regions

The correlation between age-adjusted mortality rates and population share by type of region (urban, intermediate and rural) was strongest for males in rural regions (in 14 out of 24 OECD countries) and for females in urban regions in 13 countries.

For males, the positive correlation between mortality rates and share of population in rural regions was particularly marked in Norway (0.84), Belgium (0.80), Korea and Australia (0.69) and the Slovak Republic (0.68). For intermediate regions it was strongest in Belgium (0.80), the Slovak Republic (0.76) and the Czech Republic (0.67), and for urban regions, it was strongest in Denmark (0.91) and Greece (0.80) (Figure 28.6).

For females, the strongest positive correlation between mortality rates and share of population in urban regions occurred in Denmark (0.92) and Japan (0.79), while in intermediate regions it was strongest in the Slovak Republic (0.99) and in rural regions it was strongest in Hungary (0.84) and Australia (0.58) (Figure 28.7).

28.6. The highest mortality rates for males were present in rural regions...

Correlation between male regional age adjusted mortality rates and population share by regional type, 2003 (TL2)

28.7. ... and for females in urban regions

Correlation between female regional age adjusted mortality rates and population share by regional type, 2003 (TL2)

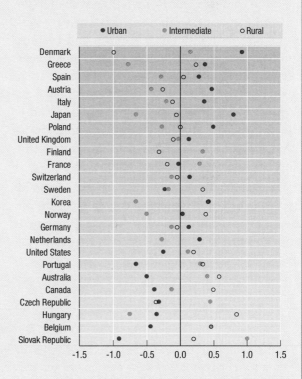

StatLink http://dx.doi.org/10.1787/520004880758

Premature mortality, measured in terms of potential years of life lost (PYLL), is often interpreted as a measure of preventable deaths. This indicator places the emphasis on deaths among younger people, in particular infant mortality and deaths due to illnesses and accidents suffered by children and young adults. Advances in medical technology, together with prevention and control, can reduce such deaths.

Many of the main causes of premature mortality in the developed world are non-medical or involve risk-taking behaviour (accidents, smoking, alcohol, drugs) but also diseases such as cancer.

Premature mortality is high in eastern Europe

Throughout the OECD area, premature deaths are more common among men than women. The OECD countries with the highest rates of premature mortality are in Central and Eastern Europe, in particular Hungary, where the number of potential years of life lost per 100 000 population is almost twice the OECD average for men and 1.6 times the OECD average for women (Figure 29.1). For Hungarian men, high mortality appears to stem from an unhealthy diet linked to the consumption of alcohol and tobacco.

Switzerland and Italy fall at the other end of the scale for women, and Sweden and Iceland for men. These countries display the least premature mortality and are among the countries with the smallest regional disparities.

One region is responsible for regional disparities in Canada...

On average, premature mortality in Canadian regions is lower than the OECD average. However, in the region of Nunavut premature mortality reaches 2.5 times the national average. For this reason, of the 23 countries for which this indicator can be calculated, regional disparities in Canada are considerably greater than in other countries (Figure 29.2). The region of Nunavut and, to a lesser extent, the Northwest Territories are the two regions with the highest level of premature deaths. The PYLL indicator for Nunavut is 15 072 years per 100 000 men and 7 478 per 100 000 women. These figures are much higher than the national figures for Hungary but also for the Hungarian region with the highest values for this indicator. One explanation for the disparities in Canada may be the number of premature deaths in the native population, many due to suicide and risk-taking behaviour stemming from social problems.

... while disparities are more frequent among regions in Europe

In European countries, a few regions in Portugal, France and Germany are characterised by higher premature mortality among men. In France, excessive alcohol consumption, a factor in several diseases (cancer, digestive disorders and cardiovascular disease, as well as road accidents), has been suggested as one explanation for such disparities, for instance in the Nord-Pas-de-Calais region.

Definition

Premature mortality is measured in potential years of life lost (PYLL). The calculation of PYLL involves summing up deaths occurring at each age and multiplying this figure by the number of years remaining to live to a selected age limit (70 years).

29.1. Potential years of life lost at the national level in the OECD area, 2004

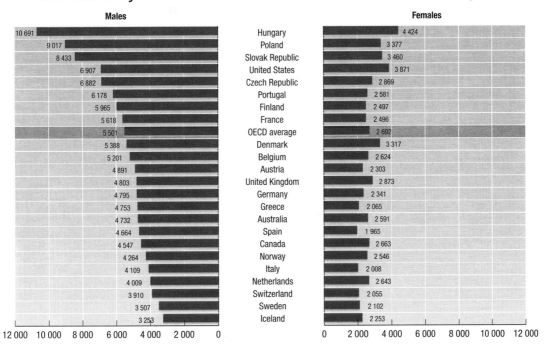

29.2. Regional disparities in premature mortality, 2004

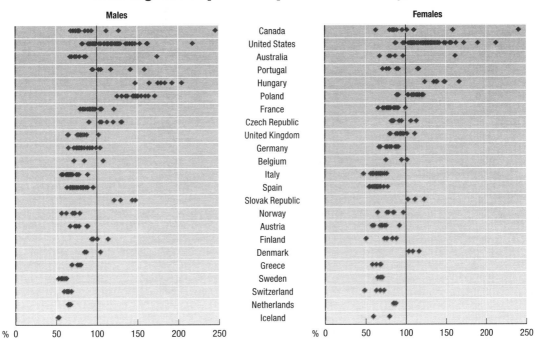

Regional variation (TL2), percentage of OECD average (23).

StatLink ⚏⊓ᴸ⅃ http://dx.doi.org/10.1787/048468323417

29.3. **Premature mortality for males: Asia and Oceania**

Potential Years of Life Lost (PYLL) per 100 000 population, 2004

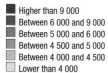

- Higher than 9 000
- Between 6 000 and 9 000
- Between 5 000 and 6 000
- Between 4 500 and 5 000
- Between 4 000 and 4 500
- Lower than 4 000

StatLink ⟨图⟩ http://dx.doi.org/10.1787/456753421474

OECD REGIONS AT A GLANCE 2007 – ISBN 978-92-64-00987-5 – © OECD 2007

29.4. Premature mortality for males: Europe

Potential Years of Life Lost (PYLL) per 100 000 population, 2004

- Higher than 9 000
- Between 6 000 and 9 000
- Between 5 000 and 6 000
- Between 4 500 and 5 000
- Between 4 000 and 4 500
- Lower than 4 000

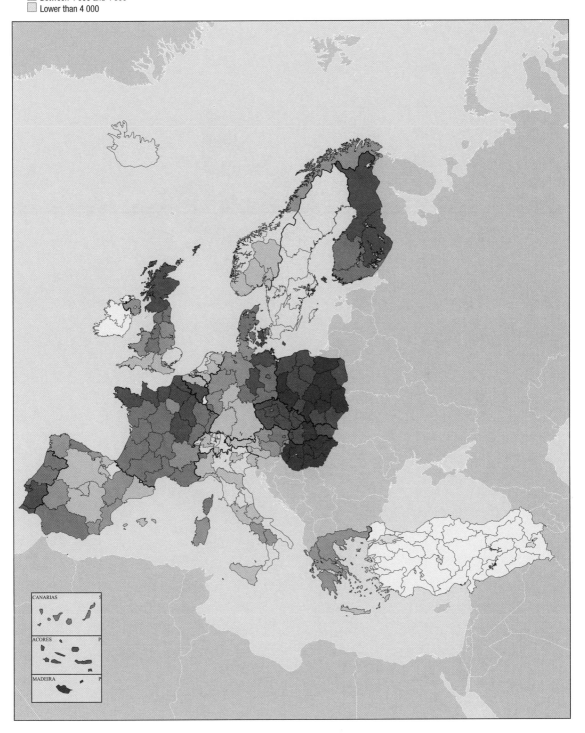

StatLink ⌗ http://dx.doi.org/10.1787/456753421474

29.5. **Premature mortality for males: North America**

Potential Years of Life Lost (PYLL) per 100 000 population, 2004

- Higher than 9 000
- Between 6 000 and 9 000
- Between 5 000 and 6 000
- Between 4 500 and 5 000
- Between 4 000 and 4 500
- Lower than 4 000

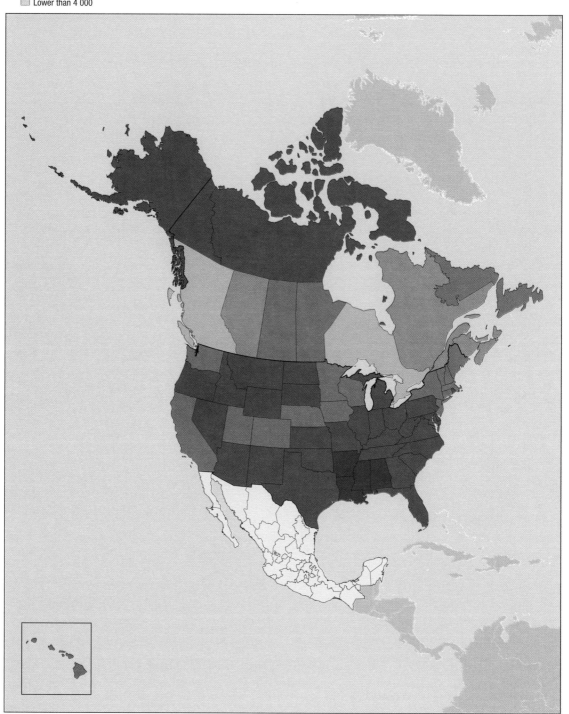

StatLink ⬛⬛⬛ http://dx.doi.org/10.1787/456753421474

OECD REGIONS AT A GLANCE 2007 – ISBN 978-92-64-00987-5 – © OECD 2007

Premature mortality affects OECD rural and urban areas differently, depending on gender

Premature deaths among men are more common in rural regions. In 19 out of 23 countries, the rate of premature mortality for males in rural regions is positively correlated with the share of population (Figure 29.6). The situation is quite the opposite for women in several countries, where premature deaths are more common in mostly urban or intermediate areas (Figure 29.7). A possible explanation for such disparities may be premature deaths due to road accidents which are more common among men and in rural areas.

Spain, Austria and Greece are the most noticeable exceptions to the preponderance of premature death among men in rural areas.

The smallest differences in premature mortality among types of regions are recorded in France and the Netherlands for men and in Sweden and the United Kingdom for women. In these countries, in fact, there seems to be no correlation between the distribution of regional population by type of region and premature mortality.

29.6. Correlation between premature mortality among men and distribution of population by type of region

Spearman correlation coefficient, 2004 (TL2)

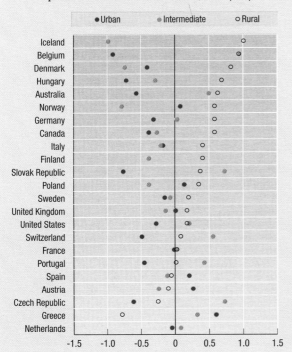

29.7. Correlation between premature mortality among women and distribution of population by type of region

Spearman correlation coefficient, 2004 (TL2)

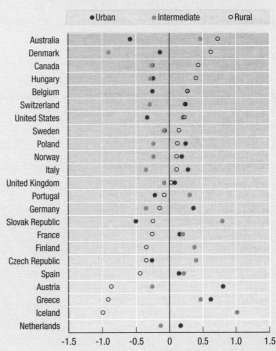

StatLink http://dx.doi.org/10.1787/048468323417

Cancer is the second highest cause of death

Cancer is the second major cause of death in most OECD countries, after cardiovascular diseases. Incidence rates of cancer can therefore be used as a partial measure of regional disparities in terms of healthcare needs.

The steady rise in the elderly population has brought an increase in the number of new cases of cancer. It will rise even more steeply if exposure to behavioural risk factors – such as smoking, alcohol and an unhealthy diet – persists.

Statistics should be interpreted with caution

The international comparability of data on the incidence of cancer can be affected by differences in medical training and practices. It should also be borne in mind that better screening, and more importantly early diagnosis, may push up the reported incidence of cancer but are efficient means of limiting deaths from the disease.

The lowest cancer incidence rates are found in Asia, southern Europe and Mexico. The United States and New Zealand report the highest numbers of new cases (Figure 30.1).

Incidence rates are highest in Australia

Among the six countries for which regional data are available, Australia shows the largest regional disparities for both men and women.

In each country, the rate of incidence and its regional variations differ according to gender (Figure 30.2). In the Slovak Republic, for instance, regional disparities in the incidence of cancer are larger for women than for men. In addition, the incidence rate for men is below the average of the six countries for which regional data are available but above the average for women.

In France and Canada, instead, regional disparities are smaller for women. In these countries, the regional rates of incidence are more frequently below the average of the six countries for women than for men.

In Iceland, the incidence of cancer among women is high on average, but far higher in the capital regional than in the rest of the country.

Definition

Annual number of new cases of cancer per 100 000 population. All of the cancers included are classed as Code C00-C97 in the ICD-10 classification of diseases and Code 140-208 in the ICD-9 classification.

OECD REGIONS AT A GLANCE 2007 – ISBN 978-92-64-00987-5 – © OECD 2007

30.1. Incidence of cancer at the national level, 2002

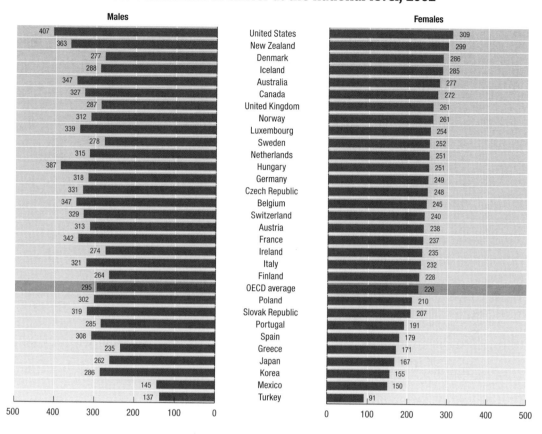

	Males	Females
United States	407	309
New Zealand	363	299
Denmark	277	286
Iceland	288	285
Australia	347	277
Canada	327	272
United Kingdom	287	261
Norway	312	261
Luxembourg	339	254
Sweden	278	252
Netherlands	315	251
Hungary	387	251
Germany	318	249
Czech Republic	331	248
Belgium	347	245
Switzerland	329	240
Austria	313	238
France	342	237
Ireland	274	235
Italy	321	232
Finland	264	228
OECD average	295	226
Poland	302	210
Slovak Republic	319	207
Portugal	285	191
Spain	308	179
Greece	235	171
Japan	262	167
Korea	286	155
Mexico	145	150
Turkey	137	91

30.2. Regional disparities in the incidence of cancer

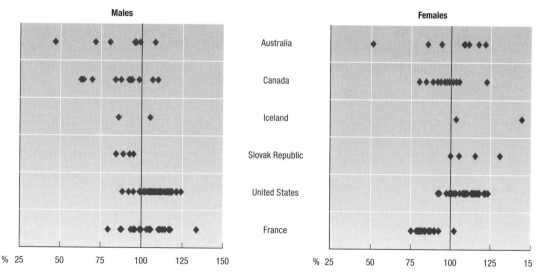

Regional variation (TL2), percentage of OECD average (6), 2003.

StatLink ᵐˢ⌐ http://dx.doi.org/10.1787/863260604803

30.3. **Incidence of cancer among women: Asia and Oceania**

Number of new cases of cancer per 100 000 population, 2003

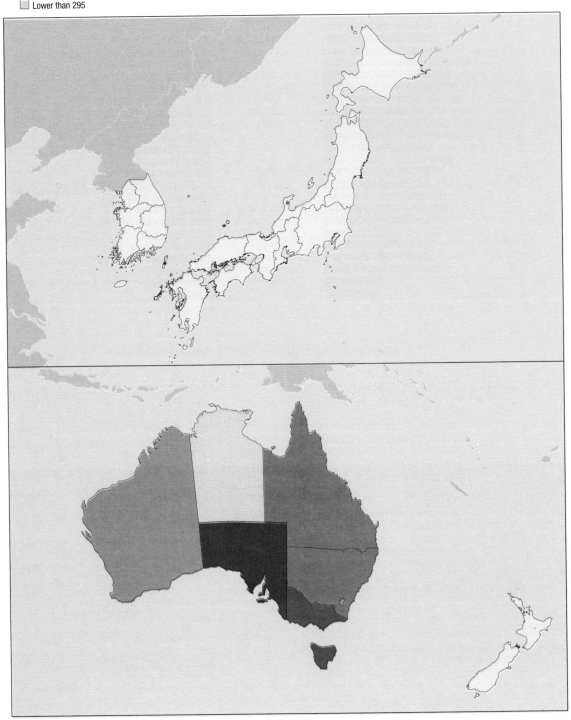

- ■ Higher than 440
- ■ Between 400 and 440
- ■ Between 370 and 400
- ■ Between 310 and 370
- ■ Between 295 and 310
- □ Lower than 295

StatLink http://dx.doi.org/10.1787/172153836678

OECD REGIONS AT A GLANCE 2007 – ISBN 978-92-64-00987-5 – © OECD 2007

30.4. **Incidence of cancer among women: Europe**
Number of new cases of cancer per 100 000 population, 2003

- Higher than 440
- Between 400 and 440
- Between 370 and 400
- Between 310 and 370
- Between 295 and 310
- Lower than 295

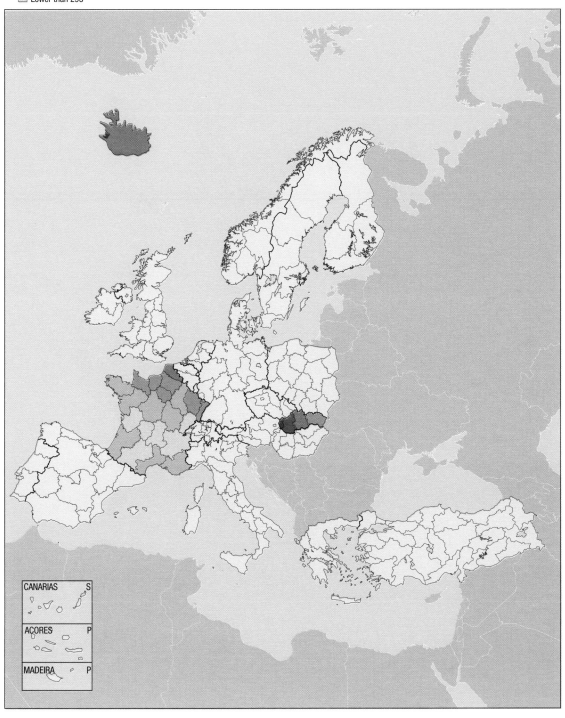

StatLink ⧉ http://dx.doi.org/10.1787/172153836678

30.5. Incidence of cancer among women: North America

Number of new cases of cancer per 100 000 population, 2003

- Higher than 440
- Between 400 and 440
- Between 370 and 400
- Between 310 and 370
- Between 295 and 310
- Lower than 295

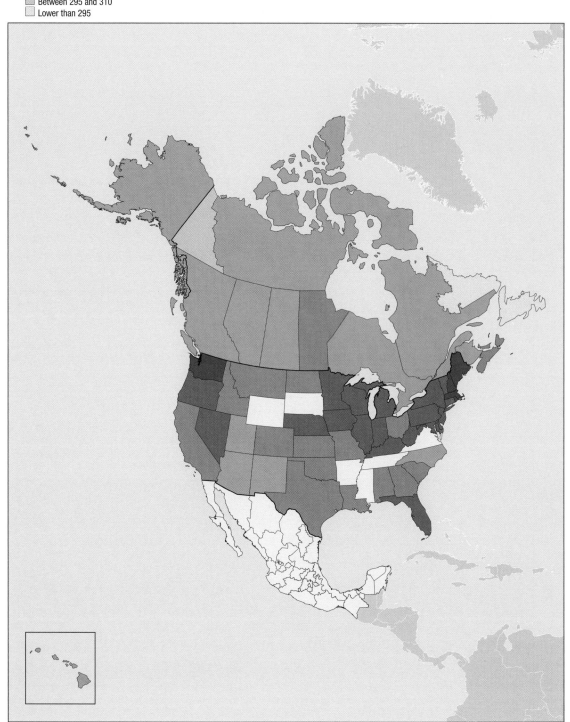

StatLink ⌐🔢 http://dx.doi.org/10.1787/172153836678

When controlling for age, the incidence of cancer tends to be lower in rural regions

Population ageing, individual risk-taking behaviour and environmental risk factors have often been cited as determinants of the increase in cancer. Individual risk factors are tobacco consumption, alcohol consumption and an unhealthy diet. Environmental risk factors include air and water pollution as well as exposure to chemicals and radiation. The link between these risk factors and the incidence of cancer has been established in a number of studies based on individual data.

Although regional data on risk factors are not available, it is commonly believed that rural regions provide a healthier environment so that the incidence of cancer tends to be lower among the rural population. To test this idea, the incidence of cancer in regions is regressed on three explanatory variables: the percentage of the regional population living in rural areas; the proportion of the regional population aged 65 years and above (to control for the effect of ageing); and country-specific dummy variables (to control for differences in risk factors among countries). Figure 30.6 compares the observed and the estimated incidence of cancer among men across the regions of the six countries for which regional data are available (Australia, Canada, Iceland, Slovak Republic, United States and France). Figure 30.7 compares the observed and the estimated incidence of cancer among women.

Overall, the three explanatory variables explain a significant proportion of the regional difference in the incidence of cancer: 56% of the variance for women and 41% for men (based on the adjusted R^2). The country-specific dummy variables are significant at the 5% level for both men and women.

The regression coefficient on the proportion of people aged 65 years and above is positive and significant at the 5% level for both sexes. As expected, regions with an ageing population tend to have a higher incidence of cancer.

The regression coefficient on the proportion of population living in rural regions is negative and significant at the 5% level for men and 10% level for women. Therefore, the incidence of cancer appears to be lower among population in rural regions.

Lack of data prevent testing the effects of risk-taking behaviour on the incidence of cancer in regions. However, to the extent that risk-taking behaviour is not systematically higher in rural regions, this should not change the above results.

30.6. Estimates of the incidence of cancer among men, 2003 (TL2)

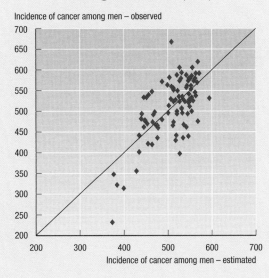

30.7. Estimates of the incidence of cancer among women, 2003 (TL2)

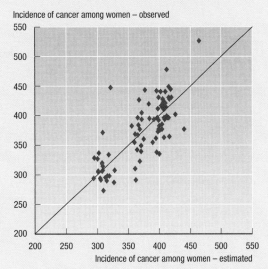

StatLink http://dx.doi.org/10.1787/863260604803

Density of physicians is frequently used as an indicator of health-care provision. An adequate number of qualified practising physicians, located according to need, helps to ensure the delivery of safe, high-quality medical services.

However, it is hard to estimate the minimum number of physicians required to guarantee adequate provision. As well as the number of physicians, the hours they work and the presence of complementary and substitute health professionals (nurses, for instance) also determine actual levels of provision. However, the density of physicians is seldom expressed in full-time equivalents.

Furthermore, the density indicator does not specify whether the physicians actually practise, nor does it reflect features specific to the region. The mix of private/hospital practice may carry a risk of double counting, depending on how the data are collected (*e.g.* by professional organisations). Another area not covered by the indicator is cross-border health-care provision.

Access to physicians varies widely among countries...

In 2004, there was an average of three practising physicians per 1 000 population in the OECD area as a whole. There were wide variations among OECD countries, ranging from over 4 per 1 000 in Italy and Greece, or 1.3 times the OECD average, to fewer than 2 per 1 000 in Turkey, Mexico and Korea, or 0.5 times the OECD average (Figure 31.1). The number of practising physicians was also relatively low in Japan, Canada, the United Kingdom and New Zealand.

... and even more among regions

The 26 OECD countries with information available at regional level have an average of 3.2 physicians per 1 000 population. The largest disparities are found in the United States and in Turkey, where the regions with the highest densities may have up to 2.5 and 2.2 times the national average, respectively (Figure 31.2). In the regions with the highest density, the numbers may be almost twice the national average. Generally, the regions with the lowest density do not have above half of the national average. Consequently, regional disparities within countries are greater than disparities among countries.

Urban areas are better provided

By and large, density of physicians is greater in regions where the population lives predominantly in urban areas. In 17 countries, it is positively correlated with the share of the regional population living in urban regions (Figure 31.3). The correlation is particularly strong in the Czech Republic, Greece, Hungary and Portugal.

Definition

The number of physicians, general practitioners and specialists, actively practising medicine in a region during the year, in both public and private institutions.

OECD REGIONS AT A GLANCE 2007 – ISBN 978-92-64-00987-5 – © OECD 2007

31.1. Practising physicians, density per 1 000 population, 2004

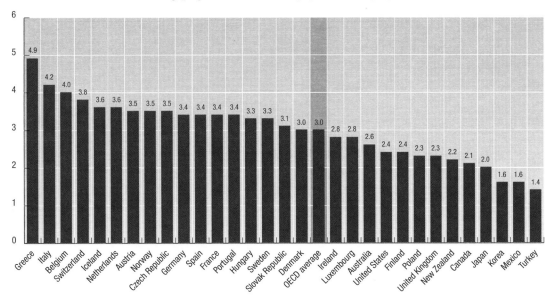

31.2. Regional variations in physician density

Percentage of national average, 2004 (TL2)

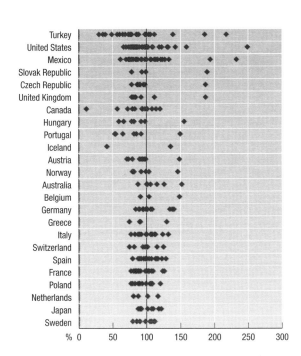

31.3. Correlation between physician density and distribution of population by type of regions

Spearman correlation coefficient, 2004 (TL2)

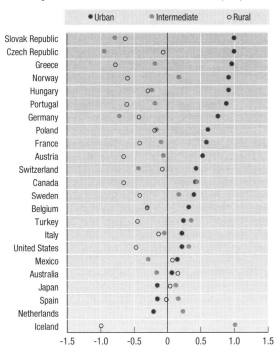

StatLink http://dx.doi.org/10.1787/684847570781

31.4. **Density of physicians: Asia and Oceania**

Percentage of national average, 2004

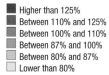

■ Higher than 125%
■ Between 110% and 125%
■ Between 100% and 110%
■ Between 87% and 100%
■ Between 80% and 87%
□ Lower than 80%

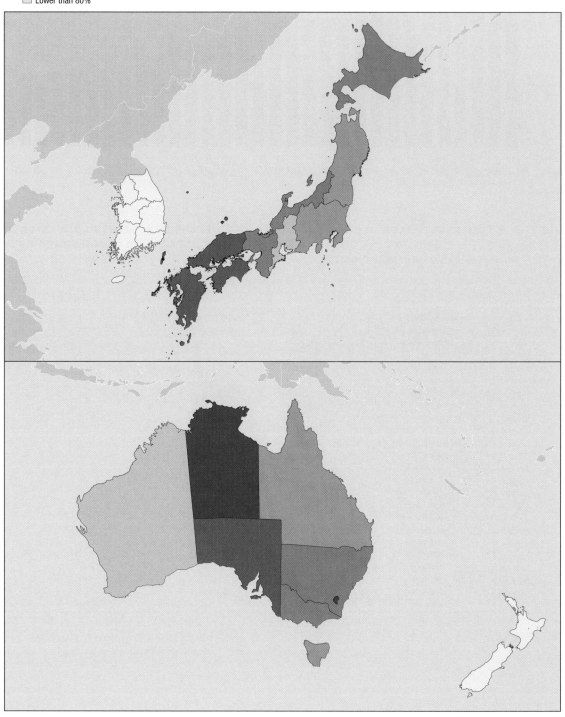

StatLink ⃗ http://dx.doi.org/10.1787/075731856241

OECD REGIONS AT A GLANCE 2007 – ISBN 978-92-64-00987-5 – © OECD 2007

31.5. **Density of physicians: Europe**

Percentage of national average, 2004

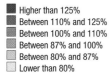

- ■ Higher than 125%
- ■ Between 110% and 125%
- ■ Between 100% and 110%
- ■ Between 87% and 100%
- ■ Between 80% and 87%
- □ Lower than 80%

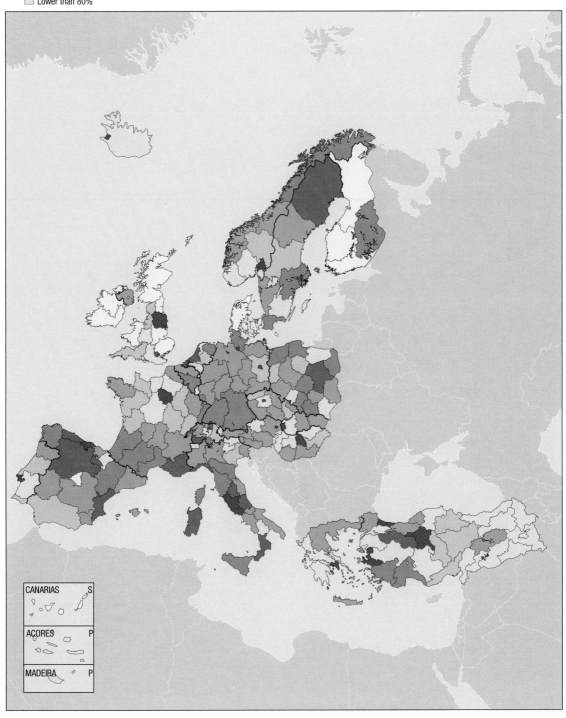

StatLink ⫘⫘ http://dx.doi.org/10.1787/075731856241

31.6. **Density of physicians: North America**
Percentage of national average, 2004

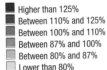

- Higher than 125%
- Between 110% and 125%
- Between 100% and 110%
- Between 87% and 100%
- Between 80% and 87%
- Lower than 80%

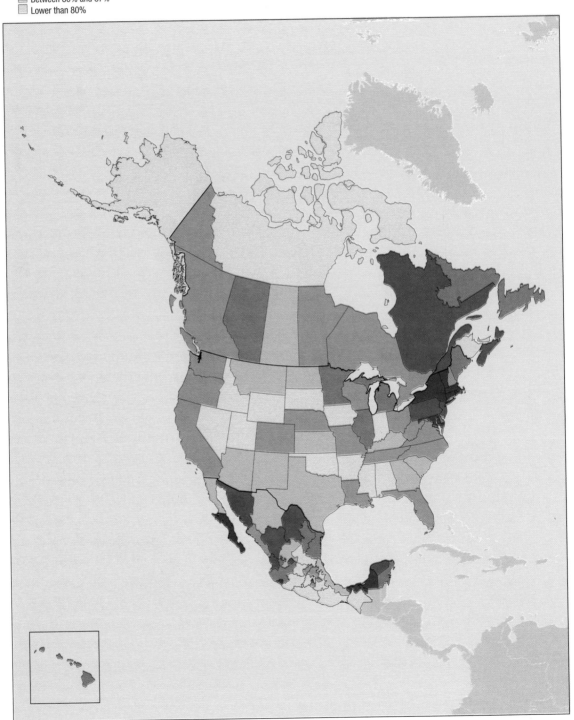

StatLink 🔗 http://dx.doi.org/10.1787/075731856241

OECD REGIONS AT A GLANCE 2007 – ISBN 978-92-64-00987-5 – © OECD 2007

Density of physicians across the country: general practitioners and specialists

The term physician covers both general practitioners and specialists. General practitioners provide primary or first-line healthcare, which is usually the first point of contact with the health system for patients in need of care or advice. It serves to co-ordinate access to other health services and consists in basic preventative and curative care, including diagnosis, simple treatment and referral of complex cases to the appropriate specialised establishments. Specialists provide secondary and tertiary care. Secondary care is specialised care requiring more complex diagnosis and treatment than that provided at primary care level (*e.g.* orthopaedics, surgery), while tertiary care is highly specialised care including diagnostic examinations and treatment such as kidney dialysis and magnetic resonance imaging (MRI). The distinction between general practitioners and specialists serves as a partial measure of access to primary care, on the one hand, and to secondary and tertiary care, on the other.

There are disparities in the density of physicians, particularly with regard to specialists (Figure 31.7). This is the case in Mexico, where the number of specialists per habitant is as high as three times the national average in one region (Distrito Federal) and about half the average in other regions (Mexico, Oaxaca). In this country, the distribution of general practitioners among regions is also very variable. In Turkey, regional disparities are large for both professions.

In general, an unbalanced distribution of specialists per inhabitant among regions is coupled with large disparities in the number of general practitioners per inhabitant. Poland, where the regional distribution of specialists is very balanced but that of general practitioners is not, it is the only exception.

In the Netherlands and Hungary, regional disparities among general practitioners are very small. They are larger for specialists in Hungary but do not exceed the OECD average.

31.7. **Regional variations in physician density by category of physician**
Percentage of the national average, 2004 (TL2)

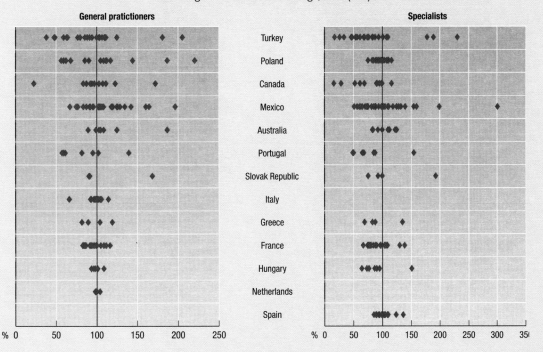

StatLink http://dx.doi.org/10.1787/684847570781

Nursing staff are involved in several ways in the provision of both primary health care and hospital care. They form the largest category of health-care providers in almost all OECD member countries.

Distribution of nurses is an important factor

A sufficient number of nurses is required to guarantee the quality of hospital care. The distribution of labour between doctors and nurses may vary, and there may be substitution for some types of care. It is therefore important to take account of both physicians and nurses per 1 000 population, to obtain an accurate reflection of care provision.

The organisation of healthcare systems and the distribution of work, duties and competencies of health-care professionals vary widely across countries. In addition, the professional categories covered by the term "nurse" in the statistics may also vary. For instance, it may include midwives.

Moreover, coverage may be incomplete for some care establishments.

In 2004, the average number of nurses in OECD countries was 8.2 per 1 000 population, but it varies substantially from one OECD country to another, in part because of the limited comparability of data (Figure 32.1).

Regional variations are high in Spain and Mexico

In Spain, Mexico and Turkey, the number of nurses per 1 000 population varies considerably across regions. Some regions in Spain and Mexico have 2.5 times more nurses per 1 000 than the national average (Figure 32.2). In parts of Turkey, the number of nursing staff per 1 000 population is only 40% of the national average. In other OECD countries, particularly the United Kingdom and Finland, the regional distribution is markedly more balanced.

32.1. **Nursing staff per 1 000 population, 2004**

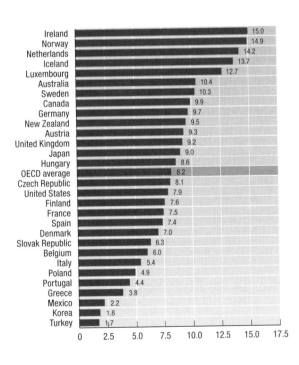

32.2. **Regional variation in nursing staff per 1 000 population, 2004 (TL2)**
Percentage of the national average

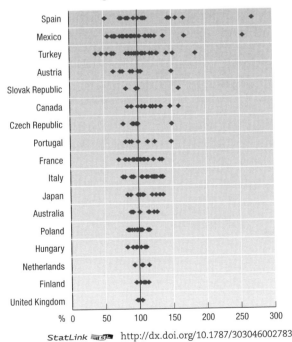

StatLink ⚌⚌ http://dx.doi.org/10.1787/303046002783

Definition

The number of nurses practicing in a region during the reference year.

OECD REGIONS AT A GLANCE 2007 – ISBN 978-92-64-00987-5 – © OECD 2007

32.3. **Density of nurses: Asia and Oceania**
Percentage of national average, 2004

- ■ Higher than 120%
- ■ Between 105% and 120%
- ■ Between 100% and 105%
- ■ Between 95% and 100%
- ■ Between 85% and 95%
- □ Lower than 85%

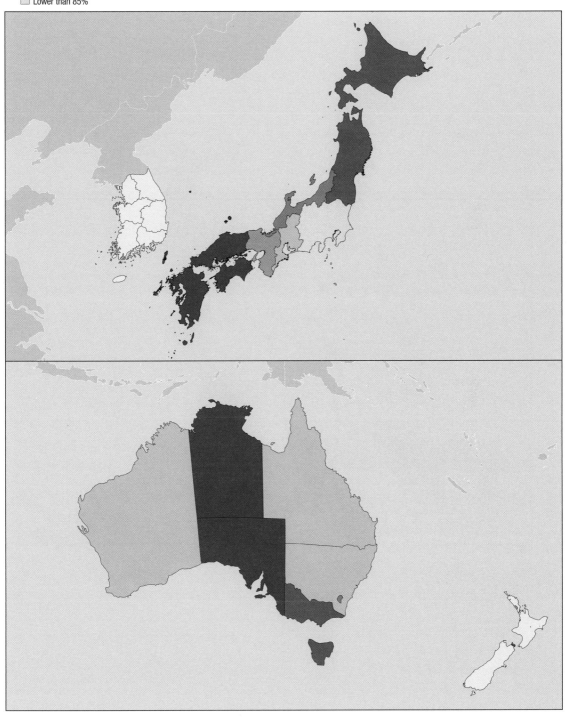

StatLink  http://dx.doi.org/10.1787/808328453414

32.4. **Density of nurses: Europe**
Percentage of national average, 2004

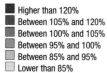

- Higher than 120%
- Between 105% and 120%
- Between 100% and 105%
- Between 95% and 100%
- Between 85% and 95%
- Lower than 85%

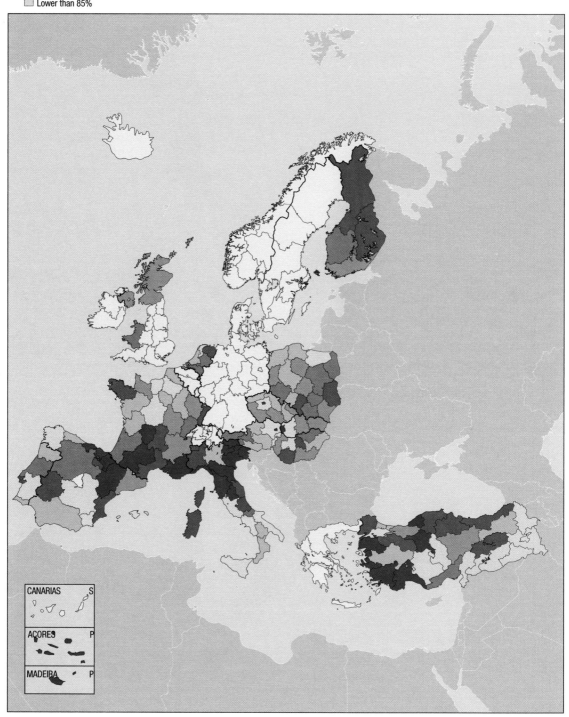

StatLink ⟶ http://dx.doi.org/10.1787/808328453414

OECD REGIONS AT A GLANCE 2007 – ISBN 978-92-64-00987-5 – © OECD 2007

32.5. Density of nurses: North America
Percentage of national average, 2004

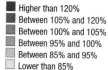

- ■ Higher than 120%
- ■ Between 105% and 120%
- ■ Between 100% and 105%
- ■ Between 95% and 100%
- □ Between 85% and 95%
- □ Lower than 85%

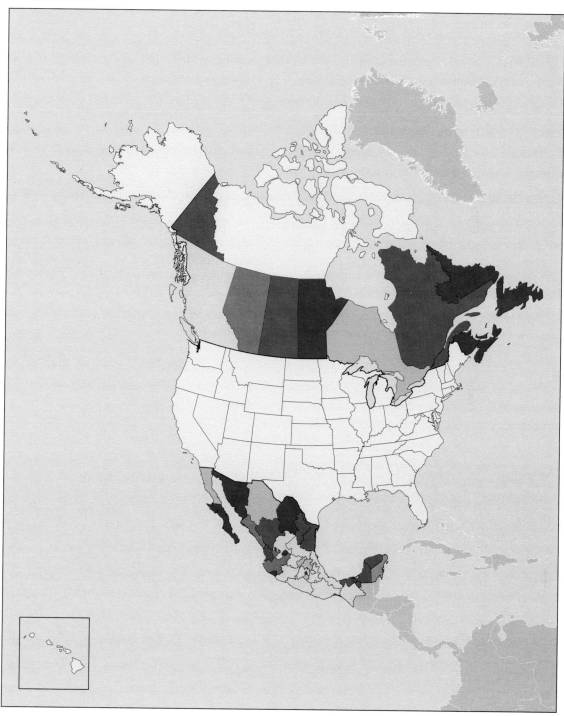

StatLink ⬛ http://dx.doi.org/10.1787/808328453414

The number of hospital beds usually provides a measure of the resources available for delivering health services in hospitals.

It does not, however, provide a comprehensive measure of capacity since it does not capture the capacity of hospitals to furnish services for non-admitted patients (*e.g.* outpatient consultations, day care and ambulatory surgery).

Nor is it a measure of physical accessibility to hospital health services. In fact, a region may have a large number of hospital beds but accessibility may be low if the hospital is located far from the population.

Japan has the most beds per capita

In 2004, there were on average 5.6 hospital beds per 1 000 population in the regions of the 20 OECD member countries for which this information is available (Figure 33.1). Japan was the country with the most beds per capita. Mexico and Turkey were at the opposite end of the scale.

Alternative approaches have reduced the number of hospital beds

The development of varying degrees of alternatives to hospital care (home health care, for instance) across countries has been accompanied by a reduction in the number of hospital beds, in particular long-term beds. In fact, a shortage of hospital beds is often a factor in transfers to ambulatory care.

Some regions have double the national average

Regional disparities were particularly large in Mexico, Portugal, Turkey, Canada and France. In some regions of these countries, the number of beds per capita was between 1.5 and 2 times the national average (Figure 33.2). In Mexico in particular, regional disparities are large although there are, on average, more hospital beds per inhabitant than the OECD average. In the under-equipped regions of Canada and Turkey the number of hospital beds per capita is less than a half the national average. The relative variation in the number of beds per 1 000 population is particularly low in the Netherlands and Hungary.

No general pattern for rural and urban areas

The distribution of hospital beds by type of region does not show any general patterns. In some countries, the number of beds per inhabitant is positively correlated with the proportion of regional population living in urban areas. The correlation is particularly strong in Hungary and the Slovak Republic (Figure 33.3). In Sweden and Germany, however, the number of beds per capita is positively correlated with the proportion of regional population living in rural areas.

Definition

Number of hospital beds (occupied or unoccupied) immediately available for use by patients admitted to all types of hospitals (general hospitals, mental health hospitals and other specialist hospitals) in all sectors (public and private).

33.1. Number of hospital beds per 1 000 population, 2004

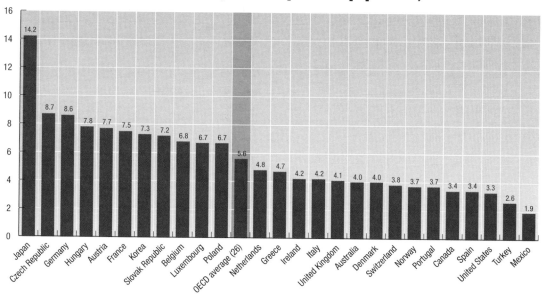

33.2. Variations in the number of hospital beds per 1 000 population

Percentage of the national average, 2004 (TL2)

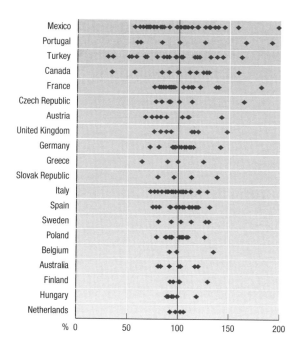

33.3. Correlation between the number of beds per inhabitant and the share of population by type of regions

Spearman correlation coefficient, 2004 (TL2)

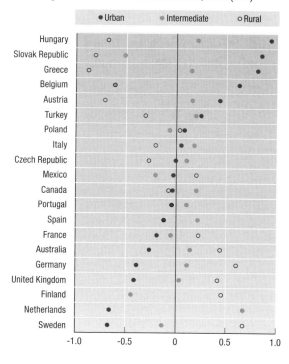

StatLink http://dx.doi.org/10.1787/088748303170

33.4. **Number of hospital beds per 100 000 inhabitants: Asia and Oceania**
Percentage of national average, 2004

- ■ Higher than 125%
- ■ Between 110% and 125%
- ■ Between 100% and 110%
- ■ Between 90% and 100%
- ▫ Between 75% and 90%
- ▫ Lower than 75%

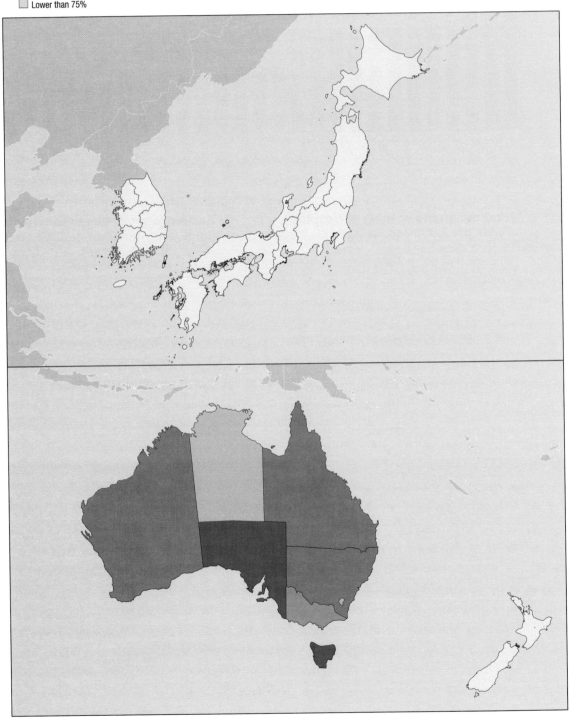

StatLink 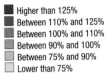 http://dx.doi.org/10.1787/782006473176

33.5. **Number of hospital beds per 100 000 inhabitants: Europe**

Percentage of national average, 2004

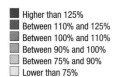

- Higher than 125%
- Between 110% and 125%
- Between 100% and 110%
- Between 90% and 100%
- Between 75% and 90%
- Lower than 75%

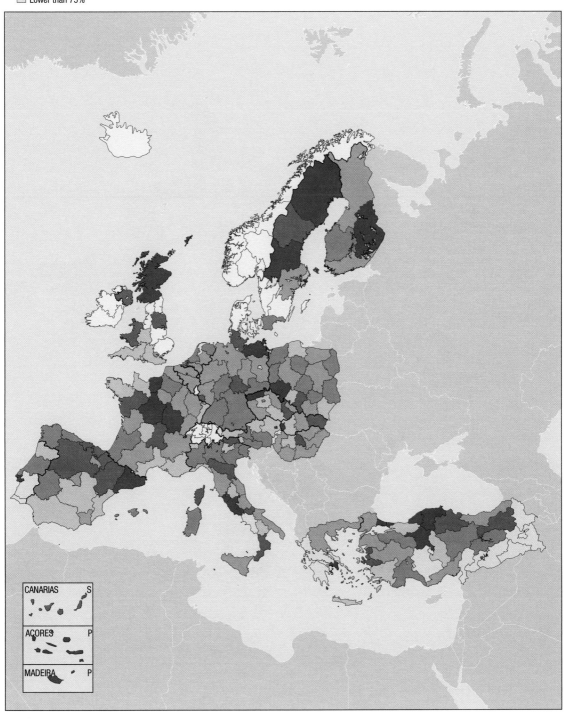

CANARIAS S

AÇORES P

MADEIRA P

StatLink http://dx.doi.org/10.1787/782006473176

33.6. **Number of hospital beds per 100 000 inhabitants: North America**
Percentage of national average, 2004

- ■ Higher than 125%
- ■ Between 110% and 125%
- ■ Between 100% and 110%
- ■ Between 90% and 100%
- ■ Between 75% and 90%
- □ Lower than 75%

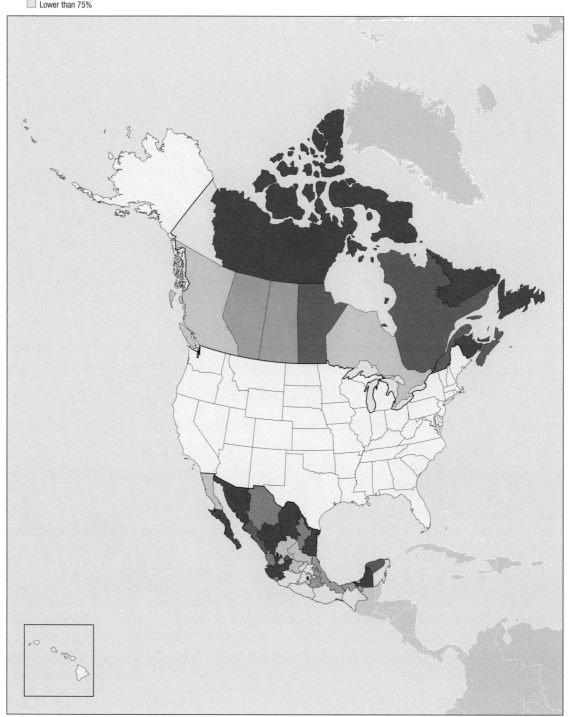

StatLink ⬛⬛⬛ http://dx.doi.org/10.1787/782006473176

OECD REGIONS AT A GLANCE 2007 – ISBN 978-92-64-00987-5 – © OECD 2007

The distribution of hospital beds for long-term and acute care

Beds for long-term care are those for in-patients who need assistance on a continuing basis owing to chronic impairments and a reduced degree of independence in daily activities. These beds are provided in hospitals, geriatric facilities or other types of medical institution. In many OECD countries, health-care policies have promoted the transfer of long-term healthcare provision from medical institutions to care in the community. Home care or housing adapted to the frail elderly results in a decrease in the number of long-term beds. Regions vary in their use of alternatives to hospital care for such patients.

Acute-care beds are those used for all types of medical services, excluding day care and long-term care.

Disparities in the distribution of total hospital beds are due to disparities affecting acute-care beds but especially long-term beds. This is because the greatest regional variations for acute-care beds range from 39% to 182% of the national average (in Canada), whereas the figures for long-term beds range from 11% to 548% of the national average (in Portugal).

There are large regional disparities in the number of long-term beds in southern European countries. The territorial distribution of acute-care beds in these countries is markedly more uniform.

By and large, the supply of acute-care beds is uniform across the regions. Only Canada stands out for its larger disparities.

33.7. **Variation in the number of long-term care and acute-care beds per 1 000 inhabitants**

Percentage of the national average, 2004 (TL2)

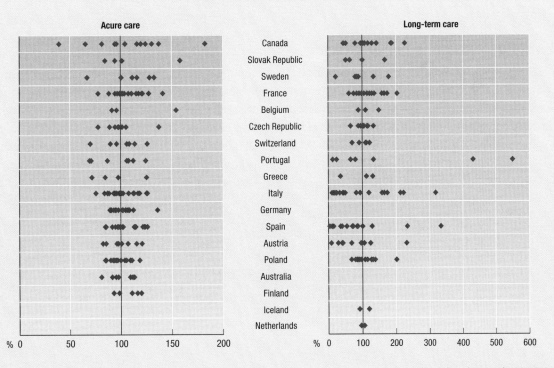

StatLink 📊 http://dx.doi.org/10.1787/088748303170

The number of computerised tomography (CT) scanners and magnetic resonance imaging (MRI) units can be used to measure the diffusion of modern medical technology and, more specifically, diagnostic techniques based on medical imaging. Both of these technologies are used to diagnose a wide range of disorders.

Technology improves diagnosis...

Modern technology provides better diagnosis, helps in selecting better treatment and enhances quality of life by avoiding the need for certain operations. Increasingly precise imaging now provides better evidence of deep or very small lesions that cannot be identified by clinical examination alone. It can also detect early signs of cancer, greatly improving the prognosis. CT scanners can detect morphological anomalies. They provide anatomical images of bones and organs. MRI units visualise details of specific tissues which are less well analysed by CT scanners. They offer the added advantage of not exposing patients to ionising radiation.

... but high costs are a limiting factor

To improve patient monitoring, radiologists often use a combination of the techniques available. These scanners are partly substitutable and partly complementary. Both are expensive but the cost of an MRI unit (some USD 1.9 million) is markedly higher than that of a CT scanner (from USD 600 000 to USD 1 million).

Availability varies widely

Figures for 2004 show significant disparities in the diffusion of diagnostic techniques. Japan has far more CT scanners and MRI units per capita than other OECD countries (Figure 34.1). The United States, Korea and Belgium also have far more CT scanners than the OECD average, although far fewer than Japan. The United States and several European countries (Iceland, Switzerland, Austria, Finland and Italy) also have a relatively high number of MRI units per capita. Mexico and Poland, on the other hand, have few of either device. In both the Slovak and the Czech Republic, the number of MRI units is particularly low. The United Kingdom and Hungary have very few CT scanners.

Significant regional variations

Turkey, at the bottom of the list for the diffusion of diagnostic technology, also suffers from a very uneven spread of such equipment across the country (Figure 34.2). And while Italy is above average for both types of equipment, it is having difficulty ensuring even access to them throughout the country. The number of CT scanners in parts of southern Italy is much higher than the national average, threefold in Campania, which has fewer MRI units, and 1.5 times more in Molise, which also has more MRI units. At the other end of the scale, the Trento area has no equipment of either type. The fact that healthcare provision is organised on a regional basis may explain these disparities, given the cost of such equipment.

Definition

Number of magnetic resonance imaging (MRI) units and computerised tomography (CT) scanners used in radiology to scan a cross-sectional plane of all or part of the body and to produce an image generated by computer synthesis of x-ray transmission data.

34.1. National diffusion of advanced diagnostic equipment, 2004

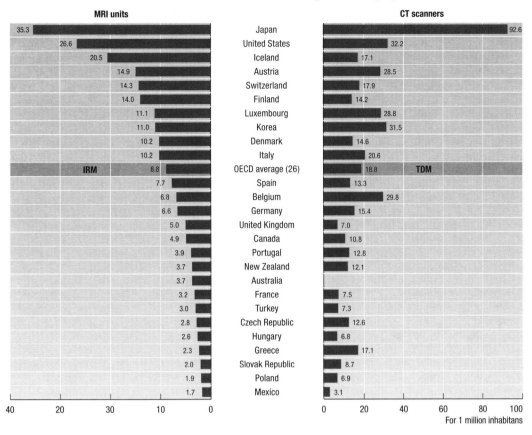

34.2. Regional variations in the number of MRI units and CT scanners, 2004

Percentage of OECD (10) average, 2004 (TL2)

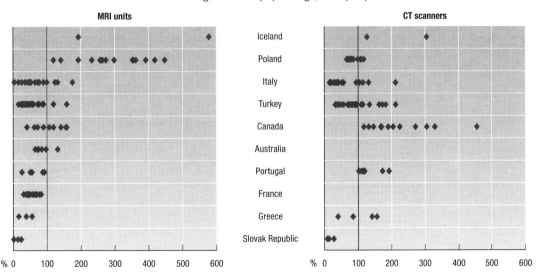

StatLink http://dx.doi.org/10.1787/814648674464

34.3. MRI units per 1 million population: Asia and Oceania, 2004

- ■ Higher than 14
- ■ Between 5 and 14
- ■ Between 4 and 5
- ■ Between 3 and 4
- ■ Between 2 and 3
- □ Lower than 2

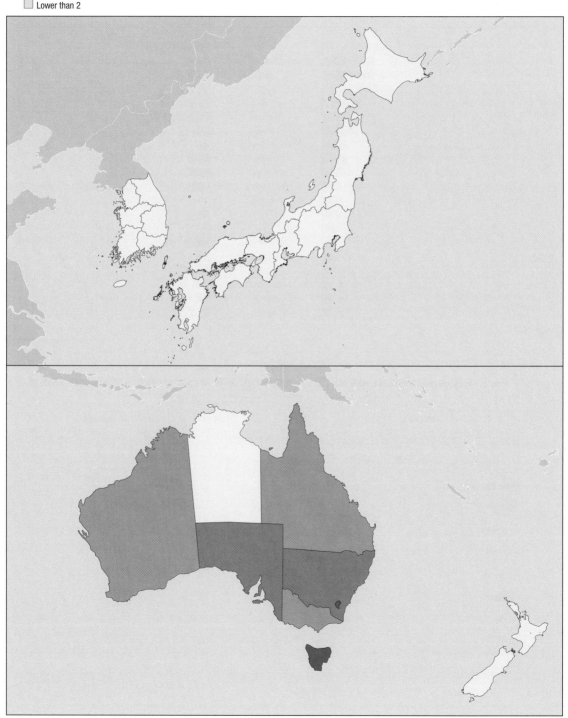

StatLink ◈◈◈ http://dx.doi.org/10.1787/658443863616

34.4. MRI units per 1 million population: Europe, 2004

- Higher than 14
- Between 5 and 14
- Between 4 and 5
- Between 3 and 4
- Between 2 and 3
- Lower than 2

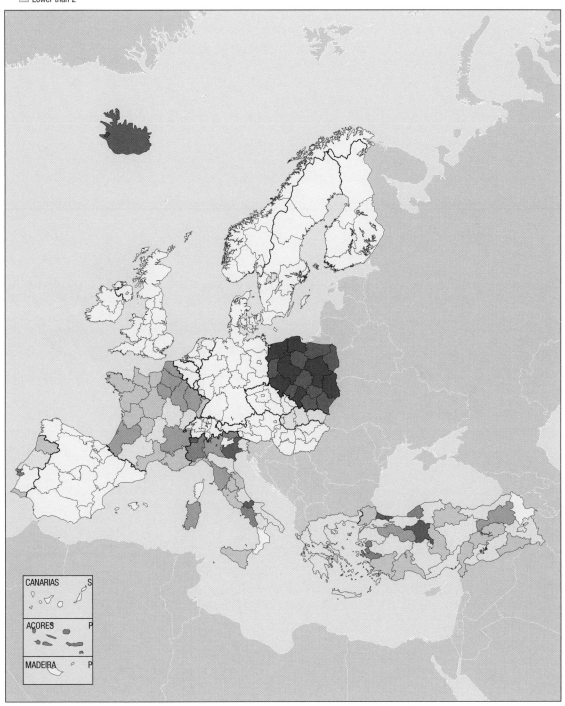

StatLink http://dx.doi.org/10.1787/658443863616

34.5. MRI units per 1 million population: North America, 2004

- Higher than 14
- Between 5 and 14
- Between 4 and 5
- Between 3 and 4
- Between 2 and 3
- Lower than 2

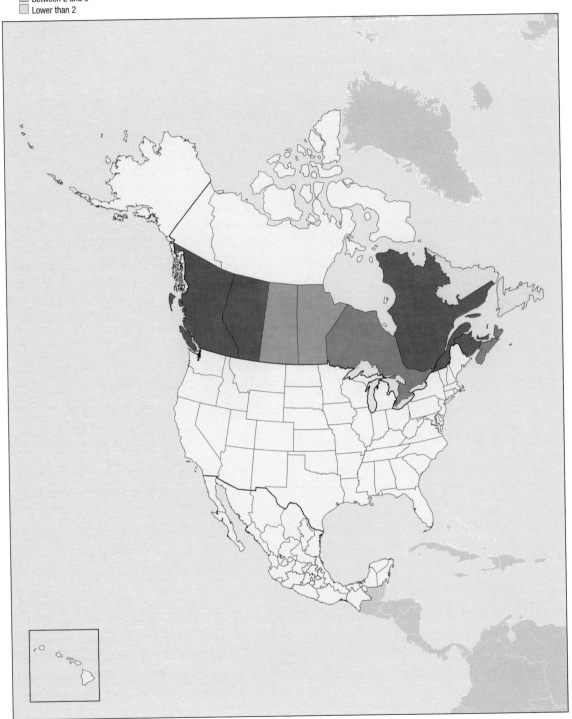

StatLink ⓢ http://dx.doi.org/10.1787/658443863616

OECD REGIONS AT A GLANCE 2007 – ISBN 978-92-64-00987-5 – © OECD 2007

Regional distribution of medical imaging technologies by type of region

The regions best equipped with medical imaging units are usually those in which the population lives primarily in urban areas. In a majority of OECD countries for which such information is available, the number of MRI units and CT scanners per capita is positively correlated with the proportion of the regional population living in urban areas (Figure 34.6 and 34.7). Canada and Italy are the only countries where the number of medical imaging units is positively correlated with the proportion of the regional population living in rural areas.

These patterns, however, do not provide a full picture of the accessibility of medical technologies. While the number of MRI units and CT scanners per capita is a measure of the resources available in regions, their physical accessibility depends on the geographical distance from patients. In fact, a region may have a high number of MRI units and CT scanners per capita but accessibility may be low if they are located far from its inhabitants. Additional indicators – such as the number of tests and the time of utilisation – would be necessary in order to measure the actual accessibility of these technologies at the regional level.

34.6. Correlation between the number of MRI units per inhabitant and the distribution of population by type of region

Spearman correlation coefficient, 2004 (TL2)

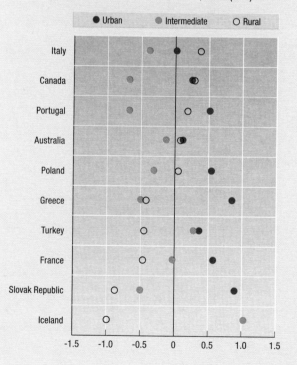

34.7. Correlation between the number of CT scanners per inhabitant and the distribution of population by type of region

Spearman correlation coefficient, 2004 (TL2)

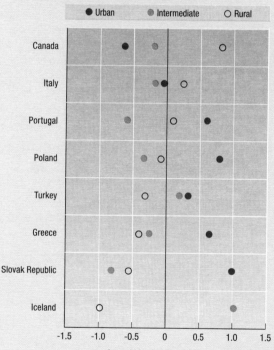

StatLink ⟶ http://dx.doi.org/10.1787/814648674464

Tobacco is considered by the World Health Organization (WHO) to be the second major cause of death worldwide. It is a major risk factor for at least two of the leading causes of premature mortality: circulatory diseases and a range of cancers. In addition, it is an important contributory factor for respiratory diseases and remains the largest avoidable risk to health in OECD countries.

Turkey suffers from high tobacco use

Self-reported daily smokers represent about a quarter of the OECD population aged 15 years and above (Figure 35.1). Greece is the country with the highest proportion of smokers (32%). In Canada, daily smokers represent only 15% of the national population aged 15 years and above. Hungary has the highest share of daily smokers of all eleven countries for which regional statistics are available. It is also one of the countries with the smallest regional disparities in the prevalence of smoking. Spain and Norway are, to a lesser extent, fairly similar, with the prevalence of smoking above the OECD average but relatively small regional disparities.

Variations are wide in Canada, the United States and Australia

In Canada, Australia and the United States, where the prevalence of smoking is on average lower than elsewhere in the OECD area, some regions are more affected and the regional disparities are greatest (Figure 35.2).

35.1. **Proportion of self-reported daily smokers**

Percentage of population aged 15 years and over, 2004

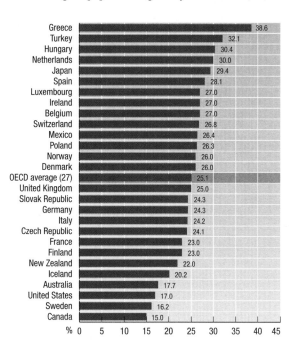

35.2. **Regional variations in the prevalence of smoking**

Percentage of the OECD (11) average, 2004 (TL2)

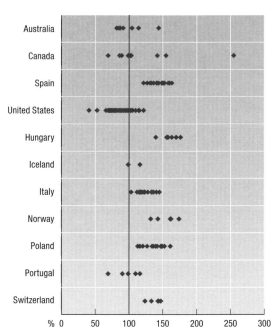

StatLink http://dx.doi.org/10.1787/301887638251

Definition

Percentage of the population aged 15 years and over reporting that they smoke every day.

OECD REGIONS AT A GLANCE 2007 – ISBN 978-92-64-00987-5 – © OECD 2007

35.3. **Prevalence of smoking: Asia and Oceania**
Percentage of national average 2004

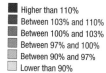

- Higher than 110%
- Between 103% and 110%
- Between 100% and 103%
- Between 97% and 100%
- Between 90% and 97%
- Lower than 90%

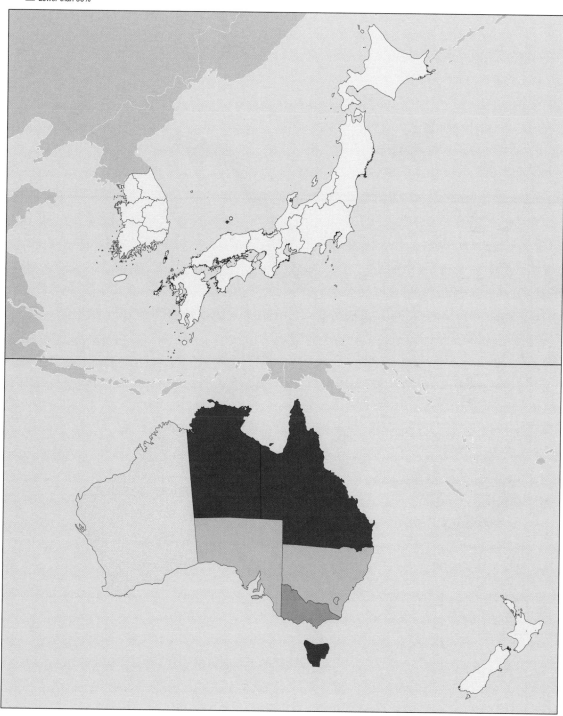

StatLink ᴍ≋ꜱ⌐ http://dx.doi.org/10.1787/417307878270

35.4. **Prevalence of smoking: Europe**
Percentage of national average 2004

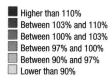

■ Higher than 110%
■ Between 103% and 110%
■ Between 100% and 103%
■ Between 97% and 100%
■ Between 90% and 97%
□ Lower than 90%

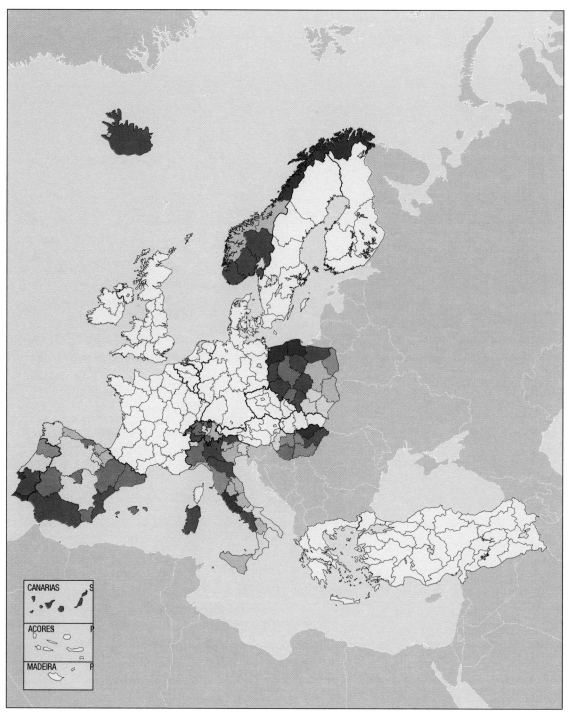

StatLink ⟪ http://dx.doi.org/10.1787/417307878270

35.5. **Prevalence of smoking: North America**

Percentage of national average 2004

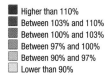

- ■ Higher than 110%
- ■ Between 103% and 110%
- ■ Between 100% and 103%
- ■ Between 97% and 100%
- ■ Between 90% and 97%
- □ Lower than 90%

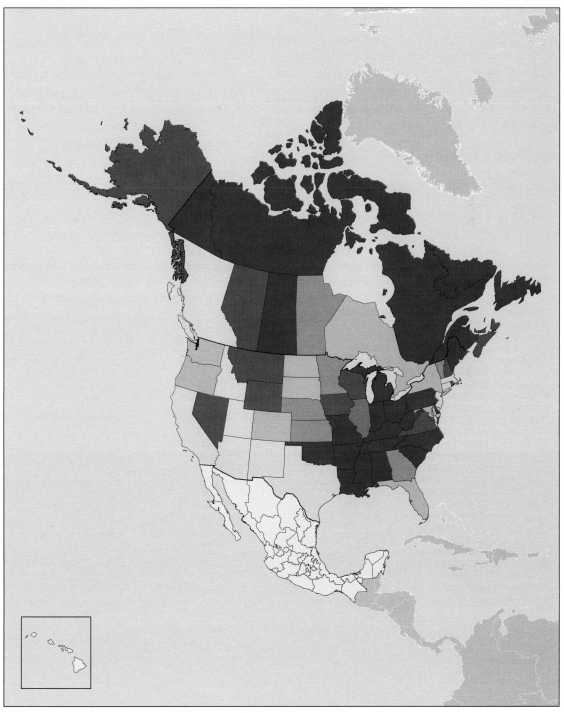

StatLink ⬛⬛ http://dx.doi.org/10.1787/417307878270

Obesity is a known risk factor for several health problems, including diabetes, hypertension and cardiovascular diseases, as well as respiratory and musculoskeletal disorders. There has been a considerable increase in obesity-related problems over the past two decades, along with an associated rise in health-care costs. Adults with a Body Mass Index (BMI) of over 30 are defined as obese. However, some ethnic groups may have equivalent levels of risk at lower or higher BMIs. Survey definitions differ significantly among countries. As a consequence, results may be quite different depending on whether obesity is self-reported (*e.g.* Australia, the United States) or measured (see Sources and Methodologies).

Obesity is highest in North America and Hungary

Of the nine countries for which this information is available at the regional level, obesity is most prevalent on average in the United States, Canada and Hungary (respectively 22%, 18% and 18% compared with the 15% average across all nine countries) (Figure 36.1). The region with the lowest prevalence of obesity in each of these countries has a a rate higher than the OECD average. At the other end of the scale, Italy, and particularly Switzerland, have far fewer cases of obesity (averaging 9% and 7%, respectively).

Regional variations are small in Australia ...

Australia has the smallest regional disparities, ranging from 15.6% to 17.6% (Figure 36.2). In Canada, which has an average incidence of obesity similar to Australia's, there are very wide regional disparities, ranging from 11.6% to 21.9%.

... but large in Spain

While obesity is below the OECD average in Spain, it displays the largest regional disparities.

36.1. **Prevalence of obesity**
Percentage of population aged 15 years and over, 2004

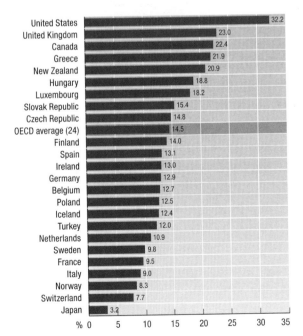

36.2. **Regional disparities in the prevalence of obesity**
Percentage of the national average, 2004 (TL2)

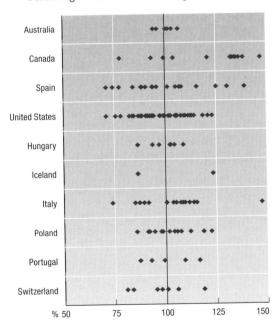

StatLink http://dx.doi.org/10.1787/433308868127

Definition

Number of people suffering from obesity in the population. Obesity is measured by the Body Mass Index (BMI). The obese population is the percentage of people aged 15 and over with a BMI over 30.

OECD REGIONS AT A GLANCE 2007 – ISBN 978-92-64-00987-5 – © OECD 2007

36.3. **Prevalence of obesity: Asia and Oceania**

Percentage of national average, 2004

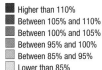

- ■ Higher than 110%
- ■ Between 105% and 110%
- ■ Between 100% and 105%
- ■ Between 95% and 100%
- ■ Between 85% and 95%
- □ Lower than 85%

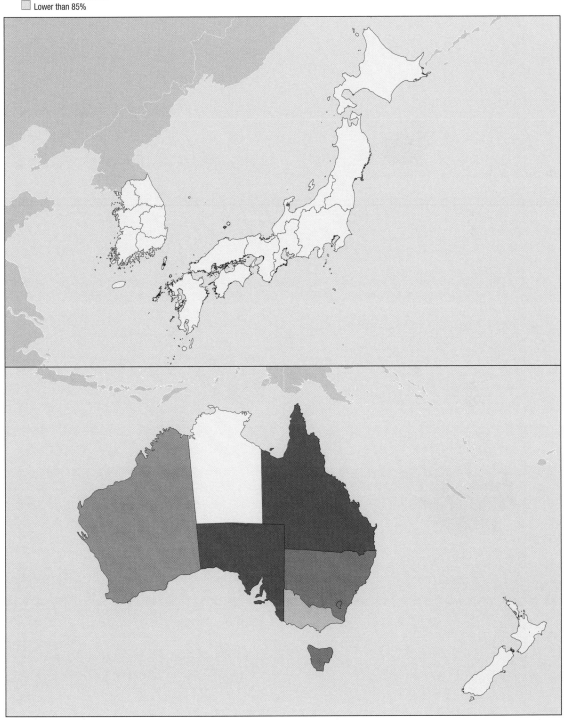

StatLink ⟲ http://dx.doi.org/10.1787/010101203614

36.4. **Prevalence of obesity: Europe**
Percentage of national average, 2004

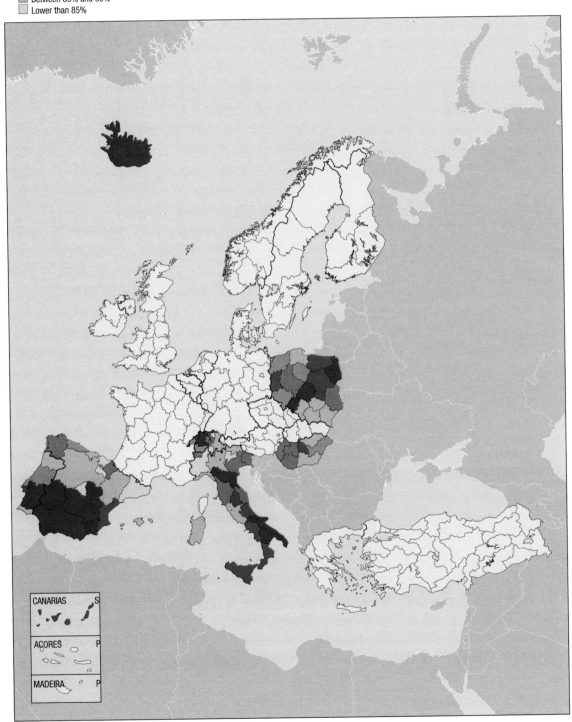

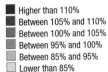

- Higher than 110%
- Between 105% and 110%
- Between 100% and 105%
- Between 95% and 100%
- Between 85% and 95%
- Lower than 85%

StatLink http://dx.doi.org/10.1787/010101203614

OECD REGIONS AT A GLANCE 2007 – ISBN 978-92-64-00987-5 – © OECD 2007

36.5. **Prevalence of obesity: North America**
Percentage of national average, 2004

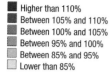

- Higher than 110%
- Between 105% and 110%
- Between 100% and 105%
- Between 95% and 100%
- Between 85% and 95%
- Lower than 85%

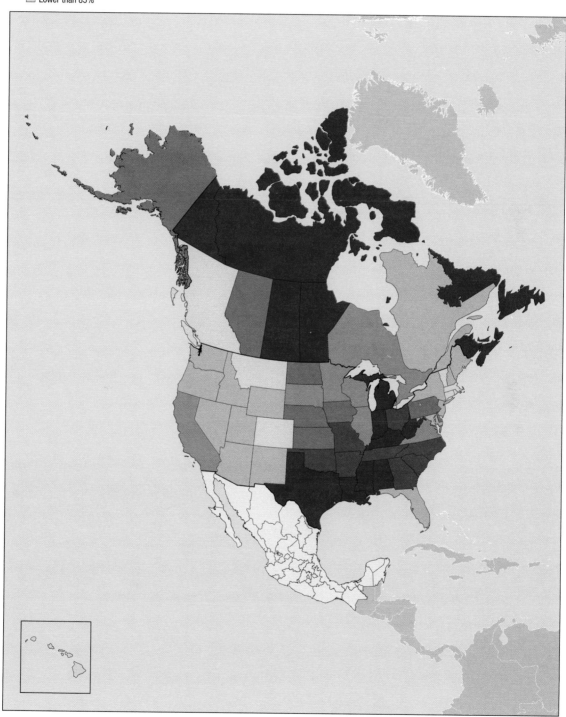

StatLink ⟨⟩ http://dx.doi.org/10.1787/010101203614

ISBN 978-92-64-00987-5
OECD Regions at a Glance 2007
© OECD 2007

Source and Methodology

Territorial Grids and regional typology

Regional grids

In any analytical study conducted at sub-national levels, the choice of the territorial unit is of prime importance. The word "region" can mean very different things both within and between countries. For instance, the smallest OECD region (Melilla, Spain) has an area of less than 15 square kilometres whereas the largest region (Northwest Territories and Nunavut, Canada) has over 3 millions square kilometres. Similarly, population in OECD regions ranges from about 400 inhabitants in Balance ACT (Australia) to more than 47 million in Kanto (Japan).

To address this issue, the OECD has classified regions within each member country (Table 1). The classifications are based on two Territorial Levels (TL). The higher level (Territorial Level 2) consists of 335 macro-regions while the lower level (Territorial Level 3) is composed of 1 679 micro-regions.[1] This classification – which, for European countries, is largely consistent with the Eurostat classification – facilitates greater comparability of regions at the same territorial level. Indeed, these two levels, which are officially established and relatively stable in all member countries, are used by many as a framework for implementing regional policies.

Due to limited data availability, labour market indicators in Canada and Australia are presented for groups of TL3 regions. Since these groups are not part of the OECD official territorial grids, for the sake of simplicity they are labelled as Non Official Grids (NOGs) in this publication (Table 1).

Regional typology

A second important issue for the analysis of regional economies concerns the different "geography" of each region. For instance, in the United Kingdom one could question the relevance of comparing the highly urbanised area of London to the rural region of the Shetland Islands, despite the fact that both regions belong at the same territorial level. To take account of these differences, the OECD has established a regional typology according to which TL3 regions have been classified as Predominantly Urban, Predominantly Rural and Intermediate. This typology, based on the percentage of regional population living in rural or urban communities, enables meaningful comparisons between regions belonging to the same type and level (Figures 1-4).

The OECD regional typology is based on three criteria. The first criterion identifies rural communities according to population density. A community is defined as rural if its

---

1. Level 0 indicates the territory of the whole country and Level 1 denotes groups of macro-regions.

population density is below 150 inhabitants per square kilometre (500 inhabitants for Japan to account for the fact that its national population density exceeds 300 inhabitants per square kilometre). The second criterion classifies regions according to the percentage of population living in rural communities. Thus, a TL3 region is classified as:

- *Predominantly rural (rural)*, if more than 50% of its population lives in rural communities.
- *Predominantly urban (urban)*, if less than 15% of the population lives in rural communities.
- *Intermediate*, if the share of population living in rural communities is between 15% and 50%.

The third criterion is based on the size of the urban centres. Accordingly:

- A region that would be classified as rural on the basis of the general rule is classified as intermediate if it has a urban centre of more than 200 000 inhabitants (500 000 for Japan) representing no less than 25% of the regional population.
- A region that would be classified as intermediate on the basis of the general rule is classified as predominantly urban if it has a urban centre of more than 500 000 inhabitants (1 000 000 for Japan) representing no less than 25% of the regional population.

Table 1. **Territorial grid of OECD member countries**

	Territorial Level 2 (TL2)	Non Official Grid (NOG)	Territorial Level 3 (TL3)
Australia	States/Territories (8)	LFS, Dissemination regions (30)	Statistical divisions (58)
Austria	Bundesländer (9)	–	Gruppen von Politischen Bezirken (35)
Belgium	Régions (3)	–	Provinces (11)
Canada	Provinces/Territories (12)	LFS, Economic areas (71)	Census divisions (288)
Czech Republic	Oblasti (8)	–	Kraje (14)
Denmark	Regions (3)	–	Amter (15)
Finland	Suuralueet/Storområden (5)	–	Maakunnat/Landskap (20)
France	Régions (22)	–	Départements (96)
Germany	Länder (16)	–	Spatial planning regions (groups of Kreise) (97)
Greece	Groups of Development regions (4)	–	Periferies (13)
Hungary	Tervezési-statisztikai régiók (7)	–	Megyék + Budapest (20)
Iceland	Regions (2)	–	landsvæi (8)
Ireland	Regions (2)	–	Regional Authority Regions (8)
Italy	Regioni (21)	–	Provincie (103)
Japan	Districts (10)	–	Prefectures (47)
Korea	Provinces (7)	–	Provinces + metropolitan cities (16)
Luxembourg	State (1)	–	State (1)
Mexico	Estados (32)	–	Groups of municipios (209)
Netherlands	Landsdelen (4)	–	Provincies (12)
New Zealand	Northern and southern Island (2)	–	Regional Councils (14)
Norway	Landsdeler (7)	–	Fylker (19)
Poland	Województwa (16)	–	Podregiony (45)
Portugal	Comissões de coordenação regional + Regiões autónomas (7)	–	Grupos de Concelhos (30)
Slovak Republic	Oblasti (4)	–	Kraje (8)
Spain	Comunidades y ciudades autónomas (19)	–	Provincias + Ceuta y Melilla (52)
Sweden	Riksområden (8)	–	Län (21)
Switzerland	Grossregionen/Grandes régions/Grandi Regioni (7)	–	Kantone/Cantons/Cantoni (26)
Turkey	Alt Bölgeler (26)	–	Iller (81)
United Kingdom	Government Office Regions; Country (12)	–	Upper tier authorities or groups of lower tier authorities (unitary authorities or districts) (133)
United States	States (51)	–	(BEA) Economic Areas (179)

Table 2. **Percentage of national population living in predominantly urban, intermediate and predominantly rural regions (TL3) and number of regions classified as such in each country**

	Percentage of population (2003*)			Number of regions (TL3)		
	Urban	Intermediate	Rural	Urban	Intermediate	Rural
Australia	55%	22%	23%	5	11	42
Australia (NOG)	–	–	–	6	7	17
Austria	23%	31%	46%	2	8	25
Belgium	83%	14%	2%	8	2	1
Canada	53%	18%	29%	27	38	223
Canada (NOG)	38%	36%	26%	6	18	47
Czech Republic	11%	84%	5%	1	12	1
Denmark	29%	32%	39%	3	4	8
Finland	26%	12%	62%	1	2	17
France	29%	40%	31%	11	30	55
Germany	49%	39%	12%	27	48	22
Greece	36%	24%	40%	1	2	10
Hungary	17%	39%	44%	1	8	11
Iceland	0%	63%	37%	0	1	7
Ireland	28%	0%	72%	1	0	7
Italy	54%	37%	10%	34	49	20
Japan	55%	31%	14%	12	21	14
Korea	52%	31%	17%	8	5	4
Luxembourg	0%	100%	0%	0	1	0
Mexico	42%	21%	38%	30	33	146
Netherlands	85%	15%	0%	7	5	0
New Zealand	43%	57%	0%	2	12	0
Norway	11%	39%	49%	1	5	13
Poland	23%	38%	40%	8	15	22
Portugal	50%	24%	26%	6	7	17
Slovak Republic	11%	63%	25%	1	5	2
Spain	35%	52%	13%	7	28	17
Sweden	21%	30%	50%	1	2	18
Switzerland	41%	50%	9%	7	12	7
Turkey	17%	48%	35%	2	31	48
United Kingdom	70%	27%	4%	81	37	15
United States	55%	21%	24%	39	25	115

* Mexico 2000.

Figure 1. **Regional typology, OECD countries: Asia and Oceania (TL3)**

Figure 2. **Regional typology, OECD countries: Europe (TL3)**

■ Predominantly Urban
■ Intermediate
□ Predominantly Rural

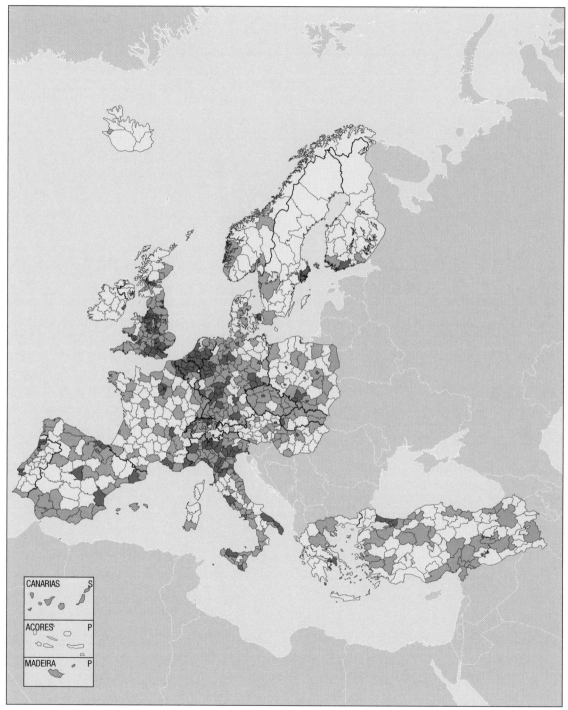

Figure 3. **Regional typology: OECD countries: North American (TL3)**

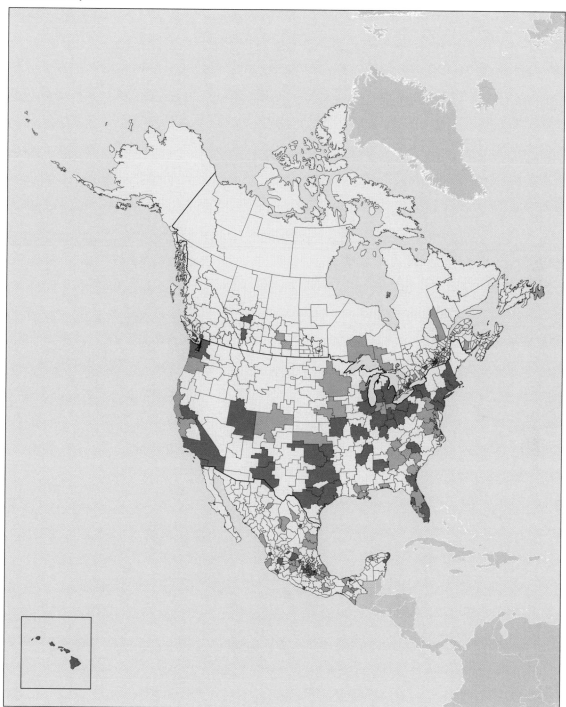

Figure 4. **Regional typology: Canada and Australia (NOG)**

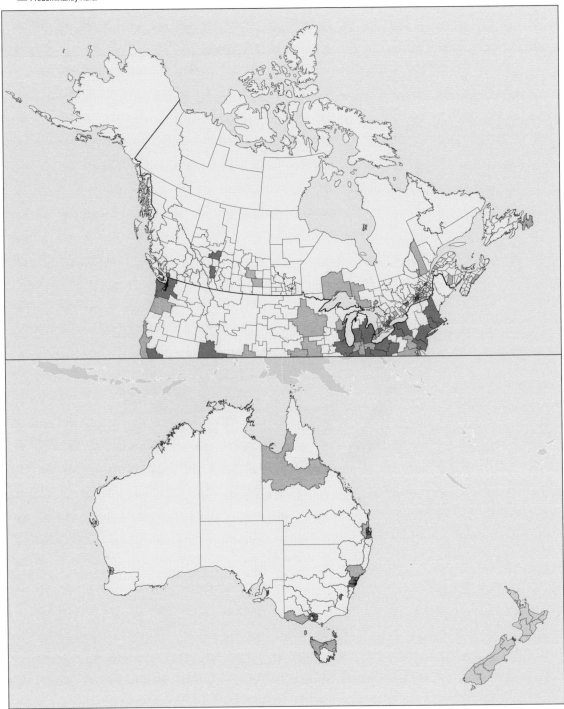

Table 3. **User guide: list of indicators and variables by chapter**

Chapters	Indicator	Variables used	Page
Chapter 1	Geographic concentration of population	Total population	223
Chapter 2	Geographic concentration of elderly population	Population by age and sex	224
Chapter 3	Geographic concentration of GDP	Gross domestic product	226
		Total population	223
Chapter 4	Regional contribution to growth in national GDP	Gross domestic product	226
Chapter 5	Geographic concentration of industries	Employment by industry	228
Chapter 6	Regional contribution to change in employment	Employment	229
Chapter 7	Geographic concentration of patents	Patent applications	232
Chapter 8	Regional disparities in GDP per capita	Per capita gross domestic product	226
Chapter 9	Regional disparities in labour productivity	Gross domestic product	226
		Employment at place of work	231
Chapter 10	Regional disparities in specialisation	Employment by industry	228
Chapter 11	Regional disparities in tertiary educational attainments	Tertiary educational attainments	233
		Population by age and sex	224
Chapter 12	Regional disparities in unemployment rates	Unemployment	229
		Labour force	229
		Long-term unemployment	229
Chapter 13	Regional disparities in participation rates	Labour force	229
		Female participation rate	229
		Population aged 15-64	224
		Female population aged 15-64	224
Chapter 14	Factors of regional competitiveness	See chapters 15, 16, 17, 18, 19	
Chapter 15	Regional growth in the OECD	Gross domestic product	226
Chapter 16	National factors and regional performances	Gross domestic product	226
Chapter 17	Regional factors: GDP per capita and population	Gross domestic product	226
		Population	223
Chapter 18	Regional factors: productivity and specialisation	Gross domestic product	226
		Employment	229
		Employment by industry	228
Chapter 19	Regional factors: Employment, participation and ageing	Gross domestic product	226
		Employment Labour force	229
		Employment by industry	228
		Population by age	224
Chapter 20	Accessibility: Time distance from the closest urban centre	Time distance to the major urban centre	235
Chapter 21	Education: Student enrolment in tertiary education	Students enrolment in tertiary education	237
		Total population	223
Chapter 22	Voter turnout in national elections	Voter turnout	238
Chapter 23	Safety: Crimes against property	Crime against property	239
		Total population	223
Chapter 24	Safety: Reported murders	Number of murders	241
		Total population	223
Chapter 25	Home ownership	Number of dwellings inhabited by the owner	243
		Total number of occupied dwellings	243
Chapter 26	Environment: Private vehicles	Stock of private vehicles	244
		Total population	223
Chapter 27	Environment: Municipal waste	Volume of produced waste	245
		Total population	223
Chapter 28	Age-adjusted mortality rates	Number of deaths by age and sex	246
		Population by age and sex	224
Chapter 29	Premature mortality	Number of deaths by age and sex	246
		Population by age and sex	224
Chapter 30	Incidence of cancer	Number of new cases of cancer	248
		Total population	223
Chapter 31	Density of practicing physicians	Number of physicians	249
		Total population	223
Chapter 32	Density of practicing nurses	Number of nurses	251
		Total population	223
Chapter 33	Hospital beds	Number of hospital beds	253
		Total population	223
Chapter 34	Medical technologies	Number of CT scanners	255
		Total population	223
Chapter 35	Prevalence of smoking	Number of smokers aged 15 and over	256
		Total population	223
Chapter 36	Prevalence of obesity	Number of persons suffering from obesity	257
		Total population	223

Population – Chapters: 1, 8, 17, 21, 23, 24, 26, 27, 30, 31, 32, 33, 34, 35, 36

Sources and year of reference

	Source	Reference years	Territorial Level
Australia	Australian Bureau of Statistics, 3201.0	1998-2003	3
Austria	Eurostat, New Cronos, Annual average population	1998-2003	3
Belgium	Eurostat, New Cronos, Annual average population	1998-2003	3
Canada	Statistics Canada, CANSIM Table 051-0036, Estimates of population	1998-2003	3
Czech Republic	Eurostat, New Cronos, Annual average population	1998-2003	3
Denmark	Eurostat, New Cronos, Annual average population	1998-2003	3
Finland	Eurostat, New Cronos, Annual average population	1998-2003	3
France	Eurostat, New Cronos, Annual average population	1998-2003	3
Germany	Eurostat, New Cronos, Annual average population	1998-2003	3
Greece	Eurostat, New Cronos, Annual average population	1998-2003	3
Hungary	Eurostat, New Cronos, Annual average population	1998-2003	3
Iceland	Statistics Iceland	1998-2003	3
Ireland	Eurostat, New Cronos, Annual average population	1998-2003	3
Italy	Eurostat, New Cronos, Annual average population	1998-2003	3
Japan	Statistics Bureau, MIC	1998-2003	3
Korea	Korean National Statistical Office	1998-2003	3
Luxembourg	Eurostat, New Cronos, Annual average population	1998-2003	3
Mexico	Secretariat estimates based on Census of population (INEGI)	1998-2003	3
Netherlands	Eurostat, New Cronos, Annual average population	1998-2003	3
New Zealand	Statistics New Zealand, Estimated Resident Population	1998-2003	3
Norway	Statistics Norway, StatBank,	1998-2003	3
Poland	Eurostat, New Cronos, Annual average population	1998-2003	3
Portugal	Eurostat, New Cronos, Annual average population	1998-2003	3
Slovak Republic	Eurostat, New Cronos, Annual average population	1998-2003	3
Spain	Eurostat, New Cronos, Annual average population	1998-2003	3
Sweden	Eurostat, New Cronos, Annual average population	1998-2003	3
Switzerland	Swiss Federal Statistical Office, Statweb	1998-2003	3
Turkey	Turkish Statistical Institute (TURKSTAT)	1998-2003	3
United Kingdom	Eurostat, New Cronos, Annual average population	1998-2003	3
United States	US Census Bureau, Intercensal estimates	1998-2003	3

Country notes

Canada: Census divisions according to Census 2001 boundaries.

Iceland: population at 1 December.

Mexico: data for 1998 and 2003 are estimated using the exponential growth function based on the period 1995-2000 and 2000-05.

Japan: population at 1 October.

Korea: data for 2001-04 are based on population projections.

New Zealand: population ats 30 June. Population estimates at 30 June 1996–2000 are based on 2001 Regional Council boundaries, whereas estimates from 2001 onwards are based on 2005 Regional Council boundaries.

Switzerland: Permanent resident population at the end of the year.

Turkey: Mid-year population estimates.

United States: Mid-year population estimates.

Population by age and sex – Chapters: 2, 11, 13, 19, 28

Sources and year of reference

	Source	Reference year	Territorial Level
Australia	Australian Bureau of Statistics, 3201.0.	1998-2003	3
Austria	Secretariat estimates based on Eurostat, New Cronos	1998-2003	3
Belgium	Eurostat, New Cronos	1998-2003	3
Canada	Statistics Canada, CANSIM Table 051-0036, Estimates of population	1998-2003	3
Czech Republic	Czech Statistical Office	1998-2003	3
Denmark	Statistics Denmark, Statbank	1998-2003	3
Finland	Statistics Finland	1998-2003	3
France	INSEE, Local population estimates	1998-2003	3
Germany	Regional statistics Germany, Spatial Monitoring System of the BBR	1998-2003	3
Greece	Eurostat, New Cronos	1998-2003	3
Hungary	KSH, Hungarian Statistical Office	1998-2003	3
Iceland	Statistics Iceland	1998-2003	3
Ireland	Central Statistics Office, Ireland (Census of population)	2002	3
Italy	ISTAT, Intercensal population estimates	1998-2003	3
Japan	Statistics Bureau, MIC	1998-2003	3
Korea	Korean National Statistical Office	1998-2003	3
Luxembourg	Eurostat, New Cronos	1998-2003	3
Mexico	INEGI, (Census of Population)	2000	3
Netherlands	Eurostat, New Cronos.	1998-2003	3
New Zealand	Statistics New Zealand (Census of population)	2001	3
Norway	Statistics Norway, Statbank	1998-2003	3
Poland	Central Statistical Office, Poland	2000-2003	3
Portugal	National Statistics Institute (INE)	1998-2003	3
Slovak Republic	Statistical Office of the Slovak Republic	1998-2003	3
Spain	National Statistics Institute (INE)	1998-2002	3
Sweden	Statistics Sweden	1998-2003	3
Switzerland	Swiss Federal Statistical Office, Statweb	1998-2003	3
Turkey	Turkish Statistical Institute (TURKSTAT)	1998-2003	3
United Kingdom	National Statistical Office, population estimates	1998-2003	3
United States	US Census Bureau, Population Estimates Program	1998-2003	3

Country notes

Austria: Data are estimated computing the share of working age population to total population for each TL2 region, and then applying the share of working age to total population to the population at TL3.

Belgium, France, Greece, Hungary, Luxembourg, Netherlands, Norway: Population at 1 January.

Canada: Census divisions according to Census 2001 boundaries.

Czech Republic and Slovak Republic: Population at 31 December.

Denmark: Population at 1 January. The source of the statistics is Statistic Denmark's population register, which receives partly an annual outdraw of the total population and partly a weekly outdraw which include information about weekly events such as removals, emigrations and immigrations, births and deaths from CPR (Central Person Register).

Italy: Resident population at 1 January.

Japan: Population at 1 October.

Korea: data for 2001-04 are based on population projections.

Portugal: Provisional estimates of resident population at 31 December for 2001, 2002, 2003 and 2004. Definitive estimates of Resident population at 31 December for 1991 to 2000.

Spain: Data for the years 1991-99 are Intercensus estimates of the population. Data for years 2000-04 are population projections.

Sweden: Conditions on 31 December for each respective year according to administrative subdivisions of 1 January of the following year.

Switzerland: Permanent resident population at the end of the year.

Turkey: Mid-year population estimates.

United States: Population at 1 April.

Gross domestic product – Chapters: 3, 4, 8, 9, 15, 16, 17, 18, 19

Sources and year of reference

	Source	Reference years	Territorial Level
Australia	Australian Bureau of Statistics, 5220.0	1998-2003	2
Austria	Eurostat, New Cronos, Economic accounts	1998-2003	3
Belgium	Eurostat, New Cronos, Economic accounts	1998-2003	3
Canada	Statistics Canada, Provincial economic accounts	1998-2003	2
Czech Republic	Eurostat, New Cronos, Economic accounts	1998-2003	3
Denmark	Eurostat, New Cronos, Economic accounts	1998-2003	3
Finland	Eurostat, New Cronos, Economic accounts	1998-2003	3
France	Eurostat, New Cronos, Economic accounts	1998-2003	3
Germany	Eurostat, New Cronos, Economic accounts	1998-2003	3
Greece	Eurostat, New Cronos, Economic accounts	1998-2003	3
Hungary	Eurostat, New Cronos, Economic accounts	1998-2003	3
Ireland	Eurostat, New Cronos, Economic accounts	1998-2003	3
Italy	Eurostat, New Cronos, Economic accounts	1998-2003	3
Japan	Economic and Social Research Institute, Cabinet Office	1998-2003	3
Korea	National Statistical Office	1998-2003	3
Luxembourg	Eurostat, New Cronos, Economic accounts	1998-2003	3
Mexico	Inegi, System of national accounts of Mexico	1998-2003	2
Netherlands	Eurostat, New Cronos, Economic accounts	1998-2003	3
Norway	Norwegian Regional Accounts	1998-2002	3
Poland	Eurostat, New Cronos, Economic accounts	1998-2003	3
Portugal	Eurostat, New Cronos, Economic accounts	1998-2003	3
Slovak Republic	Eurostat, New Cronos, Economic accounts	1998-2003	3
Spain	Eurostat, New Cronos, Economic accounts	1998-2003	3
Sweden	Eurostat, New Cronos, Economic accounts	1998-2003	3
Turkey	State Institute of Statistics	1998-2001	3
United Kingdom	Eurostat, New Cronos, Economic accounts	1998-2003	3
United States	Bureau of Economic Analysis	1998-2003	2

Country notes

Australia: Gross state product, current prices in millions of AUD.

Austria, Belgium, Czech Republic, Denmark, Finland, France, Germany, Greece, Hungary, Ireland, Italy, Luxembourg, the Netherlands, Poland, Portugal, Slovak Republic, Spain, Sweden and United Kingdom: GDP data were initially obtained in millions of EUR at current prices. The OECD Secretariat recalculated the figures into millions of national currency units (including former currencies of the euro zone) at current prices by utilising the annual average exchange rates between the euro and the national currencies.

Canada: GDP in millions of CAD at current prices (expenditure based estimates).

Japan: Real GDP in millions of JPY at current prices. Figures are based on fiscal year (Apr.-Mar.).

Korea: Gross regional domestic product in millions of KRW at current prices.

Mexico: GDP in thousands of MXN at current prices.

Norway: Gross value added (GVA) data in millions of NOK at current prices.

Turkey: GDP in millions of TRY at current prices.

United States: Gross state product expressed in millions of current USD.

For regional comparisons across counties (*i.e.* OECD total in Figures 3.1, 3.3, 3.8, 3.9), GDP is measured at constant PPP 2000 USD.

GDP data for Australia, Canada, Mexico and the United States are only available at TL2, where data by regional type carry a large bias; therefore Figures 3.3, 4.8, 4.9, 8.8 do not include data for these countries.

OECD REGIONS AT A GLANCE 2007 – ISBN 978-92-64-00987-5 – © OECD 2007

Employment by industry – Chapters: 5, 10, 18

Sources and year of reference

	Source	Reference year	Territorial Level
Australia	Australian Bureau of Statistics, LFS, Table: 6291.0.55.003	2003	2
Austria	Eurostat, Branch accounts, Employment	2003	2
Belgium	Eurostat, Branch accounts, Employment	2003	2
Czech Republic	Eurostat, Branch accounts, Employment	2003	2
Denmark	Statbank Denmark, Register based-labour force statistics	2003	2
Finland	Eurostat, Branch accounts, Employment	2003	2
France	Eurostat, Branch accounts, Employment	2003	2
Germany	Eurostat, Branch accounts, Employment	2003	2
Greece	Eurostat, Branch accounts, Employment	2003	2
Hungary	Eurostat, Branch accounts, Employment	2003	2
Iceland	Statistics Iceland	2003	2
Ireland	Eurostat, Branch accounts, Employment	2003	2
Italy	Eurostat, Branch accounts, Employment	2003	2
Japan	Statistics Bureau, Establishment and enterprise census	2004	2
Korea	KNSO-KOSIS Census on basic characteristics of establishments, Business enterprise	2003	2
Luxembourg	Eurostat, Branch accounts, Employment	2003	2
Mexico	Economic Census 1999 and 2004	2004	2
Netherlands	Eurostat, Branch accounts, Employment	2003	2
Norway	StatBank Norway	2003	2
Poland	Eurostat, Branch accounts, Employment	2003	2
Portugal	Eurostat, Branch accounts, Employment	2003	2
Slovak Republic	Eurostat, Branch accounts, Employment	2003	2
Spain	Eurostat, Branch accounts, Employment	2003	2
Sweden	Eurostat, Branch accounts, Employment	2003	2
Switzerland	Federal Statistical Office (OFS), Census of population, Table: VZ0024KD	2000	2
United Kingdom	Eurostat, Branch accounts, Employment	2001	2
United States	Bureau of Economic Analysis	2003	2

For regional comparisons across countries data have been converted into ISIC Rev. 3.1. according to UN Statistics Division correspondence tables.

Country notes

EU countries: Data provided by Eurostat according to the NACE classification.

Canada: Data for regions CA60, Yukon and CA61, Northwest Territories and Nunavut are missing.

Germany: Sections g, h, m, n, o and p are missing.

Iceland: Sections c, o and p are missing.

Italy: Data for regions ITD1, Provincia autonoma di Bolzano and ITD2, Provincia Autonoma di Trento are missing.

Japan: Data provided according the 2004 Enterprise and Census Industrial Classification. Sections l, o and p are missing

Mexico: Sections l, o and p are missing.

Korea: Data provided according to the Korean Industrial Classification.

Switzerland: Data provided according to the Switzerland Economic Activity Classification.

United States: Data provided according to NAICS.

Labour force,[1] employment, unemployment and long-term unemployment[2] – Chapters: 6, 9, 12, 13, 18, 19

Sources and year of reference

	Source	Reference years	Territorial Level
Australia	Australian Bureau of Statistics, LFS, Table: 6291.0.55.001	1998-2003	3*
Austria	Eurostat, New Cronos, LFS	1999-2003	3
Belgium	Eurostat, New Cronos, LFS	1999-2003	3
Canada	Statistics Canada	1998-2003	3*
Czech Republic	Eurostat, New Cronos, LFS	1999-2003	3
Denmark	Eurostat, New Cronos, LFS	1999-2003	3
Finland	Eurostat, New Cronos, LFS	1999-2003	3
France	Eurostat, New Cronos, LFS	1999-2003	3
Germany	Eurostat, New Cronos, LFS	1999-2003	3
Greece	Eurostat, New Cronos, LFS	1998-2003	3
Hungary	Eurostat, New Cronos, LFS	1999-2003	3
Iceland	Statistics Iceland	1998-2002	3
Ireland	Eurostat, New Cronos, LFS	1999-2003	3
Italy	Eurostat, New Cronos, LFS	1999-2003	3
Japan	Statistics Bureau, MIC	1998-2003	3
Korea	National Statistical Office	1998-2003	3
Luxembourg	Eurostat, New Cronos, LFS	1999-2003	3
Mexico	INEGI, Census of Population	2000	3
Netherlands	Eurostat, New Cronos, LFS	1999-2003	3
New Zealand	Statistics New Zealand, LFS	1998-2003	3
Norway	Statistics Norway.	1998-2003	3
Poland	Eurostat, New Cronos, LFS	1999-2003	3
Portugal	Eurostat, New Cronos, LFS	1999-2003	3
Slovak Republic	Eurostat, New Cronos, LFS	1998-2003	3
Spain	Eurostat, New Cronos, LFS	1999-2003	3
Sweden	Eurostat, New Cronos, LFS	1999-2003	3
Switzerland	Secretariat estimates based on Swiss Federal Statistical Office	1998-2003	3
Turkey	TURKSTAT, LFS	2000	3
United Kingdom	Eurostat, New Cronos, LFS	1999-2003	3
United States	Bureau of Labour Statistics, Labour Force data by county, Annual averages	1998-2003	3

Country notes

Australia: Data are based on the *Labour Force Dissemination Regions* as defined by the Australian Bureau of Statistics.

Austria: Data for regions AT125, AT222, AT226, AT321, AT333 and AT341 are obtained multiplying labour force by the unemployment rate (Eurostat LFS data).

Canada: Data are based on a grouping of TL3 regions according to the *Economic Regions* as defined in Statistics Canada (2006), *Guide to the Labour Force Survey* (Ottawa: Statistics Canada, Catalogue No. 71-543). (*www.statcan.ca/bsolc/english/bsolc?catno=71-543-G*). For female participation rates observations for regions CA056 and CA057 are missing.

1. Data on Female labour force are missing for France, Iceland, Korea, Mexico, Portugal, Switzerland and Turkey, for Spain they are available up to 2002, for the United States data are available at TL2 only.
2. Data for long term unemployment are at TL2 only. For Canada (CA60 and CA61 only), Denmark, Iceland, Japan, Korea, Mexico, New Zealand, Norway, Switzerland, and the United States data are not available. For Turkey data are available for 2004 only.

Eurostat LFS data: Employment is computed by subtracting unemployment from labour force data.

Finland: For unemployment for Aland (FI200), employment is subtracted from active population (Eurostat LFS data).

Germany: Data for labour force and employment are available from the year 2000.

Iceland: Labour force data are computed with available unemployment and unemployment rate data.

New Zealand: Data are provided by Statistics New Zealand aggregated for regions nz015-nz016 and nz021-nz021. Data for the merged regions have been estimated on the basis of census data, assuming exponential growth between census years (86-91-96-01).

Norway: Unemployment is obtained by subtracting employment from labour force (employment and labour force data come from the Norwegian LFS, Statbank Table: 05613).

Poland: Data for regions from PL121 to PL127 and from PL224 to PL227 for the years 1998-2000 are estimated from TL2 data using the share of each TL3 for the year 2000.

Switzerland: Data at TL3 are estimated from unemployment at TL2 using the share of labour force as weights.

United Kingdom: Data for working age population and labour force for regions from UKM41 to UKM46 come from the Local Area Labour Force Survey (LFS), NOMIS, Official Labour Market Statistics. For the remaining regions whenever Eurostat data are missing, estimation are made (where possible) based on the Local Area LFS data as follows: first, aggregating Local Area LFS data from TL3 into TL2. At TL2 both the Eurostat and the Local Area LFS databases have full coverage. Than ratio of the two databases is taken and applied to the Local Area LFS data to estimate the missing Eurostat values. For female participation rates data are missing for regions UK41, UK42, UK43, UK44, UK45 and UK46.

Employment at place of work – Chapter 9

Sources and year of reference

	Source	Reference years	Territorial Level
Australia	ABS, Census of Population and Housing	1998-2003	2
Austria	Eurostat, New Cronos, Branch accounts, Employment	1998-2003	3
Belgium	Eurostat, New Cronos, Branch accounts, Employment	1998-2003	3
Canada	Statistics Canada	1998-2003	2
Czech Republic	Eurostat, New Cronos, Branch accounts, Employment	1998-2003	3
Denmark	Eurostat, New Cronos, Branch accounts, Employment	1998-2003	3
Finland	Eurostat, New Cronos, Branch accounts, Employment	1998-2003	3
France	Eurostat, New Cronos, Branch accounts, Employment	1998-2003	3
Germany	Eurostat, New Cronos, Branch accounts, Employment	1998-2003	3
Greece	Eurostat, New Cronos, Branch accounts, Employment	1998-2003	3
Hungary	Eurostat, New Cronos, Branch accounts, Employment	1998-2003	3
Ireland	Eurostat, New Cronos, Branch accounts, Employment	1998-2002	3
Italy	Eurostat, New Cronos, Branch accounts, Employment	1998-2003	3
Japan	Statistics Bureau, MIC	1998-2003	3
Korea	National Statistical Office	1998-2003	3
Luxembourg	Eurostat, New Cronos, Branch accounts, Employment	1998-2003	3
Mexico	INEGI, Census of population and housing	1998-2001	2
Netherlands	Eurostat, New Cronos, Branch accounts, Employment	2001-2003	3
Norway	The Databank of the Regional Model System PANDA, SINTEF Group	1998-2001	3
Poland	Eurostat, New Cronos, Branch accounts, Employment	1998-2003	3
Portugal	Eurostat, New Cronos, Branch accounts, Employment	1998-2003	3
Slovak Republic	Eurostat, New Cronos, Branch accounts, Employment	1998-2003	3
Spain	Eurostat, New Cronos, Branch accounts, Employment	1998-2003	3
Sweden	Eurostat, New Cronos, Branch accounts, Employment	1998-2003	3
Turkey	TURKSTAT, Census of Population and Housing	2000	3
United Kingdom	Eurostat, New Cronos, Branch accounts, Employment	1998-2001	3
United States	US Census Bureau, Census of population	1998-2003	2

Country notes

Netherlands: 2003 data are provisional.

Australia, Canada, United States: Data have been estimated for the years 1998-2000, 2002, 2003 by computing the ratio of employment at place of work to employment (see indicator 11) where both variables are available for a common year. The ratio has then been applied to employment data where data on employment at place of work were missing.

Japan: Data have been estimated for the years 1998, 1999, 2001-2003; the methodology is the same as for Australia, Canada and United States, see above.

Calculation of labour productivity: GDP data are at TL2 for Australia, Canada, Mexico and United States. For these countries, therefore, the labour productivity indicator is calculated at TL2 only. The indicator is not computed for Iceland, New Zealand and Switzerland because of the lack of sub-national GDP data.

Patent applications – Chapter 7

Sources and year of reference

	Source	Reference years	Territorial Level
Australia	Intellectual Property Australia	1998-2003	2
Austria	Eurostat, patent applications to EPO	1998-2003	2
Belgium	Eurostat, patent applications to EPO	1998-2003	2
Canada	Canadian Intellectual Property Office, annual report.	2001-2003	2
Czech Republic	Eurostat, patent applications to EPO	1998-2003	2
Denmark	Eurostat, patent applications to EPO	2001	2
Finland	Eurostat, patent applications to EPO	1998-2003	2
France	Eurostat, patent applications to EPO	1998-2003	2
Germany	Eurostat, patent applications to EPO	1998-2003	2
Greece	Eurostat, patent applications to EPO	1998-2003	2
Hungary	Eurostat, patent applications to EPO	1998-2003	2
Ireland	Eurostat, patent applications to EPO	2001	2
Italy	Eurostat, patent applications to EPO	1998-2003	2
Japan	Japan Patent Office	1998-2003	2
Korea	Korean Intellectual Property Office	1998-2003	2
Luxembourg	Eurostat, patent applications to EPO	1998-2003	2
Mexico	Mexican Institute of Industrial Property	2001-2003	2
Netherlands	Eurostat, patent applications to EPO	1998-2003	2
Norway	Eurostat, patent applications to EPO	1998-2003	2
Poland	Patent Office of the Republic of Poland	1998-2003	2
Portugal	Eurostat, patent applications to EPO	1998-2003	2
Slovak Republic	Eurostat, patent applications to EPO	1998-2003	2
Spain	Eurostat, patent applications to EPO	1998-2003	2
Sweden	Eurostat, patent applications to EPO	1998-2003	2
Turkey	Turkish Patent Institute	1998-2003	2
United Kingdom	Eurostat, patent applications to EPO	1998-2003	2
United States	United States Patent and Trademark Office	1998-2003	2

Country notes

EU countries: Patent applications to the EPO by priority year.

Canada: Patent applications filed for residents of Canada only.

Mexico: Patent applications filed for residents of Mexico only.

United States: Number of patents granted as distributed by year of patent grant.

Educational attainments – Chapter 11

Sources and year of reference

	Source	Reference population	Reference year	Territorial Level
Australia	ABS Census of population and housing	25-64*	2001	3
Austria	Eurostat, New Cronos, LFS	25-64	2001	2
Belgium	Eurostat, New Cronos, LFS	25-64	2001	3
Canada	Statistics Canada, Census of population	25-64	2001	3
Czech Republic	Czech Statistical Office, Census of population	25-64*	2001	3
Denmark	Statistics Denmark, Register-based labour force statistics	25-64	2001	3
Finland	Statistics Finland	25-64	2000	3
France	INSEE, Census of population and housing	25-64*	1999	3
Germany	Eurostat, New Cronos, LFS	25-64	2001	2
Greece	Eurostat, New Cronos, LFS	25-64	2001	3
Hungary	KSH	25-64*	2001	3
Ireland	Central Statistical Office, Census of population	25-64	2002	3
Italy	ISTAT Census of population and housing	25-64*	2001	3
Japan	Statistics Bureau, Census of population	25-64	2000	3
Korea	NSO	25-64	2000	3
Mexico	INEGI, Census of population	25-64*	2000	3
Netherlands	Eurostat, New Cronos, LFS	25-64	2001	3
New Zealand	Statistics New Zealand, Census of population	25-64	2001	3
Norway	Statistics Norway, Census of population	25-66	2001	3
Poland	Polish official statistics, Census of population	25-64*	2002	3
Portugal	INE, Census of population	25-64*	2001	3
Slovak Republic	Statistical Office of the Slovak Republic, Census of Population	25-64	2001	3
Spain	INE, Economically active population survey	25-64*	2001	3
Sweden	Statistics Sweden, The Swedish Register of Education	25-64	2001	3
Switzerland	Federal Statistical Office, OFS	25-64*	2004	2
Turkey	TURKSTAT, Census of population	25-64	2000	3
United Kingdom	NOMIS, Local area labour force survey	25-64*	2001	3
United States	Census Bureau, Census of population	25-64*	2001	3

* OECD Secretariat Estimate, see Country notes below.

General notes

The International Standard Classification for Education (ISCED 97) is used to define the levels of education. Tertiary education comprises 3 ISCED levels: 5A, 5B and 6.

ISCED 5A programmes are largely theoretically based and are intended to provide sufficient qualifications for gaining entry into advanced research programmes and professions with high skills requirements.

ISCED 5B programmes are generally more practical/technical/occupationally specific than ISCED 5A programmes.

ISCED 6 is the second stage of tertiary education: This level is for tertiary programmes that lead to the award of an advanced research qualification. The programmes are devoted to advanced study and original research.

See the *OECD Handbook for Internationally Comparative Education Statistics* for a more detailed description of ISCED-97 educational programmes and their mappings for each country.

Country notes

Australia, Czech Republic, France, Hungary, Italy, Mexico, Poland, Portugal, Spain, Switzerland, United Kingdom and United States: Regional data on educational attainments were unavailable for the population 25-64. An estimate has been made based on the national educational attainment data for population 25-64.

Austria, Germany, Switzerland: Data are only available at TL2 grid.

Hungary: Budapest and Pest regions are merged (HU101+HU102).

Time distance from the closest urban centre – Chapter 20

Methodology

Choice of cities and urban agglomeration

In order to make a selection of major centres from which to calculate the distance in time to peripheral regions, the population threshold was generally established at a minimum of 300 000 for cities and a minimum of 500 000 for urban agglomerations (time/distance for a region hosting a centre is therefore nil). The thresholds have been calculated on the basis of the 1998 *UN Demographic Yearbook* data for cities with more than 100 000 inhabitants.

Time-distance calculation

To calculate the distance in time for European countries, the Eurostat Matrix was used (weighted distance-time by road and by rail). The time-distance to go through a major centre (to go from the city limit to the centre) varies according to the size of the centre or the agglomeration (centres < 1 000 000, 35 minutes; centres 1-2 million, 40 minutes; centres 2-3 million, 45 minutes; centres 3-4 million, 50 minutes; centres 4-5 million, 55 minutes; centres 5-6 million, 60 minutes; centres 6-8 million, 65 minutes; centres 8-10 million, 70 minutes; centres > 10 million, 75 minutes).

Time-distances for Australia, New Zealand, Canada, Japan, Korea, Mexico and Turkey were measured with cartographic work (GIS software). A measure of speed (km/h) was used according to the type of communication, motorway (90 km/h), national road (60 km/h), maritime transport (35 km/h).

Therefore: (km motorway × 90) + (km national road × 60) + (km maritime transport × 35) = time/road.

Owing to lack of information, time/rail has not been taken into consideration for non-European countries (for Japan, it was possible to constitute a precise temporal relation between towns with the help of the train timetable but it was decided to not take rail into account).

For the United States distances were calculated with the help of the *Zip Code Distance Wizard* software. Linear distances were calculated from each county seat (city hall) to the closest major centre (city hall). Time-distances were then calculated taking 75 km/h as the average speed of motorways and national roads (about 45 miles per hour). On the map, which is presented at Bureau of Economic Analysis (BEA) economic areas level, average distance to the major centre was calculated for the counties belonging to an economic area.

The calculations for this variable were done in 2001 (2004 for the United States) but data on population come from the 1998 *UN Demographic Yearbook*.

Country notes

Australia, Poland: The population threshold for cities is 400 000 inhabitants.

France: The population threshold for cities is 250 000 inhabitants, the population threshold for urban agglomeration is 450 000 inhabitants

Iceland: The population threshold for cities and urban agglomerations is 100 000 inhabitants.

Ireland: Belfast is included among the selected urban units >300 000 although it has 297 300 inhabitants.

Italy: The population threshold for urban agglomerations is 300 000 inhabitants, Venice is included among the selected urban units >300 000 although it has 297 743 inhabitants.

Japan: The population threshold for cities is 800 000 inhabitants.

Korea: The population threshold for cities is 1 million inhabitants.

Luxembourg: The population threshold for cities is 100 000 inhabitants.

Mexico: The population threshold for urban agglomerations is 800 000 inhabitants.

Turkey, United States: The population threshold for cities is 500 000 inhabitants, the population threshold for urban agglomerations is 800 000 inhabitants.

Poland: Data available at TL2 only.

Germany, Switzerland, Turkey, United States: The TL3 grid differs from the one used in the rest of this publication.

Student enrolment in tertiary education – Chapter 21

Sources and year of reference

	Source	Reference year	Territorial Level
Australia	Australian Bureau of Statistics, Survey of Education and Training (SET).	2005	2
Austria	Eurostat, New Cronos, Education Statistics	2003	2
Belgium	Eurostat, New Cronos, Education Statistics	2000	2
Canada	Statistics Canada	2003	2
Czech Republic	Eurostat, New Cronos, Education Statistics	2003	2
Denmark	Statistics Denmark	2003	2
Finland	Eurostat, New Cronos, Education Statistics	2003	2
France	Eurostat, New Cronos, Education Statistics	2003	2
Germany	Eurostat, New Cronos, Education Statistics	2003	2
Greece	Eurostat, New Cronos, Education Statistics	2004	2
Hungary	Eurostat, New Cronos, Education Statistics	2003	2
Iceland	Statistics Iceland	2003	2
Ireland	Eurostat, New Cronos, Education Statistics	2003	2
Italy	Eurostat, New Cronos, Education Statistics	2003	2
Japan	Ministry of Education, Culture, Sports, Science and Technology	2003	2
Korea	Ministry of Education and Human Resources Development (MEHRD), Educational Statistics	2003	2
Luxembourg	Eurostat, New Cronos, Education Statistics	2003	2
Mexico	*www.sep.gob.mx/wb2/sep/sep_Estadistica_Historica_por_Estados*	2002	2
Netherlands	Eurostat, New Cronos, Education Statistics	2003	2
Norway	Statistics Norway – Statbank	2003	2
Poland	Eurostat, New Cronos, Education Statistics	2003	2
Portugal	Eurostat, New Cronos, Education Statistics	2003	2
Slovak Republic	Eurostat, New Cronos, Education Statistics	2003	2
Spain	Eurostat, New Cronos, Education Statistics	2003	2
Sweden	Eurostat, New Cronos, Education Statistics	2003	2
Turkey	Ministry of Education	2003	2
United Kingdom	Eurostat, New Cronos, Education Statistics	2003	2
United States	Census Bureau	2003	2

Country notes

Canada: Data include all registrations in public, private and federal schools and schools for the visually and hearing impaired, as well as DND schools overseas.

Korea: Data on the following type of schools are not available at the regional level: Miscellaneous schools, schools with a curriculum similar to a formal school curriculum. (Foreign language schools and special course schools are included in miscellaneous schools.)

Voter turnout in national elections – Chapter 22

Sources and year of reference

	Source	Reference year	Territorial Level
Australia	Australian Electoral Commission	2004	2
Austria	Ministry of Interior, sect. III/6	2002	2
Belgium	www.ibzdgip.fgov.be website with electoral results	2003	2
Canada	www.elections.ca Elections Canada	2006	2
Finland		2003	2
France	Ministry of Interior	2002	2
Germany	Regional statistics Germany, Spatial Monitoring System of the BBR	2002	2
Hungary	National Election Office Hungary	2006	2
Ireland		1997	2
Italy	Ministry of Interior	2001	2
Japan	Ministry of Internal Affairs and Communication	2003	2
Mexico	Instituto Federal Electoral IFE	2006	2
Netherlands		2003	2
New Zealand	http://2005.electionresults.govt.nz	2005	2
Norway	Statistical Yearbook	2005	2
Poland	State Election Commission	2005	2
Portugal	Secretariat for the electoral process (STAPE), Ministry of Internal Administration	2005	2
Slovak Republic	SOSR	2006	2
Spain	www.congreso.es	2004	2
Sweden	Election Authority	2006	2
Switzerland	SFSO	2003	2
Turkey	TURKSTAT	2002	2
United Kingdom	www.electoralcommission.org.uk	2005	2
United States	www.census.gov/compendia/statab/elections	2004	2

Country Notes

Japan: Representatives elections.

Germany: Results for the 2005 election not published yet.

Italy: Results for the 2006 election not published yet.

Turkey: Last General Election of Representatives.

Crimes against property – Chapter 23

Sources and year of reference

	Source	Reference year	Territorial Level
Australia	ABS – Reported Crime 4510.0	2003	2
Austria	Ministry of interior	2003	2
Belgium	Statistics Belgium, Criminalité enregistrée	2003	2
Canada	Statistics Canada, CANSIM, Table 252-0013	2003	2
Denmark	The central register of reported criminal offences	2003	
Finland	Statistics Finland	2003	2
France	Ministry of Interior, Direction Générale de la Police Nationale	2002	2
Greece	Statistics Greece	2001	2
Hungary	KSH-TSTAR	2003	2
Iceland	The national commissioner of the Icelandic Police	2003	2
Ireland	Garda Síochána Annual Report	2003	2
Italy	Forze di Polizia	2003	2
Japan	National Police Agency	2003	2
Korea	The supreme public prosecutor office	2002	2
Luxembourg		2003	2
Mexico	www.inegi.gob.mx/est/default.asp?c=5044	2003	2
Netherlands	CBS-STATLINE	2003	2
New Zealand	www.stats.govt.nz/products-and-services/table-builder/crime-tables/offences/offence-calendar.htm	2003	2
Norway	Statistics Norway, Crime statistics	2003	2
Poland	Central Statistical Office, Statistical Yearbook of the Regions	2003	2
Portugal	www.ine.pt/prodserv/quadros/public.asp?Tema=C&subtema=09&ver=en	2003	2
Slovak Republic	Ministry of Interior of the Slovak Republic	2003	2
Spain	Estadística Penal Común. Audiencias Provinciales y Juzgado de lo Penal	2003	2
Sweden	National Council for Crime Prevention	2001	2
Switzerland	OFS/EFPF-choros	2000	2
Turkey	TURKSTAT	2003	2
United Kingdom	National Statistical office	2003	2
United States	FBI	2003	2

Country notes

Australia: Property crime consists of the following offences: robbery; blackmail/extortion; unlawful entry with intent; motor vehicle theft; other theft.

Canada includes breaking and entering, motor vehicle theft, theft over 5 000 CAD, theft 5 000 CAD and under, possession of stolen goods, fraud.

Denmark includes forgery, arson, burglary theft, fraud, robbery, theft of registered vehicles, theft of motorcycle, mopeds, theft of bicycles, malicious damage to property. A violation of the law committed by more than one person is registered as one offence only and if a violation of the law includes more than a single victim it will also be registered as one offence only. If more than one person has reported the violation of the law to the police, more than one reported criminal offences can in exceptional cases be registered.

Korea includes only the number of crimes in big cities of population $\geq$ 150 000 persons.

Mexico: Crimes against the property include: crimes against personal and private property (cattle thefts, burglary, damage to private property, fraud and robbery), crimes against the security of persons (robbery), and crimes against the public faith (falsification of:

documents, currencies, certificates credit and administrative documents, seals, brands and other objects).

Poland: Ascertained crimes against property in completed preparatory proceedings.

Switzerland: The statistics on reported offences are only available for Switzerland (the whole country). On the level of cantons, data are available on the number of condemnations for each type of crime. Total offences for Switzerland are distributed proportionally by large regions.

United Kingdom: The data relate to the financial year. Offences against property include: robbery, burglary in a dwelling, theft of and theft from a vehicle. Data for Northern Ireland come from the Northern Ireland Police Service and data for Scotland are from the Scottish Executive statistics.

Number of murders – Chapter 24

Sources and year of reference

National: UN Ninth United Nations Survey on Crime Trends and the Operations of Criminal Justice Systems (2003-2004), United Nations, Office on Drugs and Crime, Division for Policy Analysis and Public Affairs, www.unodc.org/unodc/en/crime_survey_ninth.html. Data refer to 2003 intentional murder rate.

Data for Austria, Belgium, Greece, Japan, Luxembourg, Mexico, Netherlands, New Zealand, Spain, United Kingdom and United States come from the UN Eight United Nations Survey on Crime Trends and the Operations of Criminal Justice Systems (2001-2002). Data refer to 2002 intentional murder rate (Greece, Japan and Spain 2000).

Regional:

	Source	Reference year	Territorial Level
Australia	ABS – Reported Crime 4510.0	2003	2
Austria	Ministry of interior	2003	2
Belgium	Statistics Belgium, Criminalité enregistrée	2003	2
Canada	Statistics Canada, CANSIM, Table 252-0013	2003	2
Finland	Statistics Finland	2000-2005	2
Czech Republic	Czech Statistical Office REGIONAL YEARBOOKS	2003	2
Denmark	The central register of reported criminal offences	2003	2
France	Ministry of Interior, Direction Générale de la Police Nationale	2002	2
Ireland	Garda Síochána Annual Report	2003	2
Italy	Forze di Polizia	2003	2
Japan	National Police Agency	2003	2
Mexico	www.inegi.gob.mx/est/default.asp?c=5044	2003	2
Netherlands	CBS-STATLINE	2003	2
New Zealand	www.stats.govt.nz/products-and-services/table-builder/crime-tables/offences/offence-calendar.htm	2003	2
Norway	Statistics Norway, Crime statistics	2003	2
Poland	Central Statistical Office, Statistical Yearbook of the Regions	2003	2
Portugal	www.ine.pt/prodserv/quadros/public.asp?Tema=C&subtema=09&ver=en	2003	2
Slovak Republic	Ministry of Interior of the Slovak Republic	2003	2
Sweden	National Council for Crime Prevention	2001	2
Switzerland	OFS/EFPF-choros	2000	2
Turkey	TURKSTAT	2003	2
United Kingdom	Coleman, K., C. Hird and D. Povey (2006), Violent Crime Overview, Homicide and Gun Crime 2004/2005, Home Office Statistical Bulletin 02/06. London: Home Office	2003	2
United States	FBI	2003	2

Country notes (regional data)

The sum of regional data on murders do not always match the UN national data.

Finland: Data refer to the 2000-05 average.

Ireland: Homicides includes murder, manslaughter, infanticide and abortion offences.

Japan: The number of arrests includes attempted murder.

Mexico: Homicides includes murders and manslaughters.

Netherlands: Data include manslaughter.

New Zealand: "Homicide" includes murder, attempted murder, manslaughter, infanticide, abortion, and aiding suicide/pact; within this, "murder" includes conspiracy to murder, and incite/counsel/attempt/ to procure murder. This variation, plus several other limitations associated with international comparisons, means that any results must be interpreted with extreme caution.

Poland: Murders in completed preparatory proceedings (include manslaughter).

Turkey: Data include manslaughter.

United Kingdom: Offences currently recorded as homicide, as at 28 November 2005. Figures are subject to revision as cases are dealt with by the police and by the courts, as further information becomes available. Data refer to the financial year.

Number of dwellings inhabited by the owner; total number of occupied dwellings – Chapter 25

Sources and year of reference

	Source	Reference year	Territorial Level
Australia	ABS Census of Population and Housing	2001	2
Austria	Statistik Austria	2001	2
Canada	Census of population	1996	2
Czech Repubic	Czech Statistical Office, Census	2001	2
Denmark	Statistics Denmark	2003	2
Finland	Statistics Finland	2001	2
France	INSEE Census	1999	2
Greece	Statistics Greece, Census	2001	2
Ireland	Statistics Ireland, Census	2002	2
Italy	General census of population and housing	2001	2
Japan	Housing and land survey	1998	2
Mexico	INEGI Census	2000	2
Netherlands	Statistics Netherlands, Census	2001	2
New Zealand	Statistics New Zealand, Census	2001	2
Norway	Statistics Norway	2001	2
Poland	Central Statistical office	2003	2
Portugal	INE Census, definitive results	2001	2
Slovak Republic	Population and Housing Census	2002	2
Spain	INE	2001	2
Switzerland	OFS	2000	2
Turkey	Census of Population, SIS	2003	2
United Kingdom	NSO, Census (England and Wales)	2003	2
United States	Census Bureau	2001	2

Country notes

Poland: Data are estimated based on the Population and Housing Census 2002, on the balances of dwelling stocks and on current reporting.

Greece, Netherlands, Japan, and Turkey: The percentage of occupied dwellings is the ratio of dwellings inhabited by the owner to the total number of dwellings (not the total number of occupied dwellings).

Number of private vehicles – Chapter 26

Sources and year of reference

	Source	Reference year	Territorial Level
Australia	BSD Motor Vehicle Census	2003	2
Austria	Eurostat, New Cronos, Transport and Energy Statistics	2003	2
Belgium	Eurostat, New Cronos, Transport and Energy Statistics	2003	2
Canada	Statistics Canada (road motor vehicle registration – annual survey)	2003	2
Czech Republic	Eurostat, New Cronos, Transport and Energy Statistics	2003	2
Denmark	Statistics Denmark	2003	2
Finland	Eurostat, New Cronos, Transport and Energy Statistics	2003	2
France	Eurostat, New Cronos, Transport and Energy Statistics	2003	2
Germany	Eurostat, New Cronos, Transport and Energy Statistics	2003	2
Greece	Eurostat, New Cronos, Transport and Energy Statistics	2003	2
Hungary	Eurostat, New Cronos, Transport and Energy Statistics	2003	2
Iceland	Statistics Iceland	2003	2
Ireland	Eurostat, New Cronos, Transport and Energy Statistics	2003	2
Italy	Eurostat, New Cronos, Transport and Energy Statistics	2003	2
Japan	Ministry of Land, Infrastructure and Transport	2003	2
Korea	KNSO	2002	2
Luxembourg	Eurostat, New Cronos, Transport and Energy Statistics	2003	2
Mexico	INEGI	2003	2
Netherlands	Eurostat, New Cronos, Transport and Energy Statistics	2003	2
Norway	Eurostat, New Cronos, Transport and Energy Statistics	2003	2
Poland	Eurostat, New Cronos, Transport and Energy Statistics	2003	2
Portugal	Eurostat, New Cronos, Transport and Energy Statistics	2003	2
Slovak Republic	Eurostat, New Cronos, Transport and Energy Statistics	2003	2
Spain	Eurostat, New Cronos, Transport and Energy Statistics	2003	2
Sweden	Eurostat, New Cronos, Transport and Energy Statistics	2001	2
Turkey	Eurostat, New Cronos, Transport and Energy Statistics	2003	2
United Kingdom	Eurostat, New Cronos, Transport and Energy Statistics	2003	2
United States	US Census Bureau	2003	2

Country notes

Australia: ABSD Motor Vehicle Census comprises: sedans, station wagons, and forward control passenger vehicles, campervans, and utilities panel vans. Motor vehicle census: 9309.0

Volume of produced waste – Chapter 27

Sources and year of reference

National: OECD, *OECD Environmental Data: Compendium 2004*. Data on municipal waste refer to the year 2002.

Regional:

	Source	Reference year	Territorial Level
Australia	ABS 8698.0, Waste management survey.	2002-03	2
Austria	Eurostat, New Cronos, Regional waste statistics	2004	2
Belgium	Eurostat, New Cronos, Regional waste statistics	1996	2
Canada	Statistics Canada	2002	2
Czech Republic	Czech Statistical Office, REGIONAL YEARBOOKS	2003	2
France	Observatoire des territoires	1996	2
Germany	Eurostat, New Cronos, Regional waste statistics	1996	2
Greece	Eurostat, New Cronos, Regional waste statistics	1996	2
Hungary	Eurostat, New Cronos, Regional waste statistics	1998	2
Ireland	Eurostat, New Cronos, Regional waste statistics	1998	2
Italy	Eurostat, New Cronos, Regional waste statistics	1998	2
Japan	Ministry of Environment	2003	2
Luxembourg	Eurostat, New Cronos, Regional waste statistics	1999	2
Mexico	INEGI. Con base en SEDESOL. DGOT	2003	2
Netherlands	–	2003	2
Norway	Eurostat, New Cronos, Regional waste statistics		2
Poland	Central Statistical Office, Statistical Yearbook of the Regions	2003	2
Portugal	INE, Environment Statistics	2001	2
Slovak Republic	Statistical Office of the Slovak Republic	2003	2
Spain	Eurostat, New Cronos, Regional waste statistics	2000	2
Sweden	Eurostat, New Cronos, Regional waste statistics	1998	2
United Kingdom	Department for Environment, Food and Rural Affairs – Municipal Waste Management Survey, Scotand data – Scottish Environmental Protection Agency, Northern Ireland data – Environment and Heritage Service, Wales data – Welsh Assembly Government	2003	2

Country notes

The sum of collected regional data on waste does not always match the OECD national data (OECD Environmental Data: Compendium 2004).

Australia: Regional data refers to the financial year.

Canada: National data refer to the year 1990.

When interpreting the results of this analysis it should be borne in mind that the definitions and survey methods employed by member countries in the collection of data on municipal waste may vary considerably.

Death by age and sex: Chapters 28, 29

Source and year of reference

National: OECD Health Data, 2006.

Regional:

	Source	Reference year	Territorial Level
Australia	ABS, Demographic Summary, Statistical areas	2001	2
Austria	Eurostat, New Cronos	2003	2
Belgium	Eurostat, New Cronos	2003	2
Canada	Statistics Canada	2003	2
Czech republic	Eurostat, New Cronos	2003	2
Denmark	WHO, Eurostat, New Cronos	2001	2
Finland	Eurostat, New Cronos	2003	2
France	Eurostat, New Cronos, INSEE	2003	2
Germany	Eurostat, New Cronos	2003	2
Greece	Eurostat, New Cronos	2003	2
Hungary	KSH	2003	2
Iceland	Statistics Iceland	2003	2
Ireland	CSO, WHO, Eurostat, New Cronos	2001	2
Italy	Eurostat, New Cronos	2002	2
Japan	WHO, Vital Statistics of Japan	2001	2
Korea	Korea NSO, Population and Housing Census	2003	2
Luxembourg	Eurostat, New Cronos	2003	2
Mexico	WHO, INEGI, *Estadísticas Vitales*	2001	2
Netherlands	Eurostat, New Cronos	2003	2
New Zealand	WHO, New Zealand Statistics	2001	2
Norway	Statistics Norway, StatBank	2003	2
Poland	Central Statistical Office	2003	2
Portugal	National Institute of Statistics, demographic statistics	2003	2
Slovak Republic	Statistical Office of the Slovak Republic	2003	2
Spain	Eurostat, New Cronos	2003	2
Sweden	Eurostat, New Cronos	2003	2
Switzerland	Eurostat, New Cronos	2003	2
United Kingdom	Eurostat, New Cronos	2003	2
United Sates	Population Estimates Program, US Bureau of the Census, NBER Vital Statistics NCHS's Multiple Causes of Death Data, 1959-2003	2003	2

Country notes

Australia: Data presented in this ABS product refer to deaths registered during the year shown. Death statistics are presented on the basis of the state or territory of usual residence of the deceased, regardless of where in Australia the death occurred or was registered. Deaths of Australian residents that occurred overseas are not included. Deaths in Australia of persons usually resident overseas are included in these statistics and are classified according to the state or territory in which the death was registered.

Canada: The geographical breakdown of deaths is based on the usual place of residence of the deceased. The data for Nunavut and the Northwest Territories (excluding Nunavut) are presented separately. As the only data available are deaths by 5-year age groups between the ages of 1 and 15, the indicator is based on the assumption that the breakdown of deaths is uniform within each age group.

Eurostat regional data: Deaths by age and sex: age reached during the year.

Ireland: Number of regional deaths by sex is estimated based on the regional share in 2004 under the assumption that regional mortality rates by sex are proportional to mortality rates for both sexes.

Korea: Deaths abroad and of unknown age were excluded.

New Zealand: Death data at regional level by sex have been estimated using the assumption that regional mortality rates by sex are proportional to mortality rates for both sexes.

Norway: Subject: 02 Population, table, tables 05377: Deaths by gender and age and 03026: Population, by gender and 10-year age groups, as of 1 January. The indicator is not based on age as in other countries but by age groups, taking the average age of death for each age group.

Poland: Estimates from the 2002 Census.

Portugal: The national figure includes all deaths in Portugal of Portuguese residents (regardless of country of birth or nationality). Deaths in Portugal of persons resident abroad are not included. Deaths of persons whose place of residence is unknown are included.

United States: Deaths by gender and age, mortality data by cause of death for any death in the United States based on death certificates in each state and the District of Columbia. (Multiple Cause-of-Death Mortality Data from the National Vital Statistics System of the National Center for Health Statistics).

Number of new cases of cancer – Chapter 30

Sources and reference years

National: OECD Health Data, 2006.

Regional:

	Source	Reference year	Territorial Level
Australia	Australian Institute of Health and Welfare. Cancer in Australia. Canberra: AIHW	2001	2
Canada	Statistics Canada – Canadian Cancer Registry	2004	2
France	FNORS	2000	2
Iceland	Icelandic Cancer Registry	2004	2
Slovak Republic	National Health Information Centre	2002	2
United States	State Cancer Registry and the National Program of Cancer Registries Cancer Surveillance System (NPCR-CSS), CDC	2003	2

Country notes

Australia: Incidence per 100 000 population, or the number of new cases averaged over five years (*e.g.* 1993-97 = 1997).

Canada: The 1976-2000 cancer age-standardised rates are based on cancer incidence data from the Canadian Cancer Registry (CCR) Database (November 2003 file), the National Cancer Incidence Reporting System and Demography Division (population estimates) of Statistics Canada. The 2001-04 age-standardised rates are estimates produced by Health Canada through extrapolation of cancer incidence data from the National Cancer Incidence Reporting System (NCIRS, 1969-91) and the Canadian Cancer Registry. Source: Statistics Canada, Table 103-0104, last update: 22/12/2005.

United States: Some data are unavailable for reasons of confidentiality and reliability. Source: *State Cancer Registry and the National Program of Cancer Registries Cancer Surveillance System* (NPCR-CSS), CDC, submitted in January 2005, as published in *United States Cancer Statistics*, November 2005 (*www.statecancerprofiles.cancer.gov*).

 France: The age-standardised incidence rate (number of new cases per 100 000 population) is the rate that would be found in the region if it had the same age structure as the European population. Cancers include all types except non-melanoma skin cancer.

Iceland: The age-standardised incidence rate (number of new cases per 100 000 population) is the rate that would be found in the region if it had the same age structure as the Segi standard world population. The cancers considered are Codes C00-C96 (not C00-C97) in IDC-10, namely all malignant neoplasms with the exception of malignant neoplasms of independent (primary) multiple sites.

Number of physicians – Chapter 31

Sources and reference year

Nationa:l OECD Health Data, 2006.

Regional:

	Source	Reference year	Territorial Level
Australia	Australian Institute of Health and Welfare 2005. Medical labour force 2003. AIHW Cat No HWL 32. Canberra: AIHW	2003	2
Austria	Eurostat, New Cronos	2003	2
Belgium	Eurostat, New Cronos	2004	2
Canada	The Canadian Institute for Health Information (CIHI): Scott's Medical Database (formerly Southam Medical Database) (SMDB)	2004	2
Czech Republic	Eurostat, New Cronos	2003	2
Finland	Eurostat, New Cronos (data available for one region only)	2002	2
France	ADELI index, Direction de la recherche, des études, de l'évaluation et des statistiques (DREES), Ministry of Health	2004	2
Germany	Eurostat, New Cronos	2004	2
Greece	National Statistical Service Of Greece	2003	2
Hungary	Központi Statisztikai Hivatal (KSH)	2004	2
Iceland	Directorate of Health: Register of Physicians	2002	2
Italy	Eurostat, New Cronos	2003	2
Japan	Statistics and Information Department, Minister's Secretariat, Ministry of Health, Labour and Welfare. Survey of Physicians, Dentists and Pharmacists; Report on Public Health Administration	2002	2
Korea	Ministry of Health and Welfare, Health Resources Division	2001	2
Mexico	INAFED, Instituto Nacional para el Federalismo y Desarrollo Municipal	2000	2
Netherlands	Nivel	2002	2
New Zealand	New Zealand Health Information Service	2002	2
Norway			
Poland	Ministry of Health	2004	2
Portugal	National Statistics Institute, health statistics	2004	2
Slovak Republic	National Health Information Centre	2004	2
Spain	Eurostat, New Cronos	2001	2
Sweden	Eurostat, New Cronos	2000	2
Switzerland	OFAS; OFS, Statistics yearbook 2002	2002	2
Turkey	Turkish Statistical Institute (TURKSTAT)	2002	2
United Kingdom	Eurostat, New Cronos	2000	2
United States	American Medical Association (AMA)	2003	2

Country notes

Australia: Data from survey of medical practitioners.

Canada: Number of active civilian general practitioners, family practitioners and medical specialists on 31 December of the reference year.

France: Metropolitan France; the data refer to both salaried and self-employed physicians, and include locums but not full-time hospital practitioners (PHTP) practising on a self-employed basis in hospitals. Figures refer to the number of professionals registered as of 1 January in the reference year.

Regional data from Eurostat for Spain, Finland and Italy refer to physicians entitled to practice (ENPAM data for Italy), irrespective of whether they are in activity. For Germany, Belgium and United Kingdom the figures refer to data on physicians with a medical practice, and those without a medical practice in industry, administration, research, etc.

There are no data for the following regions: North East, East Midlands, Eastern, Wales or Scotland.

Mexico: Municipal data have been aggregated to levels TL2. The total number of physicians corresponds to the sum of general practitioners, specialists and physicians classed as "other" (undefined).

Poland: Physicians working in health care services of the Ministry of Health, the Ministry of National Defence and the Ministry of the Interior and Administration. The data do not include persons who are engaged only in private practice. The data on specialists and general practitioners concern persons working in health-care services of the Ministry of Health only.

Portugal: Physicians entitled to practise, irrespective of whether they are in activity, according to place of residence, not declared at their place of practice.

Switzerland: Density of physicians covers only the density of physicians in private practice in 1990-2002 (Indicator BADAC, data from Table 14.2.2.2. of the *Statistics Yearbook 2002*).

Turkey: The data do not include physicians working in public/university administration. Health-care personnel working for the Ministry of Defence are included in the total numbers for Turkey.

Number of nurses – Chapter 32

Sources and reference year

National: OECD Health Data, 2006.

Regional:

	Source	Reference year	Territorial Level
Australia	Australian Institute of Health and Welfare 2005. Nursing and midwifery labour force 2003	2003	2
Austria	Eurostat, New Cronos	2003	2
Belgium	Eurostat, New Cronos	2004	2
Canada	The Canadian Institute for Health Information (CIHI): Registered Nurses Database (RNDB)	2004	2
Spain	Eurostat, New Cronos	2003	2
Finland	Eurostat, New Cronos	2003	2
France	ADELI index, Direction de la recherche, des études, de l'évaluation et des statistiques (DREES), Ministry of Health	2004	2
Hungary	Központi Statisztikai Hivatal (KSH)	2004	2
Italy	Ministry of Health	2002	2
Japan	Statistics and Information Department, Minister's Secretariat, Ministry of Health, Labour and Welfare. Survey of Physicians, Dentists and Pharmacists; Report on Public Health Administration)	2002	2
Mexico	INAFED, Instituto Nacional para el Federalismo y Desarrollo Municipal	2000	2
Netherlands	Nivel	2001	2
Poland	Eurostat, New Cronos	2003	2
Portugal	National statistics institute, Health statistics	2004	2
Slovak Republic	National Health Information Center	2004	2
Czech Republic	Eurostat, New Cronos	2003	2
United Kingdom	Eurostat, New Cronos	2000	2
Turkey	Turkish Statistical Institute (TURKSTAT)	2002	2

Country notes

Australia: Data are for employed nurse clinicians and clinical nurse managers, based on a survey of re-registering nurses.

Belgium: Includes midwives.

Canada: Includes registered nurses (RNs) and licensed practical nurses (LPNs) and registered psychiatric nurses (RPNs), but excludes part-time midwives. In the case of RNs and LPNs, the data on Nunavut are not available prior to 2001 and are combined, in 2004, with those on the Northwest Territories. The figures indicate the number of nurses as of 31 December of the reference year (*http://secure.cihi.ca/cihiweb/products/ Nurse_practitioners.pdf*).

Spain: No data on the Madrid region.

France:The data refer to metropolitan France, and cover both self-employed and salaried nurses; they also include replacements. The numbers are as of 1 January of the reference year, *i.e.* the number of nurses registered as of that date, and entitled to practise during the year, not full-time equivalents.

Japan: Number in relation to the population estimated by OECD/GOV/SIU (*i.e.* average population 2000-03). TL2 data are based on TL3 aggregates.

Mexico: Municipal data have been aggregated at TL2. The total number of nurses is the sum of general, specialised and other (undefined) nurses.

Portugal: Data from the College of Nurses, nursing staff registered with the College of Nurses, whether or not in activity, by place of work, in relation to the resident population as of 31 December estimated by the National Statistics Institute.

Slovak Republic: Number of nurses reported by the *National Health Information Center* in relation to the Eurostat population. Since 1999, the number has included midwives.

United Kingdom: The number does not include second-level nurses (private nursing homes only). There are no data on the following regions: North East, North West (including Merseyside), Yorkshire and The Humber, East Midlands, West Midlands, Eastern, London, South East, or South West.

Turkey: Includes midwives. Health-care staff working for the Ministry of Defence are included in the total.

Number of hospital beds – Chapter 33

Sources and reference year (national and regional data)

	Source	Reference year	Territorial Level
Australia	Australian Institute of Health and Welfare 2006. Australian Hospital Statistics 2004-05. Canberra: AIHW	2004	2
Austria	Eurostat, New Cronos	2003	2
Belgium	Eurostat, New Cronos	2003	2
Canada	The Canadian Institute for Health Information (CIHI): Canadian MIS Database (CMDB)	2003	2
Czech Republic	Eurostat, New Cronos	2002	2
Finland	Eurostat, New Cronos	2003	2
France	SAE file, DREES, Ministry of Health	2003	2
Germany	Eurostat, New Cronos	2003	2
Greece	National Statistical Service Of Greece for total beds and Centre of Planning et Economic Research-KEPE for acute-care beds	2000	2
Hungary	KSH	2004	2
Iceland	Statistics Iceland	2003	2
Italy	Eurostat, New Cronos for total, Istat: data from the Ministry of Health on long-term and acute care	2003	2
Mexico	INEGI, Recursos materiales seleccionados en instituciones del Sistema Nacional de Salud por entidad federativa, 2003 y 2004	2004	2
Netherlands	Statistics Netherlands	2002	2
Poland	Ministry of Health	2004	2
Portugal	National Statistics Institute, Health Statistics, Hospital survey data	2004	2
Slovak Republic	National Health Information Center	2004	2
Spain	Eurostat, New Cronos	2004	2
Sweden	Eurostat, New Cronos	2000	2
Switzerland	OFS, Statistics yearbook 2002. BADAC Indicator: Density of beds and hospital stays	2004	2
Turkey	Turkish Statistical Institute (TURKSTAT)	2003	2
United Kingdom	Eurostat, New Cronos	2000	2

Country notes

Germany, Austria, Spain, Finland, Greece, Hungary, Mexico and Turkey: No data on long-term care beds.

European Union, source Eurostat: Data for Germany include only beds used for full in-patient accommodation and not include care or rehabilitation centres. Data are annual averages. In Sweden, beds in the private sector are excluded. Beds in elderly care institutions under the responsibility of municipalities are not included either. In Spain, beds in emergency services, ambulatory haemodialysis, and beds for new-born babies are excluded.

Italy: Excludes military hospital, day hospital and nursing home beds. (cf. *Eurostat, European regional and urban statistics – Reference guide, ed. 2005*).

France: Series collected throughout France, in public and private healthcare establishments. Elles sont données au 31 décembre de l'année (définitions disponibles dans Eco-Santé Régional de l'IRDES, voir *www.ecosante.fr/DEPAFRA/3025.html* et *www.ecosante.fr/DEPAFRA/2303.html*).

Iceland and Switzerland: Long-term care beds only. Iceland: for this indicator, the regional data available do not fully match OECD regional boundaries. TL2 region "IS01: Capital

Region" covers TL3 regions "IS01: Capital Region" and "IS021: Suournes". The OECD usually includes the latter in other IS02 regions. Switzerland: Average number of hospital beds and "semi-hospital" (one-day) beds over the year (Table 14.2.3.1.2).

Australia: Data are for available or licensed beds in public acute and psychiatric hospitals, private free-standing day hospitals and other private hospitals.

Canada: The total number of beds includes the number of beds from organisations that do not submit their data to their provincial ministry of health. Includes beds staffed and in operation reported in all types of hospitals (including general, specialty, long-stay psychiatric, rehabilitation and long-term care hospitals). The total number of long-term care beds includes beds in non-acute care hospitals (including long-stay psychiatric, rehabilitation and long-term care hospitals) outside Quebec, where beds for psychiatric care are included as the average length of stay in those beds is about 40 days. Acute-care beds include paediatric and short-stay psychiatric hospitals. For long-term and acute-care beds, some provinces report beds staffed while other provinces report beds approved by the provincial health authorities.

Mexico: The data include rooms used by general practitioners, specialists, odontologists and emergency medical staff, excluding data from "IMSS-Oportunidades". The overall total does not correspond to the federal entity total. Source: SSA. *Boletín de Información Estadística. Recursos y Servicios*, 2003. Vol. I. No. 23. Mexico, D.F., 2004, *www.inegi.gob.mx, site consulté le 29 août 2006*.

Sweden: Excludes private sector beds, and beds in geriatric care homes run by municipal authorities.

Netherlands: Long-term nursing care is now provided in nursing homes instead of hospitals. Some acute-care beds are occupied by patients who should be in nursing homes, but the percentage is unknown.

Poland: Number of hospital beds of health-care services of the Ministry of Health excluding health-care services of the Ministry of National Defence and the Ministry of the Interior and Administration.

Portugal: Number of hospital beds: all hospitals; number of long-term beds: psychiatric care beds and post-detox beds for alcohol/substance-abuse care beds; number of acute-care beds: all hospital beds excluding psychiatric care beds and post-detox beds for alcohol/substance-abuse.

Turkey: Total includes Ministry of Defence hospital beds.

Number of CT scanners and MRI units – Chapter 34

Sources and reference year

National: OECD Health Data, 2006.

Regional:

	Source	Reference year	Territorial Level
Australia	Australian Department of Health and Ageing	2004	2
Canada	The Canadian Institute for Health Information (CIHI): Medical Imaging In Canada Report, 2004	2004	2
France	SAE file, DREES, Ministry of Health, available on the FNORS site – Score santé (MRI only)	2002	2
Greece	Centre of Planning and Economic Research-KEPE	1999	2
Iceland	Radiation Protection Institute	2004	2
Italy	Istat: Ministry of Health data	2003	2
Poland	Ministry of Health	2004	2
Portugal	National Statistics Institute, Health Statistics, Hospital survey data	2004	2
Slovak Republic	National Health Information Centre	2004	2
Turkey	Ministry of Health	2003	2

Country notes

Australia: the data are only for units that are Medicare-eligible.

Canada: The 2005 National Survey of Selected Medical Imaging Equipment collected data from all identifiable health-care facilities (public and private) in each province and territory in Canada that had one or more of seven specific types of equipment. The types of medical imaging equipment that were included in the scope of the survey were magnetic resonance imaging scanners, computerised tomography scanners, positron emission tomography scanners, angiography suites, catheterisation laboratories and nuclear medicine cameras. Data were also collected on a seventh type of equipment, lithotripters. The survey was carried out between 9 May 2005, and 31 July 2005, with follow-up to the end of October 2005. Participants were asked to identify the technologies, described above, which were installed and operational prior to 1 January 2005 (cf. Table 2, p. 53 of the "Medical Imaging In Canada Report, 2004" *http://secure.cihi.ca/cihiweb/products/MedImag05_e.pdf*).

France: Number of magnetic resonance imaging (MRI) units as of 31 December in both the public and private sectors.

Poland: Data concern medical equipment of health care services of the Ministry of Health excluding health care services of the Ministry of National Defence and the Ministry of the Interior and Administration.

Number of smokers aged 15 and over – Chapter 35

Sources and reference year

	Source	Reference year	Territorial Level
Australia	Australian Institute of Health and Welfare. National Drug Strategy Household Survey: State and territory supplement	2004	2
Hungary	OEK (National epidemiology centre)	2003	2
Iceland	Iceland Institute of Public Health	2004	2
Italy	ISTAT	2003	2
Norway	Statistics Norway (StatBank)	2004	2
Poland	Central Statistical Office	2004	2
Portugal	Ministry of Health, National health institute (INSA)	1999	2
Spain	Encuesta Nacional de Salud	2003	2
Switzerland	OFS, Swiss health surveys, 1997 and 2002	2002	2
United States	Centers for Disease Control and Prevention (CDC)	2004	2

Country notes

Australia: Data are for population aged 14 years and over (rather than 15).

Spain: The national health survey is conducted every two years (1997, 2001 and 2003). The regions of Ceuta and Melilla have been grouped together.

United States: Data reported by the *Centers for Disease Control and Prevention* (CDC), Behavioral Risk Factor Surveillance System Survey Data. Atlanta, Georgia: US Department of Health and Human Services, Centers for Disease Control and Prevention, 2004.

Iceland: Data from a three-year survey conducted annually on the 15-89 age group.

Norway: Table 04814 of Subject 03 Health, social conditions, social services and crime, Statistics Norway (*http://statbank.ssb.no*). The data for 2004 represent the average for 2000-04.

Portugal: Data from National Health Survey, 1998-99. Prevalence of smoking: percentage of the population aged 15 and over. This indicator is only available for 1998-99 and for the five health administrations on the mainland (Azores and Madeira regions excluded), which are the regional level of health policy implementation (including health service delivery) and do not correspond to TL2 units. The health administration units are based on district aggregates, while TL2 units (equal to NUTS II regions) are based only on municipality aggregates.

Number of people suffering from obesity – Chapter 36

Sources and reference year

	Source	Reference year	Territorial Level
Australia	Australian Bureau of Statistics National Health Survey; Summary of results. ABS Cat. No. 4364.0	2004	2
Canada	Statistics Canada	2003	2
Hungary	OEK	2003	2
Iceland	Iceland Institute of Public Health, National Survey on Nutrition 2002	2002	2
Italy	ISTAT	2003	2
Poland	Central Statistical Office	2004	2
Portugal	Ministry of Health, National Health Institute (INSA)	1999	2
Spain	Encuesta Nacional de Salud	2003	2
Switzerland	OFS, Swiss health surveys, 1997 and 2002	2002	2
United States	BRFSS	Average 1997-2003	2

Country notes

Australia: Obesity estimates are self-reported and refer to those aged 18 and over (rather than 15 and over).

Canada: The data exclude persons under 18 years of age, pregnant women, and those measuring less than 3 feet (0.914 metres) or more than 6 feet 11 inches (2.108 metres) in height. The definition for BMI was modified in 2004 to respect the latest guidelines from Health Canada. Table 105-4009, Statistics Canada; Canadian Community Health Survey (*www.statcan.ca/english/sdds/*, 3226: CCHS,), National Population Health Survey (3236: NPHS, household), National Population Health Survey (5004: NPHS, North component).

Spain: The data refer to the share of the population aged 20 and over with a BMI over 30. The national health survey is conducted every two years (1997, 2001 and 2003). The regions of Ceuta and Melilla have been grouped together.

United States: Self-reported obesity among adults aged 20 and over by state: 1997-2003. Source: BRFSS, Author: CDC/NCHS.

Iceland: The survey relates to the 15-80 age group with a BMI over 30.

Portugal: Data from National Health Survey, 1998-1999. Prevalence of obesity: percentage of the population with a BMI over 30. This indicator is only available for 1998-99, and refers to the five health administrations on the mainland (Azores and Madeira regions excluded), which are the regional level of health policy implementation (including health service delivery) and do not correspond to TL2 units. The health administration units are based on district aggregates while TL2 units (equal to NUTS II regions) are based only on municipality aggregates.

Switzerland: The survey relates to those over 18 years of age with a BMI over 30.

Indexes and Formulas

Geographic Concentration Index

Definition: The Geographic concentration index for the variable y (*e.g.* population, GDP, etc.) is defined as:

$$\left(\sum_{i=1}^{N} |y_i - a_i| \Big/ 2 \right) * 100$$

where y_i is the share of region i to the national total, a_i is the area of region i as a percentage of the country area, N stands for the number of regions and | | indicates the absolute value.

The index lies between 0 (no concentration) and 100 (maximum concentration) in all countries and is suitable for international comparisons of geographic concentration.

Interpretation: The value of the index is affected by the size of regions. Therefore, differences in geographic concentration between two countries may be partially due to differences in the average size of regions in each country.

Gini Index

Definition: Regional disparities are measured by an unweighted Gini index. The index is defined as:

$$GINI = \frac{2}{N-1} * \sum_{i=1}^{N-1} (F_i - Q_i)$$

where: N is the number of regions, $F_i = \dfrac{i}{N}$, $Q_i = \dfrac{\sum_{j=1}^{i} y_j}{\sum_{j=1}^{N} y_j}$ and y_j is the value of variable y (*e.g.* GDP per capita, unemployment rate, etc.) in region j is ranked from low (y_1) to high (y_N) among all regions within a country.

The index ranges between 0 (perfect equality: y is the same in all regions) and 1 (perfect inequality: y is nil in all region except one).

Interpretation: The value of the index is affected by the size of regions. Therefore, differences in the degree of regional disparities between two countries may be partially due to differences in the average size of regions in each country.

Specialisation Index

Definition: Specialisation is measured according to the Balassa-Hoover index, which measures the ratio between the weight of an industry in a region and the weight of the same industry in the country:

$$BH_i = \frac{Y_{ij}/Y_j}{Y_i/Y}$$

where Y_{ij} is total employment of industry i in region j, Y_j is total employment in region j of all industries, Y_i is the national employment in industry i, and Y is the total national employment of all industries. A value of the index above 1 shows specialisation in an industry and a value below 1 shows lack of specialisation.

The average degree of specialisation in region j is measured by averaging the sum of the absolute deviations from 1 of the Balassa-Hoover indexes over all industries:

$$\sum_{i=1}^{N} \left| BH_i - 1 \right| \Big/ N$$

where: BH_i is the Balassa-Hoover index of industry i

Interpretation: The value of the specialisation index decreases with the level of aggregation of industries. Therefore, the specialisation index based on a 1-digit industry (*e.g.* manufacturing) would underestimate the degree of specialisation in all 2-digit industries belonging to it (*e.g.* textile, chemistry, etc.).

Potential Years of Life Lost

Definition: The calculation of potential years of life lost (PYLL) involves summing up deaths occurring at each age and multiplying this by the number of remaining years to live up to a selected age limit (70 years).

$$PYLL_{it} = \sum_{\alpha=0}^{l-1} (l-a) \times \left(\frac{d_{at}}{P_{at}} \right) \times \left(\frac{P_a}{P_n} \right) \times 100000$$

where:

$\begin{cases} i : \text{geographical area (in terms of TL2 and TL3: region, department, county, etc.)} \\ a : \text{age} \\ l : \text{upper age limit (here 70 years),} \\ d_{at} : \text{number of deaths at age a at time } t \\ P_{at} : \text{number of persons aged } a \text{ in region i at time } t \\ P_a : \text{number of persons aged } a \text{ in the reference (national) population} \\ P_n : \text{total number of persons in the reference (national) population} \end{cases}$

Age-adjusted mortality rates

Definition: Regional age-adjusted mortality rates are defined as the ratio of the observed number of deaths in a given regions to the expected number of deaths:

$$MR_i = \frac{\sum_{i=1}^{n} d_{i_g}}{\sum_{i=1}^{n} M_{c_g} * pop_{i_g}}$$

where MR_i is the age adjusted mortality rate in region i, d_{i_g} is the observed number of deaths in region i for age group g, M_{c_g} is the age-specific mortality rate in the standard population of country c for persons in age group g, pop_{i_g} is the total population in region i in age group g.

The drivers of regional growth

The factors of regional competitiveness

The share of region i in the total GDP of the OECD can be written as:

1. $\dfrac{GDP_i}{GDP_{OECD}} = \dfrac{GDP_j}{GDP_{OECD}} * \dfrac{GDP_i}{GDP_j}$

where j denotes the country of region i. The GDP share of region i in country j is then equal to:

2. $\dfrac{GDP_i}{GDP_j} = \dfrac{GDP_i / E_i}{GDP_j / E_j} * \dfrac{E_i / LF_i}{E_j / LF_j} * \dfrac{LF_i / WA_i}{LF_j / WA_j} * \dfrac{WA_i / P_i}{WA_j / P_j} * \dfrac{P_i}{P_j}$

where P, E, LF and WA stand, respectively, for population, employment, labour force and working age (15-64) population. Therefore, the GDP share of region i in country j is a function of its GDP per worker (GDP_i/E_i), employment rate (E_i/LF_i), participation rate (LF_i/WA_i), age-activity rate (WA_i/P_i) and population (Pi), relative to, respectively, the GDP per worker (GDP_j/E_j), employment rate (E_j/LF_j), participation rate (LF_j/WA_j), age-activity rate (WA_j/P_j) and population (P_j) of its country.

By substituting equation 2 into equation 1, taking the logarithm and differentiating it, one obtains:

3.

$$(g_i - g_{oecd}) = (g_j - g_{oecd}) + (g_{\Pi,i} - g_{\Pi,j}) + (g_{e,i} - g_{e,j}) + (g_{lf,i} - g_{lf,j}) + (g_{wa,i} - g_{wa,j}) + (g_{p,i} - g_{p,j})$$

or, equivalently

Growth in the GDP share of region *i* in the OECD	=	Difference in GDP growth between country *j* and the OECD	+	Growth difference in GDP per worker between region *i* and country *j*	+	Growth difference in the employment rate between region *i* and country *j*	+	Growth difference in the participation rate between region *i* and country *j*	+	Growth difference in the activity rate between region *i* and country *j*	+	Growth difference in population between region *i* and country *j*

Labour productivity and industry specialization

Average GDP per worker in region i is equal to a weighted average of sectoral GDP per worker:

4. $$\frac{GDP_i}{E_i} = \sum_k \frac{E_{ik}}{E_i} * \frac{GDP_{ik}}{E_{ik}}$$

where k indicates the sector. A similar equation defines GDP per worker in country j:

5. $$\frac{GDP_j}{E_j} = \sum_k \frac{E_{jk}}{E_j} * \frac{GDP_{jk}}{E_{jk}}$$

By taking the logarithm of 4 and 5 and differentiating, one obtains:

6.

$$\left(g_{p,i} - g_{p,j}\right) = \sum_k \frac{GDP_{jk} / E_{jk}}{GDP_j / E_j} * \left(\Delta \frac{E_{ik}}{E_i} - \Delta \frac{E_{jk}}{E_j}\right) + \sum_k \frac{\Delta\left(GDP_{jk} / E_{jk}\right)}{GDP_j / E_j} * \left(\frac{E_{ik}}{E_i} - \frac{E_{jk}}{E_j}\right) +$$

$$+ \sum_k \Delta \frac{E_{ik}}{E_i} * \left(\frac{GDP_{ik} / E_{ik}}{GDP_i / E_i} - \frac{GDP_{jk} / E_{jk}}{GDP_j / E_j}\right) + \sum_k \frac{E_{ik}}{E_i} * \left(\frac{\Delta GDP_{ik} / E_{ik}}{GDP_i / E_i} - \frac{\Delta GDP_{jk} / E_{jk}}{GDP_j / E_j}\right)$$

or, equivalently:

Growth difference in labour productivity between region *i* and country *j*	=	Change in regional specialisation towards high-productivity sectors	+	Regional specialisation in sectors with high productivity growth	+	Change in specialisation towards sectors where the region is less productive than the country	+	Specialisation in industries where productivity growth in the region is lower than in the country

The first two components on the right-hand of equation 6 measure the growth difference in GDP per worker due to regional specialisation; the third and forth components measure differences due to lower growth in regional GDP per worker across all sectors.

OECD PUBLICATIONS, 2, rue André-Pascal, 75775 PARIS CEDEX 16
PRINTED IN FRANCE
(04 2007 02 1P) ISBN 978-92-64-00987-5 – No. 55 505 2007

Achevé d'imprimer par Corlet, Imprimeur, S.A. - 14110 Condé-sur-Noireau
N° d'Imprimeur : 104752 - Dépôt légal : mai 2007 - *Imprimé en France*